JESUS CHRIST IS LORD

JESUS CHRIST IS LORD

Adoration Viewed Through the New Testament

by

Ernest Lussier, S.S.S

ALBA · HOUSE   NEW · YORK

SOCIETY OF ST. PAUL, 2187 VICTORY BLVD., STATEN ISLAND, NEW YORK 10314

Library of Congress Cataloging in Publication Data
Lussier, Ernest, 1911
    Jesus Christ is Lord

    1. God—Worship and love—Biblical teaching.
2. Bible. N.T.—Criticism, interpretation, etc.
I. Title.
BS2398.L87   232   79-15581
ISBN: 0-8189-0382-1

Imprimi Potest:
Donald E. Pelotte, S.S.S.
Provincial Superior

Nihil Obstat:
Daniel V. Flynn, J.C.D.
Censor Librorum

Imprimatur:
Joseph T. O'Keefe, Vicar General
Archdiocese of New York
May 12, 1979

The Nihil Obstat and Imprimatur are
a declaration that a book or pamphlet is considered
to be free from doctrinal or moral error. It is not implied
that those who have granted the Nihil Obstat and
Imprimatur agree with the contents,
opinions or statements expressed.

Designed, printed and bound in the United States of
America by the Fathers and Brothers of the
Society of St. Paul, 2187 Victory Boulevard,
Staten Island, New York, 10314, as part of their
communications apostolate.

---

1 2 3 4 5 6 7 8 9 (Current Printing: first digit).

AUTHOR'S PREFACE

The theme of adoration in the Old Testament focused on God's attributes. In the New Testament its focus is on the divinity of Christ, the Incarnate Son of God. The Pauline epistles play here an essential role in divine revelation. The theme of adoration in the Bible is far from having been exhausted by what I have presented in my first volume (*Adore the Lord*: Adoration in the Old Testament, Alba House, 1978) and in this present volume. The Johannine material has not been touched. Now the Prologue of the fourth gospel, and the discourses of our Lord, especially those after the Last Supper, are essentially adoration material, or if you prefer, a proclamation of the divine attributes of the Johannine Christ. Hopefully this material could be the subject matter of a third book.

Then there is the epistle to the Hebrews which has only been lightly touched. Actually the long and admirable description of Christ's priesthood, his sacrifice, the new covenant, and the worship of God, all make this epistle in a special way the epistle of adoration. I have treated this matter at some length in my *Christ's Priesthood*, according to the Epistle to the Hebrews (1975). I have also broached the subject of adoration several times in my preceding publications, especially in five chapters of my *Living the Eucharistic Mystery*, (Alba House, 1976, pp. 151-180): prayer and worship; prayer of adoration; the divinity of Christ; adoration of Christ; prayer to Jesus.

Once again may I point out that my specific purpose is to promote liturgical worship by insisting on the personal prayer of praise, the heartfelt religion which worship should be expressing and fostering. The official manifestation of worship is clearly the Eucharistic celebration of the Mass which, however, means little without adoration in spirit and in truth.

CONTENTS

CONTENTS

INTRODUCTION

The outstanding characteristic of the secular city is the absence of the sacred. In American society, in spite of the popularity of many noncultic religious forms, a real sense for the sacred, for the holy, for the majesty and otherness of God is on the wane. God has been pushed from his throne while man is being put in his place.

In our technological society we are completely surrounded by human artifacts. Whether in the home or on the street or in our automobiles we are constantly reminded of the cleverness of man the artisan who has fashioned all of these things for his use or pleasure. Yes, we may see an occasional cross or image of a saint to remind us of God, but the competition is most intense. Unless confronted with the stark reality of a death of a loved one, we tend to look to human ingenuity for the solutions to all problems.

Contemporary scientism, rationalism and materialism are all around us. They are in the very air we breathe. They exalt man. In their neglect or denial of God they lead logically to the deification of man.

Adoration of God by man is an act that is diametrically opposed to the secular humanism of our day. To adore God means to show Him reverence, to acknowledge His absolute holiness as Creator and Lord, to submit oneself to Him in obedience, and to manifest this by certain external acts such as prostrations, kisses, sacrifices and prayers. The fully secular man recognizes no reality higher than himself and his own consciousness.

Modern man needs desperately to be reminded that he is a

mere creature, a puff of wind, a footprint in wet sand, and that his true happiness and glory flow from adoring his Creator and God. We can thank Father Ernest Lussier, S.S.S., for bringing into focus for us in this book the teaching of the New Testament on the importance of adoration.

For many years I have maintained that an excellent way to study the Bible is to take one theme and trace it through a part or the whole of the Bible. Father Lussier has done exactly that by concentrating on adoration in the New Testament.

Gradually Jesus led Mary, His Mother, and His disciples to the realization of who He was, the divine Son of the Father. When Christians began to refer to Him as the "Lord" they transferred to Him a title reserved to Yahweh—God of the Old Testament. Only the bearer of that title is worthy of adoration in conformity with the First Commandment. Thus the acclamation that "Jesus Christ is Lord" (see Phil 2:11) is the summation of the Christian faith.

Father Lussier's careful New Testament study will surely help all who read it not only to redirect their thoughts from the secular to the sacred, but it will also help them to share more deeply in the satisfying joy of true adoration of God—Father, Son and Holy Spirit.

Kenneth Baker, S.J., Editor
Homiletic & Pastoral Review

November 1, 1978
Feast of All Saints

Adoration Viewed Through the New Testament

THE FIRST ADORER OF THE INCARNATE WORD

Adoration is the keynote of the narrative of the Annunciation to Mary (Lk 1:26-38). This spirit of adoration appears also in that of the Visitation (1:39-56). Mary pondered all the events of the Nativity in her heart (2:19, 51).

The Incarnation of Christ is the central event of salvation history. It is the result of God's decisive intervention in our human history. This unbelievable novelty is at the same time in perfect continuity with the Old Testament preparation. Mary's vocation to divine maternity is the crown of all the other vocations in the course of the long centuries of the history of Israel, which have preceded it and prepared it. Mary is presented as the virgin divinely chosen in Israel to be the mother of Jesus and to experience the mystery and the spiritual benefits of his redemptive mission. She is the prefigurement of the life and destiny of the Christian community.

Adoration is the keynote of the Annunciation to Mary (Lk 1:26-38). The angel Gabriel regarded as a divine messenger of highest rank, is sent by God to the virgin Mary. He salutes her as highly favored by God, and assures her, "the Lord is with you." These last words appear frequently in biblical vocation narratives; they are a guarantee that the divine purpose will be efficacious. Mary is the recipient of God's grace in a supreme degree. The angel recognizes in her a holiness of an entirely special kind, which God has given her to fit her to be mother of the Holy One. The phrase, "highly favored," implies not only personal sanctity: Mary is endowed with grace in a permanent fashion; it also points to the source of that fullness, for the favor that makes Mary the favored one par excellence is the Messianic motherhood, the divine maternity. She is God's chosen vessel for the mystery of the Incarnation.

"Do not be afraid, you have found favor with God." Mary's fear must have had something of the sacred awe which precedes or accompanies adoration. She is troubled by the words she has just heard: "The Lord is with you." She has no doubt as to the identity of this Lord. It is the God of Abraham, Moses, David, the prophets, and he is with her. She experiences suddenly the revelation of an unexpected, invisible, particular presence of the Most High. Her wonder, her emotion is easily understood. What does this special presence mean? Moses had veiled his face; Isaiah had thought himself lost. What must she do? What is she to become? What is going to happen? Wonder and awe and adoring praise are the emotions with which Christians have always regarded the unspeakable condescension of him who "when he took upon himself human nature to deliver it, did not abhor the virgin's womb."

Gabriel's message (32-35) recalls several Old Testament passages. The radical newness of the Incarnation is rooted in the continuity of God's plan for our salvation. We are brought back to David, and with Jacob to the patriarchs. In Mary's son, the Messianic prophecies will be fulfilled. He will be called the Son of the Most High, the Son of God. His kingdom is to have perpetuity not because of a succession of kings but because the Son of the Most High now takes possession of it. The title, Son of God, is for Luke as in the Old Testament, a Messianic title; but Luke makes it the expression par excellence of the mysterious relation which unites Jesus to God. In his gospel it is never put on the lips of men. And at the end of Gabriel's message, Son of God heightens the title, Son of the Most High, and indicates the fullness of the divine filiation of Jesus.

The conception of Jesus is effected only by God and his spirit. The virginal birth is the sign of his uniqueness and mysterious filiation. "The Holy Spirit will come upon you, and the power of the Most High will overshadow you; therefore the holy child to be born will be called Son of God." The term holy indicates exclusive belonging to God. It is one of the oldest expressions of the divinity of Jesus (Ac 3:14). Already in Gn 1:2, the Spirit of God hovered over the waters, about to perform the great work of creation; here that divine power overshadows Mary and is about to perform a new and wonderful creation, a conception wrought by the direct action of God.

The power of God overshadows Mary like the Shekinah, the cloud which covered with glory the meeting tent (Ex 40:34) and later the Jerusalem Temple (1 K 8:10), or like the cloud of glory at our Lord's Transfiguration (Lk 9:34). The cloud symbolized the gracious, efficacious presence of God to his people. The Holy Spirit miraculously formed and hallowed our Lord's human body and soul at his conception; descended upon him with an abiding unction at his baptism, consecrating him for his ministry; and brought about the mystical union of the ascended Christ with his people. The birth of Jesus is brought about by the coming of the Holy Spirit, or power of God, as the beginning of the Church's mission was to be effected by the bestowal of power on the disciples through the coming of the Holy Spirit upon them (Ac 1:8).

The angel ends his message by proclaiming the divine omnipotence: "nothing is impossible with God. And Mary said, 'Behold I am the handmaid of the Lord; let it be done to me according to your word.' " At these words the conception of the humanity of Jesus took place. More than humility there is question here of faith (1:45) and love; in the Bible to be the servant of God is a title of glory. Mary accepts but recognizes her human condition which remains unchanged. Her humble acceptance is manifested in profound adoration. The scene and its dialogue are surely worthy of the creator and the most perfect of his creatures. The mother of the Son of God is the servant of the Lord. The Incarnation of God is the occasion for the most profound adoration that ever went up to God from the heart of a human creature.

This sacred moment which marks the beginning of our

Lord's incarnate life should be contrasted with Gn 3:6. There the disobedience of a woman brought sin into the world; here the obedience of a woman brought salvation, reversing the effect of the fall. Mary is the second Eve: so second century Fathers loved to call her. Her obedience reverses Eve's disobedience. The only legitimate attitude of man to God is represented in her answer; and as always the divine purpose of God for man waits for man's assent and correspondence.

The spirit of adoration found in Luke's narrative of the Annunciation to Mary, appears also in that of the Visitation (1:39-56). The Magnificat, Mary's canticle of thanksgiving is the exterior expression of her praise and profound adoration. This beautiful lyric is presented as a meditation expressing deep personal emotions, experiences, and strong convictions. It is a very old hymn celebrating God's goodness to Israel. We can feel confident that whoever actually gave it its ultimate form, the poem really expresses Mary's mind.

The Magnificat reads like a triumph song of Israel (frequently pictured in the Old Testament as mother Zion e.g., Is 51:1-12) rejoicing at the birth of the greatest of her sons who will bring in what was promised to Abraham. It suggests to the reader that the real significance of Jesus is that he embodies in himself the mission of the old Israel.

Mary's song is rich in Old Testament reminiscences and allusions, particularly recalling the song of Hannah (1 S 2:1-10). It develops two characteristic Old Testament ideas: God comes to the help not of the rich and powerful but of the poor and simple; ever since Abraham received the promises, Israel has been God's favorite people. This glorious song of praise tells us more than anything else in the New Testament of the character of our Lord's mother, and of her spiritual fitness for her exalted dignity. She was one who diligently searched the Scriptures and was able to enter into their deepest spiritual meaning.

The deep reverence of Elizabeth at the presence of her young cousin is rooted in her realization of being in the presence of the mother of her Lord. Mary is attuned to this feeling and gives it free expression in her need to exalt God as much as she is able. Her basic feeling is that affirmed before Gabriel, a disposition of service. She sings of God the almighty, the holy one, the master of history through the ages, the God of Abraham, the protector of Israel, the just judge of individuals, of kings as well as of humble folk. Actually she is repeating the great themes of the adoring praise of the patriarchs, of Moses, and of the prophets. She makes her own the adoration of her country, of her people, of her Son, who is her God, and brings it to its summit, its highest point. Full of grace, the mother of God gives her adoration a perfection that no creature will ever equal.

The hymn is a meditation on the goodness of God and his saving deeds of mercy toward his people throughout history. It sings the personal gratitude of the mother of Jesus, then that of all God's people for the fulfillment of the covenant promises. The exultant praise of the holy mother, for the signal favor which God has shown her, is followed by a presentation of the character of God's kingdom as a moral revolution, and a reversal of all existing standards of goodness and greatness. The poem may be divided into three strophes. The first (46-50) expresses sentiments of joy and of praise of God's power, holiness, and mercy; it extols the fruits of faith and of lowly dependence on the merciful God. The second (51-53) gives a general principle: the goodness of God for the lowly; it insists on the great reversals of salvation history. The conclusion (54-55) gives homage to the fidelity of God who by his Son fulfills the promises he made to Abraham and his descendants; it interprets the events in the light of the Servant theology of the Old Testament.

The glory of the Magnificat lies in its public-spiritedness. After an expression of thankfulness for the unique divine favor shown to herself, Mary loses thought of herself in the wider thought of the fulfillment of the divine promise, long nourished through evil times in the heart of the "humble folk who do God's bidding" (Zp 2:3), constantly made sport of by the proud, the princes, the rich, but now at last coming to its triumph in Israel. It is a psalm of thanksgiving. Mary praises God for his goodness to her and to all men, in vindication of his way for the fulfillment of his promises. The ideas of the song are those of Old Testament piety. We might think that Jesus began his ministry with the echo of these feelings in his soul (Lk 4:18-19).

Elizabeth, as an inspired prophetess, greets Mary as the mother of her Lord, and is blessed for her acceptance in faith of God's promise; actually as more blessed than all women (42). Elizabeth calls Mary, "the mother of my Lord," giving to Jesus the title typical of early Christian adoration.

The fruit of Mary's faith and unselfish humility redounds to her everlasting glory. "Henceforth all generations will call me blessed" (48). She has become the pattern of womanhood and motherhood to the whole Christian world. Reverence to our Lord's mother has had its elevating effect on humanity. It is remarkable that one of whom we know practically nothing except her gentleness and her sorrow, should have exercised such a magnetic power upon the world, to elevate and purify the ideal of woman and soften the manners of men.

The poem closes with insistence on the manifestations of God's power, holiness, goodness and fidelity to his promises; and it links the fulfillment of the Messianic hope of Israel with the original covenant promise to Abraham. The past tenses indicate what God always is doing. A kingdom based on humility and love has entered into the world, more powerful than all earthly kingdoms, and destined to revolutionize them all. It is to the lowly and the hungry that the mercy of God has been shown; these were by now consecrated terms for the faithful clients of the Lord, in whom the people of God could be epitomized. Among these Mary takes a chief and culminating place.

No word of Mary concerning the birth of Jesus has been preserved for us, but twice (Lk 2:19, 51), after the visit of the shepherds at the end of the infancy narratives, we read that "Mary kept all these things, pondering them in her heart" a statement which underlines her quiet, reflective nature. Mary is rapt in awe and wonder. Luke presents reflective recollection as characteristic of Mary. The events of the infancy were the subject matter of her meditation.

Three great Christian claims about Jesus are revealed to the shepherds: that he is Savior, Christ (Messiah), and Lord. "To you is born this day in the city of David, a savior who is Christ, the Lord" (2:11). The sacred fear they experience when the glory of the Lord shone around them (9) prepared them to render homage "glorifying and praising God for all they had heard and seen" (20). This incident was the first that Mary treasured in her heart (19). The angels and the shepherds went away but Mary's immaculate adoration never ceased in her heart.

The angels sang a song of adoration. "A multitude of the heavenly host praised God saying: Glory to God in the highest, and on earth peace to men with whom he is pleased" (2:13-14). The angels proclaim the mystery of the Savior, Christ the Lord, the glory he gives to God, and the peace he brings to men. Peace in Bible thought means more than absence of strife. It is entire harmony of life, something which, in its perfection, only God has. But the good news of the gospel is that God intends human beings to have a life similar to his in its freedom and satisfaction. God's peace is God's alone, and, it is his favor to men to bring about in them a peace which has some resemblance to his own.

In Luke, everyman's gospel, Jesus is born in a stable and his birth is first announced to peasants, in token that the gospel is meant for the poor and ignorant, as well as for the rich and learned. In Matthew, the regal gospel, wise men from the east visit the infant. In Matthew's story of the Magi, the Gentiles join in Mary's and Joseph's adoration. "They fell down and worshipped him" (Mt 2:11). The homage of the Magi included something of religious worship; they must at least have understood that the child stood in unique relationship to God. They worshipped even though they would not have full understanding of the one who was God with us. Mary was touched by their reverence and the generosity of their gifts. In her heart she joined them and richly complemented their devotion.

The Magi brought to Jesus the most costly products of the countries in which they lived; such gifts were customary in the Orient as signs of homage. They point to the kingly rights of the child and to the worldwide acknowledgement that he is ultimately to receive. The Fathers see in the gifts of the Magi symbols of the royalty (gold), divinity (incense), and passion (myrrh) of Christ. The adoration of these wise men fulfills the Messianic prophecies of the homage paid by the nations to the God of Israel (Is 49:23).

The nativity scenes are essentially expressions of adoring love, the attitude of the primitive Christian Church towards its Head, an attitude which is a reality of the most precious kind. The infant Jesus is presented as not only human but divine; he constitutes a link between the world of history and the spiritual sphere which is the originating center of the creative process. The events recorded by Luke and Matthew as attending the birth of Jesus symbolize the sacredness of his personality, and the scope and quality of his mission.

Finally, Mary knew that the child she had conceived was divine. She was not fully enlightened but understood sufficiently well to accomplish her special vocation. Her fiat was essentially an act of adoring faith (Lk 1:45) which included in its object, the divinity of Christ, but seen in the darkness that is a necessary feature of faith.

MARY'S PIERCED HEART

Simeon foretold that a sword would pierce Mary's heart (Lk 2:35). Her first anguish was experienced at the loss of the boy Jesus at Jerusalem (Lk 2:48); anxiety also is in the background of Mt 12:46-50; but it is especially at the foot of the cross (Jn 19:26-27) that Simeon's prophecy was fulfilled. Mary shows us that Christian fellowship begins at the foot of the cross and is maintained by prayer and the Eucharistic breaking of the bread (Ac 1:14, 2:42).

Mary surely performed the ceremony of the presentation of Jesus in the Temple (Lk 2:22-38) in the spirit of adoration it supposes. All first-born were regarded as holy or consecrated to God (Ex 13:2, 12); the first-born of animals were sacrificed, but the first-born of men were redeemed when they were one month old, by the payment of five shekels (Nb 18:15). By buying back, symbolically her child from God, as all Jewish women did, Mary recognized God's absolute right on every creature. Her act, moreover, formalized and externalized what was and would remain always true, her son's consecration to God. For Luke this first cultual act of Jesus in the holy city has great importance. Throughout Luke's writings Jerusalem occupies a place of honor. It is where the paschal event will take place and is the point of departure of the Christian mission.

The old man Simeon may well be considered as the best of

the Old Testament welcoming the best in the New. The consolation of Israel he expects (Lk 2:25) is the salvation which the Messiah brings. His adoring praise (2:29-35) comes quite unexpected. He reveals to Mary a grandiose but terrible perspective which could not yet have been in her heart. Prophetically he thinks of the grown man, while her thoughts are concentrated on the child in her arms. Jesus' mission of light for the pagan nations will be accompanied by hostility and persecution even from his own people. The Messiah's mission will not be accomplished without suffering. He will meet with opposition, rebuke, and scorn. The child's coming will bring judgment as well as salvation, for men will be revealed as they really are in their hearts, and Mary herself will suffer anguish at the treatment meted out to her son.

"This child is destined to be the fall and rising of many in Israel, and a sign that will be opposed (and a sword will pierce you to the heart also) that the thoughts of many hearts may be laid bare" (Lk 2:34-35). These figures make important points: the coming of the Messiah means decision and judgment and suffering. A parenthesis associates Mary with the sad and painful aspect of the career of her son. True daughter of Sion, Mary will carry in her own life the painful destiny of her people. With her son she will be in the center of contradiction where hearts will be revealed, for or against the Lord and his Messiah. This prophecy was fulfilled especially when Mary saw her son rejected, condemned, insulted, scourged, and crucified. Her adoration receives an orientation leading to a mysterious holocaust. The sword that will pierce her soul confers on her a victimal character. Here was new food for meditation. It was in the Temple where the Old Testament sacrifices were offered that the shadow of the sacrifice of Calvary already marked the heart of the victim's mother.

Every year the holy family went up to Jerusalem for the feast of Passover. This was the occasion for Mary to renew her spirit of adoration. She passed unnoticed among the pilgrims, but God surely saw in the holy family a beginning of that new heartfelt religion of which the prophets had spoken and which pleased him more than all sacrifices. Mary's first anguish was experienced at the time of Passover when Jesus was twelve years old and stayed on in Jerusalem without the knowledge of his parents. Her sorrow would be much more soul-rending at the time of another Passover when Jesus died on Calvary.

Mary's reproach to Jesus is the spontaneous expression of the pain she had suffered: "Son, why have you done this to us? Your father and I have been searching for you in great anxiety" (2:48). The mother, as always in history, stands for the claims of home and family. Jesus' answer gives the first manifestation of his conscience of being God's Son. From an early age Jesus was aware of an intimate filial relationship to God, and of the divine mission that lay before him. "How is it that you sought me? Did you not know that I must be in my Father's house?" (2:49). The text could also be translated, "about my Father's business." In any case, in the presence of Joseph, Jesus asserts that God is his Father and claims relations with him which take precedence over those of his human family. Jesus is asserting his personal duty to his Father, and in the interest of that duty, an absolute independence from creatures. The first word of Jesus in Luke's gospel, as also his last (23:46) mentions his heavenly Father.

His parents, however, did not understand what he meant (2:50). They knew that he was predestined of God, but they might still fail to understand this and much else in his conduct and words. The mystery of Jesus' filiation surpasses human intelligence, even the most open to God's word. One of a parent's greatest sorrows afflicts Mary: not to understand her own child. Jesus' mysterious answer gave Mary fresh food for thought and prayer.

Separation from his family was one aspect of the cross that Jesus had to bear. The passage dealing with the true kinsmen of Jesus (Mt 12:46-50) gives us an inkling of how this separation affected his mother, Mary. She apparently had heard the common report about him and with a mother's anxiety she thought that overwork was the cause and came with some relatives to take him home to rest. Jesus answers that his work must be done at all costs. "Whoever does the will of my Father in heaven is my brother and sister and mother" (Mt 12:50). The relationship that counts is not physical, but moral and spiritual. It is to belong with him to the family of the one Father in heaven and to do his will. The claims of physical relationship come after those of spiritual. Jesus does not reject the bonds of kinship but raises all who believe in him to an intimacy of kinship. The ties that bind the spiritual family are even deeper and dearer than family ties, and are based upon obedience to God's will. This is the germ truth out of which grew the early Church. Luke puts it another way: "My mother and my brothers are those who hear the word of God and do it" (8:21). Read this against the background of the infancy narrative, where Mary ponders the word. This verse might point to Mary as the supreme example of the receptive bearer.

As time went by Jesus became more and more engrossed in his Father's affairs. Mary knew about the coming passion at least when our Lord announced it to his disciples. Formerly Abraham had been told that he should offer his son in sacrifice. As the public life progressed, the thought of the sacrifice of her son to his Father must have occupied more and more the heart of our blessed Lady. She must have known that no substitution was to be expected here. Abraham had walked three days to reach the place of sacrifice. During the three years of the public life, the adoring soul of Mary, seeing the hatred of the enemies of Jesus constantly growing, prepared herself for the ascent of Calvary.

Mary's stand at the foot of the cross of her dying son remains the most pathetic scene in human history. Who can fathom the depths of suffering, love, and adoration of the hearts of Jesus and Mary? The father of believers, Abraham, did not have to sacrifice his son Isaac. The mother of Christians assisted at the immolation of hers, a most agonizing experience.

Nothing escapes the attention of a mother. Mary saw the wounds of his flagellation, the nails that pierced his hands and his feet. She heard his moans and groans, his gasps, his death rattle. What is more she joined in the sentiments of his soul submerged in sorrow before the sin of the world, people's refusal to love and adore. Her son's torments were her torture; her heart bled with his wounds. Now were fulfilled Simeon's words.

Jesus chose a terrible expiation to impress on us the horrible nature of man's rejection of God. Jesus on the cross in a spirit of total homage and expiation, offered himself to God in the complete holocaust of his whole being. Mary saw it all and understood it well. Silently Jesus was asking his mother to join in his sacrifice, to enter into the views of his Father, and unite herself to his offering. And Mary answered with all the fibers of her being to God's expectation. A very pure, very loving, very heart-rending adoration went up to God, the mother and her son living together the summit of human history. At the foot of the cross the mother of dolors could not give us a more provocative, contagious example of observance of the first commandment.

John alone mentions the presence of Jesus' mother on Calvary and her relationship to the beloved disciple. The expression "the disciple whom he loved" explains why Jesus committed the two to one another. Jesus was not so much taken up with a sense of his sufferings as to forget his friends, all whose concerns he bore in his heart. A great depth of meaning is indicated by means of very few words composed with the utmost restraint. There is no hint of emotional aspects. Apparently Jesus is making sure that his death will not leave his mother desolate, and so he arranges that his filial duty should be done by this disciple. His mother loses her son, but she gains a new son, one who most fully knows the mind of the son whom she has lost. "When Jesus saw his mother and the disciple whom he loved standing near, he said to his mother, 'Woman, behold your son!' Then he said to the disciple, 'Behold your mother!' And from that hour the disciple took her to his own home" (Jn 19:26-27).

This act of filial piety characteristic of Jesus is also a sign of the spiritual motherhood of Mary, the new Eve, the mother of the faithful. The passage indicates Jesus' real humanity and concern for human values but above all for spiritual values. The evangelist sees more in this than the gesture of a dutiful son: namely, a declaration that Mary is the spiritual mother of all the believing community here represented by the faithful disciple. The beloved disciple bears the character of the true Christian who is in the heart of Christ as Christ is in the heart of God (Jn

1:18, 13:23). It is altogether fitting that this proclamation be made at the moment of Jesus' expiration, the beginning of the saving work of the Church through the power of the Spirit. Notice that John also has a role, that of providing for Mary. A mutual causality is involved. Thus in his final act on earth Jesus entrusts to those who love him and believe in him the care of his Church.

The theological meaning of the passage is suggested by the revelatory formula, "Behold." The sonship and motherhood proclaimed from the cross are of value for God's plan and are related to what is accomplished in the elevation of Jesus on the cross. This action of Jesus completes the work that the Father has given Jesus to do, and fulfills the Scriptures. There is something more profound than filial care, the starting point. The beloved disciple symbolizes the Christian. Mary is the new Eve bringing to life a new people. The imagery flows over into the idea of the Church who brings forth children modeled after Jesus and the relationship of loving care that must bind children to their mother. Jesus provides for those who believe in him a communal context of mutual love in which they will live after he is gone. Jesus' mother and the beloved disciple are established in a new relationship representative of that which binds the Church and the Christian.

The resurrection of our Lord infused Mary's adoration with an indescribable and definitive joy. Mary shared the sufferings of her crucified son, but also the joy and triumph of his resurrection. Mary's pondering adoration of the mystery of Christ's resurrection and ascension has been passed on to the Church which ultimately has s l i m a x   of   Mary's   complete assimilation of the Paschal mystery in her glorious Assumption into heaven.

The unique moment of Jesus' death on the cross was not to be without tomorrow. On the preceding evening Jesus had made its prolongation possible throughout the centuries. In the Eucharist, in a bloodless manner, his sacrifice would be perpetuated and applied to the redeemed. It was Mary's mission to show her children the sure way to salvation: in spite of all our crosses, to love and adore to the end, in union with the divine adoring victim himself the adorable Lord. Christian fellowship begins at the foot of the cross and is maintained in prayer and the breaking of the Eucharistic bread (Ac 1:14, 2:42).

The last time Mary is mentioned in Scripture she is in the Cenacle, in prayer with the nucleus of the primitive Church, expecting the coming of the Holy Spirit. "All these with one accord devoted themselves to prayer, together with the women and Mary, the mother of Jesus" (Ac 1:14). The expectancy of the great event of Pentecost was naturally expressed by a spirit of prayer which identified the yearnings of the waiting company with God's declared purpose. These prayers in the upper room fulfilled Jesus' own conditions for effective prayer (Mt 18:19). Mary's central presence is noted before she disappears from the pages of Holy Writ. It is fitting that she should have shared in the experiences of the birth of the spiritual body of Christ.

Prayer is the setting for the major events of the gospel in Luke. This is the prayer of expectation of the coming of the Spirit parallel to the prayer of Jesus at his baptism. "With one accord" is a favorite expression of Luke's, serving to emphasize the unity of the Christian community. Those closest to Jesus are involved in the mission of the Church. Mary is mentioned to distinguish her from the other women, and to link the beginning of the Acts with the opening of Luke's first volume.

There are remarkable parallels between the story of the infancy of Christ and that of the infancy of the Church. In particular, the descent of the Holy Spirit on Mary at the Annunciation, whereby she was made the type and instrument of definitive salvation, preludes his descent on Pentecost. By her fiat Mary opened the era of grace. It is fitting, then, that she should be found in the upper room, preparing by her prayers the descent of the Holy Spirit, the birth of the Church. Here Luke suggests what John made explicit, Mary's maternal role as the new Zion, engendering the Messianic people of God.

WORSHIP IN SPIRIT AND IN TRUTH

Our Lord's encounter with Satan climaxed in a temptation to idolatry (Mt 4:8-11). Jesus, as Son of Man is the point of contact, the true mediator between heaven and earth (Jn 1:49-51), the focus of worship in spirit and in truth (Jn 4:21-24).

Our Lord's retreat in the desert of Judah and his trial there is the beginning of his public life. It should not surprise us that after his baptism Jesus sought the solitude of the Judean wilderness where he could be alone with himself and his God, in order to meditate on his Messianic mission. He acted under a strong spiritual impulse to spend his time in fasting and prayer which were always connected with Israel's practice of religion.

Our Lord's encounter with Satan climaxed in a temptation to idolatry. "The devil took him to a very high mountain and showed him in a moment of time, all the kingdoms of the world and their splendor and said to him, 'All this authority and their glory I will give you, for it has been delivered to me, and I give it to whom I will. If then you will fall down and worship me, it shall be yours.' Then Jesus replied, 'Begone Satan, for it is written, You shall worship the Lord your God and him only shall you serve.' Then the devil departed biding his time" (Mt 4:8-11, Lk 4:5-8).

It is not surprising that this temptation to idolatry runs through all the centuries of human history. To the permanent basic will of the Creator is opposed the permanent refusal of

Satan, his adversary, who exerts untiring efforts to draw men into his revolt. It is natural that Satan should face Jesus, a solitary penitent, a mysterious personality, with this decisive question. In the gospel tradition the devil is waging an unsuccessful effort to wrest final control of the creation from God; the movement of history is the conflict between the kingdom of God and the kingdom of Satan. The devil is pictured as trying to trick Jesus into submitting to his ways. Jesus is asked to acknowledge subservience to the devil. He answers that he will offer worship to God alone and serve only the coming of God's kingdom.

The temptation is to sacrifice God's design of a humble and suffering Messiah, for a world empire. The temptation parallels that of the Israelites (Dt 6:10-11), who were tempted upon entering the promised land to forget God before the blandishments of worldly prosperity and to turn to idolatry. This is often equated with devil worship in late Jewish tradition. This is a temptation to secular Messianism, the use of political power to accomplish the ends of the Messianic mission. The quotation of Dt 6:13 places secular Messianism on the level of worship of false gods. It expresses the basic attitude of worship which every man should have toward God. Our Lord's answer echoes the words heard by Moses in the wilderness of Horeb. At this key moment of history, before the beginning of Christ's public mission, it is the precept of adoration that rings out.

This is the culminating temptation to the soul, to be dissatisfied with God himself and to embark on a program of unscrupulous manipulation to achieve one's ends. Jesus is asked to sacrifice and deny the perfect love which worships and serves God alone. To obtain an earthly rule over the world, he must yield to the tempter and worship him. But Christ's kingdom is not of this world. It is a spiritual kingdom of obedience to God's sovereignty. The world is conceived as under Satan's power until God's kingdom is realized. Satan is ruler of the world not in the sense that the world is irremediably evil, but in the sense that by sin the world and its ways have become subject to his direction. Whoever chooses as his own the route of worldly wisdom, rather than the ends foreordained by God, has thereby chosen the false gods of this world, as St. Paul protested to the Corinthians (1 Cor 2:6-16).

This temptation may be related to the promise of world-wide dominion given to the Davidic king in Ps 2:8, which continues the first part of the declaration of the voice from heaven at Christ's baptism (Lk 3:22). If the Messianic sovereignty is asked of God (Ps 2:8) it must be won by the way of the cross. The devil's dominion over the world is one of the key ideas of John's gospel. Although the ruler of this world (Jn 14:30) may have been in temporary occupation, the authority and glory that he offered had already been promised to the Messiah and were his for the asking (Ps 2:8). This promise must have been much in the mind of Jesus since the baptismal voice had quoted the preceding words, "You are my beloved son." That which was God's to give he would not accept from another. Later as he missioned his apostles he states, "All authority in heaven and on earth has been given to me" (Mt 28:18).

Being the Son of God, the observance of the first commandment ultimately would have to include Jesus Christ himself in its object. On this point Jewish monotheism presented a formidable obstacle. The providence of God worked its way with great prudence. Jesus himself became constantly more conscious of his divine personality which was discreetly and progressively manifested during the public life until it appeared in its definitive glorious light after the resurrection with the help of the Holy Spirit.

Nathanael recognizes Jesus as the Messiah: "Rabbi, you are the Son of God, you are the King of Israel" (Jn 1:49). Jesus directs him discreetly to the adoring attitude of Jacob by alluding to the patriarch's famous dream. "You shall see greater things than that. Amen, amen I say to you, you will see heaven open and the angels of God ascending and descending upon the Son of Man" (Jn 1:50-51). In these first words to his disciples Jesus establishes a link with the dawn of revelation and its realization in his person. The scene he evokes and applies to himself has adoration as its conclusion.

Jacob's vision of God's angels mediating between heaven and earth provides this image about the Son of Man. What Jacob

saw in vision (Gn 28:12) is now a reality in Jesus. Because of
Jesus' presence on earth, the heavens are opened and the
communication with God announced in Jacob's dream becomes
a permanent reality for believers.

Jacob's dream will be fully realized when the Son of Man is
lifted up (Jn 3:14) on the cross, as the symbol of his lifting up in
the resurrection and ascension. "Greater things" refer to the
unfolding of Jesus' glory throughout the gospel. The point of
departure for this saying is the promise that the disciples will see
Jesus risen and glorified as the Messianic king. The series of
signs to follow in the gospel, reaching a climax in the supreme
sign of the cross, *is* the vision of the opened heavens, an
unveiling in history, that is, in the life, death, and resurrection of
Jesus, of the glory of the eternal God.

The vision means that Jesus as Son of Man has become the
locus of divine glory, the point of contact between heaven and
earth. The use of the motif of the angels suggests the
inauguration of vital contact between heaven and earth. The
point is that Jesus is on earth and the revelation of his glory as
Son of Man does not have to wait for his exaltation to heaven.
The angels go up and down on the Son of Man who forms a
ladder between heaven and earth. In Jesus will be granted the
revelation of God's glory. The man Jesus is the place of
revelation, the place over which the heavens are opened. The
historical Jesus is the one true mediator between God and men.
Jesus himself is the ladder connecting heaven and earth. Within
his soul there was a continuous celestial traffic. Jesus is the type
or center of mankind on earth, quickened by heavenly powers to
do God's will. In the light of his resurrection we might think also
of our prayers taken up to God through Christ, and the answer
sent back in him, seeing that he is ever present to his Church (Mt
28:20).

Heaven is now open for continuous communication with
men; the representative of whom is Christ. It is remarkable that
the title, Son of Man, is substituted for Nathanael's Son of God.
The link between heaven and earth depends as much on the
mediator's human character as on the divine. As contrasted with
Son of God, the title Son of Man emphasizes the reality of

Christ's human nature; as with son of David, the universality of his nature and message; as with sons of men, his perfect representation of human nature and realizing its original ideal. It designates our Lord as the ideal or representative man, the man in whom human nature was most fully and deeply realized, and who was the most complete exponent of its capacities, warm and broad in his sympathies, ready to minister and suffer for others, sharing to the full the needs and deprivations which are the common lot of humanity, but conscious at the same time of the dignity and greatness of human nature, and destined ultimately to exalt it to unexampled majesty and glory.

Son of Man is a title Jesus used of himself. It stresses his humanity yet suggests glory because of its use in Dn 7:13. Its use is characteristic of Jesus to speak in such a way as to oblige his hearers to determine their own personal attitudes toward him as part of the process of understanding his words. In applying the title to himself, Jesus designated himself as the very embodiment of salvation: a man who yet lives with the glory of God, a mediator in whom heaven and earth meet. The Son of Man is a messenger from heaven to make God known (Jn 3:13). He is a heavenly figure who enters the earthly realm yet whose abode is ever in heaven. His appearance on earth is but part of a journey which ultimately will take him back into heaven.

Jesus is the Son of Man, the representative or heavenly man, who, as the figure of the ascending and descending angel shows, forms the place of mediation between heaven and earth. This representation of the unique mediatorship of Jesus depends on Gn 28:12, but also on the traditional picture of the Son of Man coming in glory with the angels (Mk 8:38). Not at the last day only, but always, to the eye of faith, Jesus united God and man. The rest of John's gospel with its signs is intended to confirm this belief.

Our Lord makes his conversation with the Samaritan woman the occasion for revealing the true object of worship and the true approach to God. He draws a sublime picture of the religion of the future. "Jesus said to her, Woman, believe me, the hour is coming when neither on this mountain nor in Jerusalem will you worship the Father. You worship what you do not know; we worship what we know, for salvation is from the Jews. But the hour is coming, and now is, when the true worshippers will worship the Father in spirit and in truth, for such the Father seeks to worship him. God is spirit, and those who worship him must worship in spirit and in truth" (Jn 4:21-24). On Mount Gerizim, an ancient holy place, the Samaritans had built a rival to the Jerusalem Temple. They included among the ten commandments the obligation to worship on Mount Gerizim. They accepted Yahweh as the true God, but knew little about him. Holding only the first five books of the Old Testament to be inspired scripture, they denied themselves the revelation given through prophet and psalmist.

The contrast between worship in Jerusalem or on Gerizim and worship in spirit and in truth is part of the familiar Johannine dualism between the earthly and heavenly, from below and from above, flesh and spirit. In Jn 2:21 it was Jesus himself who was to take the place of the Temple, and here it is the Spirit given by Jesus that is to animate the worship that replaces worship in the Temple. Notice that it is a question of worshiping the Father in Spirit. God can be worshiped as Father only by those who possess the Spirit that makes them God's children (Rm 8:15-16), the Spirit by which God begets them from above (Jn 3:5). This spirit raises men above the earthly level, the level of the flesh, and enables them to worship God properly.

Jesus means that the place of worship is not of primary importance. The aspect which gives genuineness to worship is spiritual not local. The true worship of the future will be inspired by the right thoughts of God, which flowed out of the depth of Jesus' own personal knowledge of God as divine Father. When once the full meaning of God's Fatherhood is known, there will no longer be separation and intolerance between his children. Local religious rivalries will yield to a universal worship of the Father, a worship that will be spiritual, inward and real.

Worship to be genuine must be offered in spirit and in truth. In spirit it is opposed to all that is carnal, material, and of this earth earthly. Limitations of time and place are not wrong, but they are not of the essence of religion, and become wrong when they are mistaken for the essence of religion. In truth, that it is in harmony with the nature and will of God. In the sphere of the intellect, this means recognition of his presence and omniscience; in the sphere of action, conformity to his absolute holiness.

Such worship is in virtue of the new birth and in the light of the revelation of truth in Christ. Spirit denotes both the supernatural essence of the Christian life, and the means, that is, the Holy Spirit through whom it is imparted. There can be no separation of the two; the former follows the acceptance of the latter. The Spirit who makes a new creature of man is also the inspiring principle of the new worship of God. This worship is in truth because it is the only worship that meets the conditions revealed by God through Jesus. The place where God and man are united is neither Zion nor Gerizim, but the person of Jesus (2:21). The contrast is not between the forms and ceremonies of the Temple and the spiritual worship of the Church, but between worship apart from Jesus, and worship within the filial response to the Father, soon to be revealed in the passion. This is worship in spirit, for it is the response of the man who, by belief in Jesus, is open to the influence of the spirit (Jn 3:6). It is also in truth, for it accords with the truth revealed in Jesus (1:17).

Spirit and truth are coupled. In Jn 17:17-19 truth is an agent of consecration and sanctification, and thus also enables man to worship God properly. The Johannine themes of Spirit and truth intertwine: Jesus is the truth (14:6) in the sense that he reveals God's truth to men (8:45); the Spirit is the Spirit of Jesus and is the Spirit of truth (14:17) who is to guide men in the truth.

The basic reason why true worship must be spiritual is found in God's nature: "God is spirit." The point is that like requires like: the Father demands such worshipers because he is himself spirit. Through their birth from above (Jn 3:3, 5) men have the Spirit and worship in spirit and in truth is the outcome.

When we think of God as spirit we should think not of an infinite spiritual essence in repose but of an infinite spiritual essence in action. God is spirit does not define so much his immaterial essence as his life-giving activity as sender of the Spirit into the hearts of believers. The insistence is not on the immaterial nature of God but on the fact that he is the source of the spiritual gifts which transcend all created things. God is spirit and as such unlimited in time and space: a supernatural energy communicating itself to man and lifting worship into reality. *God is spirit* is a character description. Worship expresses a relationship between God and man. This should be a spiritual relationship, because God is spirit and therefore men too must have the Spirit. This, according to John's theology, is precisely what has been established in Jesus. It follows that when Jesus says that the new worship is coming now, and that men of the Spirit are required, he is making a Messianic claim and demanding personal allegiance to himself. Worship in spirit and in truth is the very essence of our awareness of membership in the living Christ.

4

THE TRANSFIGURATION

Our Lord's miracles provoked reactions of reverence and awe: after a miraculous catch of fish (Lk 5:8-9); at the resurrection of the son of the widow of Naim (Lk 7:16); at the calming of the storm (Mk 4:35-41); at his walking on the water (Mt 14:32). Peter's confession is a profession of adoring faith (Mt 16:16-17); it is corroborated by our Lord's Transfiguration (Mt 17:5-6).

By his miracles Jesus provoked very significant spontaneous reactions. The definitive vocation of the first four apostles, after a miraculous catch of fishes, is preceded by the homage of Peter. "He fell at the knees of Jesus saying: 'Leave me Lord, I am a sinful man.' For he and all his companions were astonished at the catch of fish they had made. Jesus said to Simon, 'Do not be afraid; henceforth you will be catching men' " (Lk 5:8-9). Peter feels that he is before a holy, powerful personality. Jesus accepts Peter's devotion and calls him to his service.

Luke's longer account of this episode is focused on Simon Peter. He shows that the call took place only after Jesus had won the friendship of Peter and revealed his heavenly power to him. Although Peter, as an experienced fisherman, knew that there was little likelihood of a catch, he was already sufficiently impressed by Jesus to obey his command. When the full manifestation of Jesus' power came to him, he was overcome with a profound sense of fear and unworthiness in the presence of one who displayed heavenly power. Although the great, unexpected catch is not clearly described as a miracle, Peter sees in Jesus' guidance a more than human power, and responds by personal self-judgment. The change from Master (5) to Lord, reflects Peter's religious fear before the awesome presence of the divine. "Fear not" is a phrase usually associated with a theophany.

Our Lord revealed himself to Peter along the line of his calling, and catching fish is made symbolic of the Christian mission. Peter, the leader of the twelve is called to be a fisher of men, and the success which is to attend his mission is foreshadowed in the draft of fishes which he secured under the direction of Jesus. The realized nearness of the divine power generates a sense of terror and sinfulness. But it passes into the will of surrender and renunciation: "They left everything and followed him" (Lk 5:11).

If there be any difference of degree where there is miraculous, the resurrection of the son of the widow of Naim was one of the greatest miracles of our Lord. It was a miracle of compassion. Jesus, meeting a funeral cortege is moved at the grief of the widowed mother at the death of her only son. One could suspect a very personal reaction of Jesus, thinking of himself and his mother. The result again is reverential fear. "Fear seized them all; and they glorified God saying, 'A great prophet has arisen among us, and God has visited his people' " (Lk 7:16). Jesus, for this crowd, is just a prophet, but his power is remarkable. By his intermediary it is God who intervenes.

From 7:13 on, Luke refers to Jesus by the post-resurrection title, the Lord, strictly reserved for Yahweh himself. Kyrios (Lord) is the Greek translation for the divine name, Yahweh. It is very appropriately used on this occasion when Jesus appears clothed with exalted power over life and death, by which he becomes the object of the Church's faith and worship.

Fear indicates recognition of the limits of human understanding and power before God. Fear is the normal reaction to a manifestation of divine power, quickly followed by praise of God. The people see in Jesus a great prophet, like Elijah and Elisha who also raised people from the dead. His deed is a merciful intervention of God in favor of his people. The Old Testament often speaks of the visits of God for his gracious interventions or for his punishments.

The miracle of the calming of the storm (Mk 4:35-41) again provokes reverence and awe. On this occasion the disciples go a bit further; they wonder about the personality of Jesus. "And they were afraid and marveled saying to one another, 'Who then is this that he commands even wind and water, and they obey him?' " (Lk 8:25). Their question is understandable. The prophets and the Psalms speak of Yahweh as the one who commands wind and sea. The answer is that God rules the waves and his power was at work in Jesus. The rest of the gospel is taken up with the revelation of this answer. The point of the story is to reveal to the disciples one of the mysteries of the kingdom: the power of Jesus. Power over nature must mean that he has divine power and authority; indeed he does the very thing that God can do (Ps 107:25).

The incident illustrates first the divine authority of Jesus over the forces of nature; he is superior even to a storm which caused experienced fishermen to panic with alarm. It also shows his true and real humanity, for he had evidently toiled up to and almost beyond the limit of his strength. On no other occasion is his sleep mentioned. The sleep of Jesus, however, is not only the sleep of exhaustion but also the sleep of trust in the Lord. The intent of the narrative is to show that God's authority at work through Christ is victorious not only over human disease and disorder, but also over the destructive powers of nature as well. Man is called to a life of faith and trust under such authority. The disciples' lack of faith was the cause of their fear, and the strengthening of their faith was a greater miracle than the stilling of the storm. Christian thought has seen in the ship, the symbol of the Church.

After the multiplication of the loaves, Jesus walks on the water and climbs in the boat with Peter, and all are amazed: "And as they got into the boat, the wind ceased. And those in the boat worshiped him saying, 'Truly you are the Son of God' " (Mt 14:32). Jesus is greater than a political leader (Jn 6:15), he is

Lord of the elements. As Jesus in a veiled way had manifested himself as Messiah by feeding the multitudes, so he now manifests himself openly to the disciples in the storm, and they hail him as the Son of God. Jesus is represented here as Lord of all the forces of life and death. Triumphant over all difficulties and dangers, he sees men's distress from afar, comes to them, enters their boat, and the wind ceases. The disciples felt more or less clearly that this one must stand in wonderful relation to him of whom the psalmist wrote (Ps 77:19).

Jesus shares the power of God as the Lord of the mysteries of creation. A subsidiary theme is the assurance of the Lord's presence with his own even in the darkest hour. Symbolically interpreted, the episode represents the struggles of the soul and of the Church with the troubles of the world, and the succor which Christ gives in the darkest hour of temptation and adversity. The disciples in the boat represent the Church, from which Jesus is never far, even when the situation is threatening, and he is invisible. The presence of Christ puts an immediate end to danger and conflict. Finally, the attempt of Peter to walk on the water illustrates both the power of faith and the way fear threatens faith.

Peter's confession at Caesarea-Philippi is the crisis-point of the teaching of Jesus, and the watershed which divides the synoptic gospel record in two. It is a profession of adoring faith. "You are the Christ, the Son of the living God." And Jesus answered him, "Blessed are you Simon Bar-Jona! For it was not flesh and blood that revealed this to you but my Father who is in heaven" (Mt 16:16-17). In his parallel passage Mark has, "You are Christ;" and Luke says, "the Christ of God." The scene in Jn 6:69 recalls the confession at Caesarea; there Peter says, "You are the Holy One of God." He is God's envoy, his elect, his consecrated emissary, and united to him in an eminent manner. The Johannine thought is not so much of personal holiness as of consecration for his task.

Matthew's addition contributes a certain verbal solemnity but does not really alter the Messianic sense. "Sons of the living God" is a title used by the prophet Hosea (2:1) for the eschatological Israel, a text quoted by Paul in Rm 9:26; its use here is doubtless in the same sense, that is, applicable pre-eminently to the Messiah of Israel. Peter sees summed up in Jesus the realization of Israel's salvation hope.

Peter's confession is not made in the terms of the other answer: it is not some say, we say, or I say, but "You are." It is the expression of an inward conviction wrought by God's spirit. Understanding spiritual realities involves God's disclosure. It was God himself who led Peter to faith through his experience of the Lord; and his blessedness did not rest only upon the faith itself, but upon the divine purpose manifested in bringing him to it. The expression "flesh and blood" indicates man, emphasizing his material limited nature as opposed to that of the spirit world. Peter has received a divine revelation but the context (Mt 16:22-23) shows that he did not comprehend it completely. Post-resurrection faith will understand better that Jesus' relation to God is unique and decisive; that his filial relation to God is unmatched, and his mission for the salvation of men un-paralleled.

At the Transfiguration, "a bright cloud overshadowed them, and a voice from the cloud said, 'This is my beloved Son, with whom I am well pleased; listen to him.' When the disciples heard this they fell on their faces and were filled with awe" (Mt 17:5-6). In the Old Testament the cloud was the sign of the divine presence. It covered Sinai and later the Tabernacle. This high point in the education of the apostles, inserted them in the great millenary tradition of adoration recalled by the presence of Moses and Elijah, who attest that Jesus fulfills the promises of the Old Testament.

Matthew sees the Transfiguration as a proclamation of Jesus as the new Moses. Mark sees it as a glorious epiphany of the hidden Messiah, according to the dominant theme of his gospel; transitory as it is, this scene of glory manifests who Jesus really is and will soon be, though he will know for a while the humiliations of the suffering servant. Luke insists on the coming passion for which the disciples are being prepared. The Transfiguration is a personal experience of Jesus during a fervent and transforming prayer; he is enlightened by heaven on his exodus, his departure and his coming death which will be accomplished at Jerusalem, the city that kills the prophets.

The Transfiguration in all the synoptic gospels follows Peter's confession and is a foretaste of the glory of the Messiah. There are connecting links back to the baptism, and forward to the resurrection, exaltation, and parousia of Christ. What the baptism was to the ministry as a whole, that the Transfiguration was to the second and concluding part of it. This is a repetition of the baptism scene for the benefit of the disciples. And just as the baptism brought to Jesus an experimental awareness of his awesome ministry, so now he learns the full extent of his suffering.

The position of the Transfiguration after the confession of Peter and the prediction of the passion, makes it a reaffirmation of the Messiahship of Jesus and of the Messianic glory in which he will be revealed. He is no less a Messiah when his Messianic glory is hidden in the incarnation and passion. The Transfiguration counterbalances the prediction of the passion by affording the disciples insight into the divine glory which Jesus possesses. His glory will overcome his death and that of his disciples. The heavenly voice prepares the disciples to understand that in the divine plan, Jesus must die before his Messianic glory is made manifest. The purpose of the heavenly revelation is to show that the passion is something decreed by God. It also serves to corroborate Peter's profession of faith and is a means of strengthening the disciples for the road that lies ahead.

At his baptism the heavenly voice indicated Jesus as God's servant; here it presents him also as prophet whom all should listen to. The true significance is presented at the scene of the Father's voice. This assured the disciples that the Jesus whom they confessed to be the Messiah was indeed Son of God, was indeed their Messiah, not despite his coming passion but because of it. They were to obey him and him alone. "Listen to him," this is the all important phrase in the scene. Hear him especially in what he will say of his suffering and death, the way to glory and salvation. The same words were the divine answer to the prayer of Jesus at his baptism. If the words are here repeated, we may conclude that they have been the very heart of Jesus' prayer on the mountain. It was as he prayed that Jesus was transfigured. It was in the act of communion with his Father that the divine glory flowed out into visible brightness. Prayer has a transforming, transfiguring force. There is a depth of meaning in the simple words so often spoken: let us pray.

The Transfiguration played an important part in the formation of the disciples and profoundly impressed the early Church (2 P 1:16-18). The scene takes its full meaning in the perspective of Christ's glorious resurrection which it anticipates. It was a visible anticipation of the eschatological glory of the Son of Man, even as the life of grace is an invisible anticipation of the glory of the children of God.

5

THE GREATEST COMMANDMENT

Jesus repeats the Old Testament teaching which states positively and practically the first command-ment as love for God, and he insists on hearfelt religion. He stresses the ethical consequences of the Christian religion (Mk 12:31-46). The apostolic preaching followed closely in his footsteps (Rm 13:9-10, Jm 1:26-27).

Already in Dt 6:4-5 the first commandment had been restated in a positive form and specified practically as love for God. The prophets also, since Amos (5:21-27), rejecting cultic formalism, insisted on hearfelt religion. Our Lord repeats this teaching while stressing the ethical consequences of the Christian religion. The apostolic religion followed closely in his footsteps (Rm 13:9-10, Jm 1026-27).

Jesus answers the question, "What is the greatest commandment of all?" (Mk 12:18-33) by putting in the forefront the supreme contribution of Judaism to the history of religion in the world, faith in one, only God; and interpreting the whole duty of man to the one God and to his fellow-men, in terms of the single verb, to love. The question for Luke (10:26) concerns eternal life ("What shall I do to inherit eternal life?") rather than the foremost of the commandments and was thus of interest to Hellenistic readers who knew little about scribes and cared less about the Jewish law. That keeping the law was essential to eternal life was already suggested in the Old Testament (Dt 30:15-20).

Both the great commandments in their original meaning rest upon the special covenant relation of God to Israel. Jesus shows that love is at the heart of the Old Testament. The two commandments are summed up in one word, love, first toward God then toward man; love conceived not as an emotional sentiment but as an active principle embracing the entire personality. In modern times men lay great emphasis on love to man, or philanthropy, but are inclined to forget the requirement of love to God. Our Lord links the two and gives primacy to the latter. What is new in Our Lord's teaching is how love manifests itself, and who is a man's neighbor. In the expansion of man's horizon of obligation, as well as in the mode of life that accompanied and exemplified his teaching, lay the revolutionary, new element of Jesus' ministry.

The answer of Jesus penetrates into the very heart of the whole law as an expression of God's will. "You shall love the Lord your God with all your heart, and with all your soul, and with all your mind, and with all your strength. This is the greatest commandment. And the second is like it, You shall love your neighbor as yourself. On these two commandments depend all the law and the prophets" (Mt 22:37-40). Jesus quotes two texts of the Law that forms the foundation of the new morality of the gospel. The commandments are quoted from Dt 6:5 and Lv 19:18. The text of Dt 6:5 forms part of the Shema, the Jewish profession of faith. Mark quotes Dt 6:4 the introductory verse: "Listen, O Israel, the Lord our God, the Lord is one." The novelty consists in placing Lv 19:18 on the same level of importance as Dt 6:5.

We are directed to love God as ours. To love God as ours is to love him because he is our creator, owner, and ruler, and to conduct ourselves to him as ours, with obedience to him and dependence on him. We must love him as made ours by covenant: that is the foundation of this "your" God. The proper act of love being complacency, contentment, satisfaction, good is its proper object. Now God being good infinitely, originally, and eternally, is to be loved in the first place, and nothing beside him but what is loved for him. Love is the first thing that God demands of us, and therefore the first and greatest thing that we should devote to him.

The commandment to love God begins by stressing the unity of Godhead, and then insists on the worship of God with the whole personality. God's choice of Israel was not a privilege without a corresponding duty. To love includes three things: to admire, approve, recognize the worth of, or take pleasure in the person who is loved; to desire to possess love in return; and to do all things possible to show that one cares. All our powers of will and mind are to be given to God. We need not exactly distinguish between heart, soul and mind. The great point is that love is not primarily a matter of emotion but of total self-devotion. Taken together heart, soul, mind, and strength indicate the totality of one's being. The heart was considered the center and seat of all physical and spiritual life, and the meaning is that one must love God with all one's thoughts, passions, desires, appetites, purposes, and endeavors. It requires man to rest his whole existence upon God, to trust him without reserve, to hate and despise all evil, to get rid of all hindrances and even to love his enemies.

He loves God with all his heart who loves nothing in comparison of him, and nothing but in reference to him, who is ready to give up, do, or suffer anything in order to please and glorify him. He loves God with all his soul, or rather with all his life, who is ready to give up his life itself for his sake, to endure all sorts of torments, and to be deprived of all kinds of comfort, rather than dishonor God; who employs life with all its comforts and conveniences to glorify God in, by, and through all. He loves God with all his mind who applies himself to know God and his holy will; who receives with submission, gratitude, and pleasure the sacred truths which God has revealed to man. He loves God with all his strength who exerts all the powers of his body and soul in the service of God; who for the glory of his Maker spares neither labor nor cost; who sacrifices his time, body, health, ease, for the honor of God, his divine Master; who employs in his service all his goods, talents, power, credit, authority and influence.

A commandment might be first without being the greatest, but love of God is both: not only of necessity, extension, or actuality, but also of nature, order, time and evidence. It is of profound importance to recognize in this connection that although the second commandment is like the first in that it demands the development and exercise of the spirit of love, yet it comes second not first. The resemblance concerns not identity but the nature and equal importance of the two commandments. In the Christian life two things must be remembered: Christian conduct has two foci. Though the love of God and the love of man are intimately connected, we should think of them separately as well as together. Devotion to God, however real, in no way relieves us of the duty of serving men; and the service of men, however devoted, in no way relieves us of the duty of loving God. The love of God comes first since our debt to him is far the greater of the two. Moreover, love of God, if we understand anything of his character, always brings love of men in its train; while love for men has not the same power to bring about love for God.

Love of man can exist without conscious love of God, but it is the love of God which alone can universalize and moralize and spiritualize the love of man. In short, the love of God is the only secure and permanent basis for a love of man which strives to secure the well-being, both temporal and eternal, of the object of its love. A love of man which is not based on the love of God is always liable to succumb to the temptation of self-gratification, self-interest, and sentimentality. The love of our neighbor springs from the love of God as its source; it is found in the love of God as its principle, pattern, and end; and the love of God is found in the love of our neighbor as its effect, representation, and infallible mark. This love of our neighbor is a love of equity, charity, succor, and benevolence. We owe our neighbor what we have a right to expect from him. This is the religion of Jesus.   Just as Jesus' first great commandment sums up the first table of the Decalogue, which deals with man's duties to God, so "You shall love your neighbor as yourself" sums up the second table, man's duties to man. But the word second does not mean that love of one's neighbor is of secondary importance (1

Jn 4:20). And this love is not a matter of vague sentimentality but a matter of actual cases in everyday life. This love requires to put oneself into the other person's place so as to see his situation with all its anxieties, hopes, fears, defeats, aspirations, success and promise, through the other person's eyes. To love one's neighbor is to practice the Golden Rule in both its negative and its positive forms. Love must become ever more strict with itself, more aggressive in forgiveness, more intense after the manner of Jesus' love.

The law contains many ways of applying to life the principle of love; good works have value only as acts of love of God and of neighbor. The two commandments are like the first and last link of a chain; all the intermediate ones depend on them. True religion begins and ends in love to God and man. These are the two grand links that unite God to man, man to his fellows, and men again to God. All law is fulfilled in one word and that is love. All obedience begins in the affections and nothing is done right, that is not done there first. Man is a creature cut out for love; the law written in his heart is a law of love.

Observe the weight and greatness of these commandments. They are the sum of all that was written in men's hearts by nature, of the written Mosaic Law, and of all the preaching and writing of the prophets. Rituals and ceremonials must give way to these, as must all spiritual gifts, for love is the more excellent way. Love is the spirit that animates the law, the cement that holds it together; it is the root and spring of all other duties, the compendium of the whole Bible, not only of the law and the prophets, but of the gospel too, only supposing this love to be the fruit of faith, and that we love God in Christ, and our neighbor for his sake. All hangs on these two commandments as the effect does both to its efficient cause and its final cause.

Jesus puts personal devotion, to God and to man, right in front; and the student of the law agrees (Mk 12:22-24). The scribe repeats the substance of Jesus' words adding the primacy of love over even ritual sacrifice. In line with 1 S 15:22 and the Old Testament tradition, he draws the important conclusion that love of God and love of one's neighbor as oneself are "far more important than any holocaust or sacrifice." The whole Jewish sacrificial system is nothing compared with this. Without in any way belittling the importance of offering sacrifices, he comments that to love God and one's neighbor is a higher duty still. Love is a more necessary and important duty than the offering of the most noble and costly sacrifices.

Paul (Rm 13:10) sees the love of our fellow-men as the fulfillment of the law as far as human duties are concerned. Love not only contains every single commandment of God to serve men, but surpasses them all because it sets no bounds to goodness. It is love that keeps the law; and the law is the yardstick of love. This love is no feigned emotion but an active continual attitude fostered by the Spirit, by which the love of God in Christ, having once been poured out in the Christian's heart, proceeds through his whole life and beyond him to every man he meets.

In the famous last judgment scene (Mt 25:31-46) men are judged according to their works of mercy. The parable should be understood as Jesus' farewell speech, his testament to his disciples. Like the last discourse in John, the theme is love based on the identity of Jesus with men. The presence or absence of practical love for one's neighbor is the determining factor in the judgment passed upon all men. The evasion that this does not include man's duties toward God is met in verses 40-45: Jesus identifies himself with those to whom the service is given or refused. Jesus is not merely reiterating the venerable prophetic tradition that God is less impressed by what we do for him than by what we do for one another (Is 58:3-7). He not only singles out the poor and the wretched as objects of his special solicitude, he identifies himself with them. Before he had taught that the total dimension of neighbor is man (Lk 10:29-37). Now he teaches that he who serves man serves Christ.

James, following the teaching of the prophets and of Jesus, makes it clear that mere formal ritual observance is worthless; that love of neighbor and interior moral purity belong to the essence of religion. "If anyone thinks he is religious and does not bridle his tongue, he is self-deceived, his worship is pointless. Religion that is pure and undefiled before God the Father is this: to visit orphans and widows in their affliction, and to keep oneself unstained from the world" (Jm 1:26-27). The spiritual worship agreeable to God takes the concrete form of right conduct and the service of the defenseless and oppressed. True religion is defined not as doctrine or knowledge or ritual, but as moral action. Religion consists of more than devotional exercises. Punctiliousness in outward observance is not the sum total of religion. God is Father and he demands above all the worship of love towards his needy children, and of purity from the world's wickedness. If we know God as our Father, we shall be concerned about his children.

The pure religion that is acceptable to God is marked by practical and personal purity. In order that the service and worship of God may be acceptable, the man who offers it must show practical love and sympathy, and strive after personal holiness. Ritual purity and spotlessness was universally required in ancient religions. These qualities, usually ritual and cultic, are aptly applied to the practice of external works of charity and to inner integrity. No complete definition of religion is attempted here, but only an emphasis on certain aspects without which the practice of religion has no meaning.

The best order of cultus is not to be found in cultus but in practice. James' definition refers rather to the effects of pure religion than to its nature. This is not the secularist's paradise. James is not thinking of religion without God. He is manifesting the spirit of protest. Moral duty is being neglected and so the ethical is put forward as the true ritual. Both worship and morality are essential expressions of Christian faith (Heb 10:23-25). Christianity is not merely a code of ethics. Organized worship, the outward cultus, is essential, but worship is to show its fruits in morality. The standard is the divine character; it is that which is before our God and Father.

Religion does not consist in speculations and theological notions, however just and orthodox; not in forms or modes of worship, however scriptural and necessary to be observed; not in warmth of affection or ardor of zeal during worship. True religion consists in repentance towards God, faith in our Lord Jesus Christ; in justification by faith and regeneration by the influence of the divine Spirit; in the possession and exercise of that love for God and all mankind which is the source of the various branches of practical religion, of mercy as well as of justice towards men, and of holiness towards God.

"If you really fulfill the royal law, according to the scripture, 'You shall love your neighbor as yourself,' you do well" (Jm 2:8). Evangelical love is a master principle, well-called the royal law, being one which comprehends all duties and embraces all objects. Royal is used to signify that it is of general concern, is suitable to all and necessary for all. The royal law, like the perfect law (1:25) refers to the whole law of God revealed in the Old Testament and interpreted by Jesus and in Christian tradition. It is kingly as coming from God, the king, to be observed by the subjects of his kingdom; it has royal rank over the other commandments.

6

THE CRUCIAL QUESTION

People were impressed by the authority of our Lord's teaching (Jn 7:46, Mt 7:28-29). The man born blind worshiped Jesus (Jn 9:38) but the Sanhedrin refused to recognize him (Mt 26:63-66). After the resurrection his disciples gave him the homage of their adoration (Mt 28:9, Jn 20:28, Lk 24:51-52). The crucial question in each of the four gospels is the identity of Jesus of Nazareth.

Before Christ's miracles and the authority of his speech, a sacred reverence, more or less close to adoration, was experienced by those who approached him. The fact that even the Temple guards were impressed by Jesus' teaching to the extent of failing to execute their commission of arresting him, underlines the obduracy of his enemies. They are impervious to the word of God. The police of the chief priests and Pharisees reported, "No man ever spoke like this man" (Jn 7:46). They were impressed and realized that Jesus' teaching had won support, and feared a dangerous situation.

"The crowds were astonished at his teaching for he taught them as one who had authority and not as their scribes" (Mt 7:28-29). The scribes, the official interpreters of the written and oral law of Judaism, appealed to legal precedent to lend authority to their interpretation. But Jesus did not appeal to authorities; he had authority. Our Lord did not reject the authority of the law but he spoke as having authority from God to enunciate and enforce the principles that underlay the law, and to carry them into a new expression and a more complete correspondence to the will of God in the coming kingdom. "You have heard . . . but I say to you" (Mt 5:21 22). Jesus spoke in his own name. This places him within the Messianic realm of fulfillment and power.

He taught as one who had his authority directly from God. His own life with God was the deepest source from which all his words sprang, and this gave his teaching not only its inimitable charm, but also its penetrating and imperishable power, so that his words shall not pass away (Mt 24:35). The words of Jesus thrilled the hearts of his hearers and have moved the world and are still gripping us because they are "spirit and life." They captivate us because of their inner truth. The real secret of their power lies in the fact that they are the words of him who is in the bosom of the Father and declares the Father unto us (Jn 1:18). Whenever we are confronted with the words of Jesus, we stand in the presence of God himself.

The teaching of Jesus was the product of his own direct insight into God's nature and will. What he taught was creative. When he saw that the men of old had been wrong he said so (Mt 5:22, 28). He was a prophet, and a prophet's business is to criticize ancient beliefs and practices to see where they are out of line with God's will for the present and the future. Hence men were astonished because he taught with authority, as one who has the power not only to teach but to do what he teaches. His teaching was from God (Jn 8:28-29). The original and creative element in it made it natural, picturesque, and clear, and the common people heard him gladly.

After the cure of the epileptic demoniac, St. Luke notes, "All were astonished at the majesty of God" (9:43). Stress is put that the miracle is accomplished by the power of God, a power which Jesus possesses and which eludes the disciples.

The man born blind, after his cure, tells Jesus: "Lord, I believe; and he worshiped him" (Jn 9:38). Jesus discloses his identity: the man believes and worships. There can be little doubt that John intends us to see here the spiritual counterpart of the physical cure which has already been performed. The man has believed in the light and become a son of light (Jn 12:36). It is faith which worships, that is, devotion and dedication of the whole being. The man's faith was necessarily imperfect but wholehearted.

His attitude contrasts with that of those who oppose Jesus. Before curing him Jesus had declared in the Temple: "Amen, amen I say to you, before Abraham was, I am. So they took up stones to throw at him; but Jesus hid himself, and went out of the temple" (Jn 8:58-59). The "I am" is the divine name, a claim to pre-existence and oneness with God. The claim of Jesus to live on the divine plane is for the Jews blasphemy, for which the penalty is stoning. In Christ's claim the contrast is between an existence begun by birth and an absolute existence, denoting timeless existence. The pre-existent Christ preceded Abraham. This is one of Jesus' most emphatic affirmations concerning his divine nature.

His opponents do not change their attitude on the day of the feast of Dedication when Jesus in the Temple, claims that he is the Christ and equal to the Father. "The Father and I are one." The Jews took up stones again to stone him . . . "We stone you because being man, you make yourself God" (Jn 10:30-33). The Son's power is none other than the Father's. The context shows that this is the primary meaning but the statement is deliberately undefined and hints at a more comprehensive and a profounder unity. The Jews do not miss the implication; they sense a claim to Godhead. The moral relationships of love and obedience are primary, but essential relationship is also implied, and it is this that enrages the Jewish audience.

The Father and Son are one in mind, will and action, a unity which presupposes the even more essential one of which John speaks in 1:1. "If the power is the same, so is the being" (Chrysostom). It is a unity which is conceived first and foremost in ethical terms. A further explanation waits to be given in verse 38, and that is the ideal of mutual indwelling: "The Father is in me and I am in the Father." This suggests that the unity of the Father and the Son is no passing and temporary concurrence of mind and purpose, but is essential and permanent. John's attempt to express what he means in metaphysical terms comes in the Prologue (1:1-3).

Thus during our Lord's earthly life, the dividing line between his disciples and his enemies was the crucial question of his divinity and of adoration. During his trial before the Sanhedrin, Jesus clearly maintained his position. "The high priest said to him, 'I adjure you by the living God, tell us if you are the Christ, the Son of God.' Jesus said to him, 'You have said so. But I tell you, hereafter you will see the Son of Man seated at the right hand of the Power and coming on the clouds of heaven.' " The judgment of the tribunal was, "He has blasphemed, he deserves death" (Mt 26:63-66).

The blasphemy lay not in Jesus' claim to be Messiah but in his claim to divine rank. A simple carpenter of Nazareth, the Son of Man sitting at the right hand of God and coming again on the clouds of heaven, what a monstrous blasphemy! Between adoration and the death sentence, the supreme tribunal chose condemnation. Refusal to acknowledge Jesus as God's Son decided his fate. At the end of Jesus' mission the first commandment occupies the first place. It is impossible to go further both in its violation and in its observance. The infamous execution of his sentence was his means, as man, of giving his Father the unique, outstanding act of adoration.

The question of the high priest probably did not go further than Messiaship. At this critical moment Jesus unequivocally acknowledges, as he had acknowledged to his intimates (Mt 16:16), that he is the Messiah. But he goes much further and reveals himself not as the human Messiah of traditional expectation, but as the Lord of Ps 110 and the mysterious personage of heavenly origin whom Daniel had seen in vision. Henceforth the Jews will not see him except in his glory which will be manifest first in the victory of the resurrection and subsequently in the victory of the Church.

After the resurrection the apostles and the disciples present our Lord the homage of their total adoration. "Jesus met the women and greeted them, and they came up and took hold of his feet and worshiped him" (Mt 28:9). Jesus greets them in his familiar voice, dispels their fear and confirms the message of the angel. Holding his feet is an action which expressed deep reverence mingled with strong affection. They worshiped now with more than merely human reverence. It is noticeable that Jesus never repelled any mark of reverence shown to him, however, profound.

The doubting Thomas is won over by our Lord's kindness and makes his profession of faith: "My Lord and my God!" (Jn 20:28). The Jesus who has appeared to Thomas is a Jesus who has been lifted up in the crucifixion, resurrection, and exaltation at his Father's right, the Jesus who has received from the Father the glory that he had with him before the world existed (17:5), and now Thomas has the faith to acknowledge this. He has penetrated beyond the miraculous aspect of the appearance and has seen what the resurrection reveals about Jesus. My Lord refers to the Jesus of history, and my God is a theological evaluation of his person: "It is Jesus and he is divine." Thomas makes it clear that one may address Jesus in the same language in which Israel addressed Yahweh (Ps 35:23, Rv 4:11). Lord and God are two Old Testament titles for God. Jesus' response accepts as valid Thomas' understanding of what has happened (Jn 20:29).

At a single bound Thomas rose from the lowest depths of faith to its very pinnacle. His confession is the supreme Christological pronouncement of the fourth gospel. The wheel of the gospel has come full circle. The note struck in the beginning rings out in its ending. This final response is the believer's answer to the initial proclamation, "The Word was God" (1:1). It provides a fitting conclusion to John's record of the path of faith. Paradoxically it is the doubter who makes the most complete affirmation of Christ's nature to be found on the lips of anyone in the gospel. We are brought back to the first line of the gospel, as Thomas speaks the language that became the common Christian confession concerning Jesus (Ac 2:36).

It should be noted, however, that the account of Thomas' doubt and ensuing faith invites belief which is not dependent on physical evidence. John's type of faith, like Mary's, was deeper and surer. With only Thomases there could be no church, for the church is dependent upon the testimony of faith. Confessions of faith on which the church is founded (Mt 16:16) are the testimony of those who have laid hold of the inner life of Jesus in that report which has come down to us in the Christian brotherhood. True faith in the risen Lord is not really based on the evidence of the physical eye or ear, but on experience, attested to by thousands upon thousands down the centuries, of those who have testified, "Christ is alive, and I have known the secret of his presence."

Mark's gospel, the first to be written, begins with a summary of the Christian faith: "The beginning of the gospel about Jesus Christ, the Son of God" (1:1). This title revealed by God (1:11, 9:7), divulged by the demons (3:11, 5:7), is kept by Mark as a Messianic secret. Jesus accepts it during his trial (14:61-62) and a pagan centurion pronounces it after Jesus' death (15:39). Note how nearly this summary of our earliest gospel corresponds to the symbol, found in many of the earliest Christian sepulchral inscriptions, of a fish; the fish being chosen as consisting in Greek (ichthys) of the initial letters of the five words, "Jesus Christ, Son of God, Savior."

At the end of Luke's gospel, Jesus about to leave this earth. "As he blessed them, he withdrew from them and was carried up to heaven. They worshiped him and returned to Jerusalem with great joy; and they were continually in the Temple praising God" (Lk 24:51-52). Luke's gospel ends where it started, in the Temple; its last words are of joy and praise. An act of adoration marks the end of our Lord's mission on earth. It echoes the other act of adoration which marked the beginning of revelation and Abraham's entry into the promised land. Right through salvation history God always asks that his creatures manifest absolute dependence on him. It is God's Son who in our name answered best this demand, and it is that Son whom God presents at the same time for our adoration.

Worship is still the most universal way in which the church recognizes the divinity of Christ. The apostles give us the example. The risen Christ, having accomplished his work, provoked their adoration before sending them on their mission.

Their act of adoration fits in the great tradition of the patriarchs, of Moses, and of the prophets. Like them it is after having adored that they set out to work fulfilling their own vocation.

The crucial question in each of the four gospels is the identity of Jesus of Nazareth. Matthew emphasizes the authoritative teaching of Jesus, presenting him as the Messianic king. Mark lays his emphasis on the deeds of Jesus, and places before his readers a gospel of action. Luke presents Jesus the man, and John the Son of God.

Mark presents Christ as the Isaian Servant of God. Several features suggest this, such as the absence of genealogy and the predominance of deeds over teaching. Nevertheless, as Mark asserts in his very first verse, the lowly Servant is also beyond doubt the Son of God, whose ministry was authenticated by mighty works. The divine attestation of this at the baptism and transfiguration (1:11, 9:7) is unequivocal. This is the most fundamental element in Mark's Christology.

The two metaphors of 10:45 and 14:24 indicate the two main lines of Mark's teaching. Our Lord's life laid down sacrificially is a "ransom for many" and "the blood of the covenant." The former effects deliverance from sin and judgment, while the latter provides covenant relationship and fellowship between God and man.

For Luke the keynote of the ministry of Jesus is the gospel of salvation. Two of Luke's favorite words are preach the gospel and salvation. The former sums up the character of the ministry of Jesus; his teaching, healing, and acts of compassion were all part of the proclamation of the good news that God was visiting his people. The latter word sums up the content of Jesus' message; it is contained in a nutshell in 19:10, "The Son of Man is come to seek and save that which was lost."

Luke has reserved for his second volume the story of the Church, but already in his gospel, he has indicated the characteristic of that period. It is the time during which Jesus, having ascended to heaven, sits at the right hand of God. His disciples must continue his work of preaching the gospel of salvation to all nations, and they are enabled to do this by the power of the same Holy Spirit who equipped Jesus for his ministry, and by calling upon God in prayer, just as Jesus prayed.

John has many characteristic features, particularly in his presentation of Christ. His major purpose was theological and indeed Christological. His focus of attention was on Messiahship and Sonship. To him Jesus was the fulfiller of all the Messianic hopes of the Jewish people. But Jesus as Son of God is far more characteristic of John's gospel. Many times Jesus brings out his own filial relationship with the Father. Whereas this aspect is not absent from the synoptics, it is specifically noteworthy in John because of the frequent occurrence of the term Son without further description.

The most characteristic feature of the synoptic gospel is Jesus as Son of Man, and although it is not quite so prominent in John, it is still basic to his presentation. It is the Son of Man who not only reveals the Father but who will be lifted up (3:13, 14). John's exalted Christology is never allowed to detract from the perfect humanity of Jesus.

Jesus himself was the Word of God. He did not write his gospel on paper but on the tablets of the human heart, with the ink of his Spirit (2 Cor 3:3). The books of the New Testament are the product of the Spirit of Jesus in the lives of his followers.

7

LORD AND MESSIAH

Peter preaches the resurrection of Jesus on Pentecost day (Ac 2:36), to the crowd in Solomon's portico after the cure of the lame man (3:13-16), and before the Sanhedrin (4:11-12). Stephen affirms before the Sanhedrin that the prophecy Jesus made before them has been fulfilled (7:55-56). In his address in the house of Cornelius Peter repeats the essential of his message to the Sanhedrin (10:34-43).

The apostolate of the apostles begins on the day of Pentecost. Peter, in his address to the crowd, preaches the resurrection of Jesus. "Let all the house of Israel therefore know for sure that God has made him both Lord and Messiah, this Jesus whom you crucified" (Ac 2:36). They have not recognized him when he was performing miracles. They must now acknowledge their dependence on him and be baptized in his name if they want to be saved.

What Peter's hearers have done to Jesus is set in striking contrast to what God did to him making him both Lord, sovereign, having all authority (Mt 28:18) and worthy of universal worship (Ph 2:5-10); and Christ, the Savior in whom all God's promises of salvation have been fulfilled. Peter's sermon gives a summary of the gospel as the first preachers proclaimed it (1 Cor 15:3-4). It is a model sermon in its form. In its matter it is even more so, focusing the truths about Jesus so as to make an irresistible appeal to the consciences of his hearers.

Prophecy and contemporary fact are welded into a strong argument which is the basis of Peter's appeal. God has constituted Jesus, the crucified one, both Lord and Messiah for his people, despite their tragic rebellion. Jesus has been constituted the Lord of whom Ps 110 speaks, and the Messiah to whom Ps 16 refers. The resurrection is the act of God which David predicted (Ac 2:25-35). Ps 16:6-11 speaks of one whose soul would not see corruption. Moreover, God swore an oath to David that one of his descendants would occupy his throne, and David recognized the Christ as his Lord (Ps 110:1). Jesus is one who was raised and whom God has made both Lord and Christ. By his resurrection and exaltation at God's right, Jesus gets to enjoy the divine prerogatives which he had by right since his birth. The true meaning of the death and resurrection of Jesus is that he is the divinely enthroned Messianic king of Israel.

After the miraculous cure of the lame man, wrought by Peter in the name of Jesus (Ac 3:1-10), Peter addressed the crowd in Solomon's portico (11-16). He develops the full significance of the miracle (11-16), and concludes with an appeal to repent and accept Jesus as Christ (17-26). "God glorified his servant Jesus . . . You denied the Holy and Righteous One, and asked for a murderer to be granted to you, and killed the Author of life whom God raised from the dead. To this we are witnesses. And it is the name of Jesus which, through faith in it, has strengthened the limbs of this man whom you see and know" (3:13-16). The details of the healing stress the hopeless lameness of the beggar and the material poverty of the apostles. But the name of Jesus was invoked, and by its power the man's feet and ankles were strengthened so, that he could enter the Temple courtyard leaping and praising God. Solomon's porch was a colonnade or cloister on the east of the Temple area. It became the regular meeting place of the Christian community (Ac 5:12). Jesus often walked there and spoke to a less patient audience than Peter had (Jn 10:23).

The cure serves as an occasion for presenting the power of Jesus, in whom alone salvation is to be found. After an introduction Peter contrasts the rejection of Jesus by the Jews with the honor shown to him by God in raising him from the dead, to which the apostles bear witness, and by granting this cure to a believer in his name. Peter's discourse takes its starting point in the amazement of the people. It is designed to show that it is the power of the name of Jesus alone which has made the lame man strong. This is because Jesus, though rejected and killed, has been vindicated and glorified by God. His suffering was really in accordance with God's plan made known by the prophets. The ancient promises of God to his covenant people are fulfilled in Jesus, and to that people the blessing of repentance is now offered. This is the principal summary, given us by Luke, of the verbal proclamation of the gospel to Israel, accompanying and interpreting the acted sign of healing. The people are challenged in the very heart of their religion, the Temple itself.

The general theme of the discourse is that the work of healing proves the abiding presence and power of Jesus. The titles applied to him all serve to bring out the truth of his Messiahship. Thus he is the Holy and Righteous One. Both terms have their roots far back in the Old Testament. They characterize Jesus as Messiah, emphasizing his sinlessness and extraordinary religious dignity, which are placed in sharp contrast with the guilt of those who rejected him in favor of Barabbas. Yahweh is above all, holy and righteous. Israel as God's people is called to be holy and righteous. The Messiah must possess both these qualities in the highest degree. He sums up in his person the character and vocation of Israel.

Jesus is the source of Messianic benefits, the prince, leader, originator, founder of our faith. He is the author of life as being raised from the dead; the one who leads his subjects to full life by imparting his own life to them The miracle was wrought by the authority of the name of Jesus, to which corresponds the faith of the patient, as in the gospel's miracles. There it was faith in Jesus in person; now it is faith in his name, that is, his continuing and present power and authority. As the risen Savior is the efficient cause of this miracle of healing, so the faith of the lame man is the instrumental cause, symbolic of the way in which perfect soundness and complete salvation can be attained by all men.

The doctrine on Christ contained in these verses reflects the prophecies of the suffering servant of Isaiah, rejected of men but glorified by God. These prophecies are a major source for the Christology of Acts. The early chapters of the book especially, manifest the joy of the understanding that the crowning event of Jesus' passion and resurrection manifest him as Messiah, not only suffering (4:24-30), but also triumphant, inaugurating the new age of the Spirit. Thus he accomplishes the promises to the fathers and fulfills the hope of Israel. But besides this Messiah-Christology Acts contains also a clear though implicit realization that Jesus enjoys divine powers and prerogatives. His divinity is shown in a way far more forceful to the Semitic mentality than mere prediction. He is invoked by the title Kyrios (Lord) reserved for God in the Old Testament. It is by calling on the name of Jesus that men are cured (3:16) and are to be saved (2:21), as in the original passage of Joel, it is by calling on the name of God. "Those who call on the name of Jesus" (9:14) becomes indeed a designation of Christians. This phrase is itself a hint of Jesus' divinity recalling as it does the Old Testament blessing by calling on the name of Yahweh.

The Christology of the period is especially revealed by the names applied to the Savior: servant, holy one, righteous one, author of life, prophet, Lord's anointed. Each title focuses Messianic prophecy fully on the person of Jesus of Nazareth. At this stage there is no reference to the pre-incarnation Son and creator as in Ph 2:6-11 and Jn 1:1-3.

Before the Sanhedrin, Peter comes back to the same theme and concludes categorically: "This is the stone which was rejected by you builders, but which has become the keystone. And there is salvation in no one else, for there is no other name under heaven given among men by which we can be saved" (Ac 4:11-12). The name Jesus means God saves. Peter again witnessed to the death and resurrection of Jesus. The crucifixion is the act of men; the resurrection is the accomplishment of God. Christ's power extends beyond healing a lame man to giving salvation to the whole world. Indeed no other means of salvation is possible. The apostle uses a beautiful gradation from the temporal deliverance which has been wrought for the poor cripple by Christ's power, to that of a much nobler and more important kind which is wrought by Jesus for sinful souls.

The stone rejected by the builders has mysteriously become the keystone in the building of the Church. This passage from Ps 118 already applied by Jesus to himself (Mk 12:10-11) became one of the common places of early Christian apologetics. In its original context it applied to Israel. Israel, which the heathen builders of the world's great empires rejected and despised, was nevertheless destined to play the chief part in the world's history. The text was easily transferred to the Messiah in whom the destiny and purpose of Israel was summed up.

Stephen's discourse before the Sanhedrin is a summary of salvation history. His face shining with celestial light (Ac 6:15), he spoke in his own defense. He underlines the infidelities of Israel climaxed by the murder of Jesus. In conclusion, "Full of the Holy Spirit he gazed into heaven and saw the glory of God, and Jesus standing at the right hand of God; and he said, I see the heavens opened, and the Son of man standing at the right hand of God" (Ac 7:55-56). His stoning is his punishment for his adoring profession of faith. His vision is to be related to his transfiguration (6:15).

Stephen affirms to the Sanhedrin that the prophecy Jesus made before them has been fulfilled. Many members of the Sanhedrin must have been reminded of the words of Jesus himself (Mk 14:62) which drew their verdict of blasphemy. The claim to see Jesus exalted and sharing the glory of God was, of course, blasphemous in the ears of the Sanhedrin. Jesus rises from the throne on which he is represented as eternally sitting (Mt 26:64), to succor the martyr in his extremity (Jb 16:19), and to welcome his soul into bliss. It is important to observe not only that Stephen prays to Jesus (Ac 7:59) but also the character of his prayer. While Jesus himself had commended his spirit to the Father, Stephen commends his to Jesus, who in effect is treated as divine.

At Caesarea before the centurion, Cornelius, Peter repeats the essential of his message to the Sanhedrin: Jesus is risen and God has established him judge of the living and of the dead. He must then be honored and be believed in, according to the testimony of the prophets. "The truth I have come to realize is that God shows no partiality, but that anybody of any nationality who fears God and does what is right is acceptable to him . . . Jesus Christ is Lord of all men . . . God anointed Jesus of Nazareth with the Holy Spirit and with power, and because God was with him, Jesus went about doing good and curing all who had fallen into the power of the devil . . . God raised him on the third day and made him manifest . . . And he commanded us to preach to the people and to testify that he is the one ordained by God to be judge of the living and the dead. To him all the prophets bear this witness: that every one who believes in him receives forgiveness of sins through his name" (Ac 10:34-43). Cornelius was a member of the class referred to by Luke as God-fearers, who attached themselves to the Jewish religion without becoming full converts. When Peter entered his house and began to proclaim the divine action in the cross and resurrection of Christ, a further proof of divine guidance was afforded in the sudden possession of the gentile household by the Holy Spirit, manifested by the same outward signs as on the day of Pentecost (10:44-46).

This last great discourse of Peter in Acts is the classic proclamation of the gospel to the Gentiles. It sums up the gospel, beginning with the baptism of John and ending with the statement that Christ is judge. It gives a resume of Jesus' ministry which is very close to the synoptic presentation of the gospel. The problem of social relations between Christians converted from Judaism and Christians converted from paganism underlies the narrative. The revelation of his choice of Israel to be his people does not mean that God withholds his divine favor from other men. To us this is a truism, but it was a revolutionary thought to Peter.

What makes a person acceptable to God is not ritual purity or impurity but the fear of the Lord, righteousness, and still more deeply, faith in Jesus which purifies the heart of both Jew and pagan (Ac 15:9). God accepts from every nation those whose manner of life is like that of the devout Cornelius. Peter is not, as the words are sometimes understood, preaching a salvation by each one following his own religion or sense of right, but is declaring that caste, racial or color differences do not stand before God.

The apostolic preaching to the Jews appealed to their Messianic hope, while the appeal to the Gentiles stressed the coming divine judgment. This role will be exercised by the risen Jesus, precisely as Kyrios. Thus the risen Christ fulfills the role of the triumphant Son of Man (Lk 22:69). By raising Jesus, God has solemnly invested him as supreme judge; to proclaim the resurrection is therefore to invite men to repentance. The content of the gospel is forgiveness of sins through faith in Jesus. The Old Testament prophets testify to this, their witness confirming the apostolic preaching. The chief Old Testament prophecy promising remission of sins through Christ is Is 53. This forgiveness is open to all men and not only to Jews.

After the conversion of the pagans, a rather important problem presented itself: must circumcision and the observance of the Mosaic Law be imposed on pagan converts? The council held at Jerusalem declared: "It has seemed good to the Holy Spirit and to us, to lay upon you no burden beyond these essentials: that you abstain from food sacrificed to idols, from blood, from the meat of strangled animals, and from fornication" (Ac 15:28-29). Thus the condemnation of idolatry figures as a basic consideration of the Jerusalem assembly. It is significant that three of these four interdictions deal with the first commandment. To eat idol-meats implies sharing in sacrilegious worship. Blood symbolizes life, and that belongs to God alone. The severity with which the law forbids its use (Lv 1:5) explains the Jews' reluctance to dispense pagans from this prohibition. As blood remains in strangled animals, this is part of the prohibition for blood. The reference is to meat not ritually butchered.

The observancce of these rules would make possible table fellowship for Hellenistic Jews with law abiding Jewish-Christians. The inspiration of the Holy Spirit is unhesitatingly claimed for the Church's decision. The mind of the Spirit finds expression through the counsels of a Spirit-filled Church.

8

A HOLY PRIESTHOOD

The Christian life is a life of holiness (1 P 1:15-21), a rebirth effected by acceptance of the gospel message (1 P 1:22-25). 1 P 2:4-10 sets forth the origin, nature, and function of the Church. 2 P 1:1:4 describes the plenitude of our new life in Christ.

The apostles took up the message of Christian holiness and adoration. Recalling the divinity of Jesus, Peter exhorts his readers to fidelity to their Lord, especially in time of trial. The living hope of the Christian demands from him a new way of life, a holiness showing itself in obedience (1 P 1:14), fear of God (17), and sincere love of the brethren (22). Such a life is based on the holiness of God himself (15:16), on reverence for him as Father (17), on the redemption wrought by the blood of Christ (18-19), and on the rebirth effected by acceptance of the gospel preaching (23-25).

"Be holy in all you do since it is the Holy One who has called you, and scripture says, Be holy for I am holy . . . You know that you were ransomed from the futile ways inherited from your fathers, not with perishable things like gold and silver, but with the precious blood of Christ, like that of a lamb without blemish. He was predestined before the foundation of the world but was made manifest at the end of the times for your sake. Through him you have faith in God, who raised him from the dead and gave him glory, so that you would have faith and hope in God" (1 P 1:15-21).

The standard for Christian living is holiness of character and conduct. The new Israel, as the old, must be holy. This holiness is encouraged by hope (13), enforced by the character of God (14-17), and reinforced by the sacrifice of Christ (18-21). Holiness means dedication to God's service. The covenant relationship was the foundation of the holiness expected of Israel as a dedicated people set apart for the service of Yahweh. The meaning of holiness in terms of human behavior was, of course, made plain in the life of Jesus (Jn 1:18).

Redemption through Christ was not a sudden whim of God, but was planned before the foundation of the world; it was according to the eternal plan of the Father who thus consecrated his new people of believers. The mention of blood refers to the poured out, or spilled blood, as in ceremonial sacrifices. The central thought in redemption is liberation from captivity rather than of payment of a price. Christ is the true Paschal Lamb, the true expiatory victim, the true convenant victim; the Eucharist, as the Christian Paschal rite, fulfills these Old Testament images.

The Christian is born anew by the creative word of God. Man is frail, but God's word that works in him abides forever. "By your obedience to the truth you have sanctified your souls, to love sincerely like brothers. With a pure heart earnestly love one another. You have been born anew, not of perishable seed but of imperishable: the living and abiding word of God. . . That word is the good news which was preached to you" (1 P 1:22-25). Faith is obedience to the truth, not truth in the philosophical sense, but God's revealed message. Faith supposes adherence of the intelligence and submission to God's plan.

The equivalence between the word of God and a seed recalls the parable of the sower (Mt 13:3-9). Seed of life, the word of God is the principle of our divine rebirth, and gives us the possibility of acting according to God's will, because it is endowed with power. For James the word is the Mosaic Law (Jm 1:25); for Peter it is the evangelical preaching; for John it is the person of the Son of God (1:1). Paul sees in the Holy Spirit the principle which makes us sons of God (Rm 6:4), but the Spirit is the dynamism of the word of God.

By the use of figures of speech, Old Testament references, and personal appeals, 1 P 2:4-10 sets forth the origin, nature, and function of the Church. To come to Christ involves incorporation into that community which belongs to him, shares his election, and is the living temple of which he is the living foundation stone. This community is the new Israel whose twofold function is to offer to God through Jesus Christ the sacrifice of its obedience, and to show forth God's mighty works. "Come to him, to that living stone rejected by men but in God's sight chosen and precious; and like living stones be yourselves built into a spiritual house, to be a holy priesthood, to offer spiritual sacrifices acceptable to God through Christ... You are a chosen race, a royal priesthood, a holy nation, God's own people, that you may declare the wonderful deeds of him who called you out of darkness into his marvelous light" (1 P 2:4-10).

God's people in the Old Testament were constituted at Mt. Sinai but could not approach it (Ex 19). The new people are constituted around another rock which they can approach. So also to the sacrifices which sealed the old covenant (Ex 24:5-8) are superposed the spiritual sacrifices of the Christians. Moreover the image of growth replaces that of construction. Jesus (Mt 21:42) had compared himself to the stone rejected by men but chosen by God. The Christians, living stones like Jesus himself, are built up into a spiritual dwelling, where they render to God in Christ, an adoration worthy of him.

Through long years Judaism had its glorious physical Temple in Jerusalem. Early Christianity had no material temple but is itself a temple not made of physical stones, but a spiritual house constructed of living stones. Individual Christians are priviledged to be these living stones of which the chief is Christ. The cornerstone or keystone is to be understood of Christ as the stone holding the building together. The words of Ps 118:22 are applied to the risen Christ, who was rejected but whose precious quality in God's sight is found in the new life he shares with those who come to him. Christ is the rock of destiny: to those who believe, he is chosen and precious; to those who reject him, he is a rock that makes them fall. Christ's resurrection proclaims God's choice, the approval of his mission. It is also what makes him the living stone which gives life to believers. Christ is the basis and standard on which God erects his building, stone by stone. The Church is presented as God's temple, based on Christ and partaking of his preciousness or honor.

Since Christ is a new temple replacing the one in Jerusalem (Jn 2:21), Christians are its living stones, forming a spiritual house, and are a new priesthood replacing the Jerusalem priests. The building is spiritual not in the sense of a symbolic or invisible reality but of a house built and inhabited by the Holy Spirit. Believers are joined by the Spirit to Christ the cornerstone. They themselves become living stones and constitute the spiritual edifice, the Christian community. They form a new temple which elsewhere is called the body of Christ.

The purpose of stones is not to be kept in isolation, but so to be joined together as to form a building. This, however, describes only one aspect of the corporate life of the Church, and by itself is insufficient as a description, for once built into the edifice, the stone's role is passive. So Peter switches thought from the structure, presumably of the temple, to those who actively function inside the building in corporate worship; here is the active side of the life of the Christian community. God's people are not passive. The image changes to present the Church as a consecrated priesthood, offering to God through Jesus Christ a spiritual sacrifice, which is a life based on Christian faith. Obedience to faith, not privilege of race, is the means by which union with Christ in the new temple is effected.

Among all peoples it was regarded as a high honor to belong to the priestly class. The sacrificial system was the heart of Jewish worship and it was a high privilege to represent the Jewish congregation before the altar of God. Peter understood that the Jewish sacrificial system had, since Calvary, been superseded by another in which the sacrifices were to be spiritual. Christians are a holy priesthood whose function is to offer spiritual sacrifices acceptable to God through Jesus Christ. The essential part of any sacrifice, even under the Old Testament, lay in the dispositions of the offerers. Such was the value of the sacrifice of Christ, and the Christian sacrifice can only be acceptable to God so far as they are united with him and bear his character. This does not exclude the offering of the body and blood of Christ which gave full expression to his will; nor does it exclude any holy action by which Christians identify themselves with his action.

The Church is the spiritual heir of God's ancient people. In Christ the Church comes into the good of the Old Testament revelation. The gentiles were no people (Ho 2:23); now they are God's own people, chosen, holy, a royal priesthood admitted into the marvelous light in which God dwells (1 P 2:9-10). These descriptive terms all come from the Old Testament (Ex 19:5-6). The Church is the new people inheriting the role of the chosen people. As Jesus is Messiah, king of a new kingdom, so his subjects are a royal people. This series of Biblical allusions attributing to the Church the titles of the chosen people, underlines both its relation to God and its responsibility to the world. Christians are chosen not simply that they may enjoy their exalted privileges but also that they may tell the excellence of God to others.

The prerogatives of ancient Israel are now more fully and fittingly applied to the Christian people. A chosen race indicates our divine election (Ep 1:4). A royal priesthood, a kingdom of priests (ex 19:6), designates the people of God as a nation dedicated to the worship and service of Yahweh, their king. Their conduct among the nations is expected to be such as to manifest them as his courtiers and priestly servants. The baptized Christian is empowered and expected to live his whole life as a cultic act, continuing in a sense the sacrifice of Christ, but also manifesting to the world that he is marked for the service of Christ. Christians are a holy nation reserved for God. By baptism we are set apart and dedicated to the sacral order of things. We are a people God claims as his own, in virtue of our baptism into Christ's death and resurrection. This transcends all natural and national divisions, and unites us into one community, to glorify God who led us from the darkness of sin to the light of faith in Christ. From being no people we have become the very people of God, the recipients of his best graces. The explanation of God's creation of the Church is his gratuitous love. We are God's people because of God's mercy and loving kindness.

The idea that the whole Christian people make up a royal priesthood does not exclude certain men from being designated for cultic, ritual service, anymore than the fact that all Israel being a royal priesthood prevented the existence of the Levitical priesthood. And since Christians come from different races, nations, and peoples, Peter uses race, nation, and people to designate the new unity that we have in Christ, a unity transcending all barriers and distinctions.

Reverence for Christ should transcend all fears that might invade the Christian heart. "Have no fear of them (persecutors) nor be troubled, but in your hearts reverence Christ as Lord" (1 P 3:14). The positive antidote to fear is to be found in giving Christ the special place that is his due, right at the center of our lives, where he is to reign as Lord. The Christian makes his heart a consecrated dwelling for Christ, where his worship is carried out undisturbed.

All through St. Peter's second epistle Christ is proposed as the object of a Christian's knowledge. This knowledge includes moral discernment and the practice of virtue (2 P 1:5-8). "May you have more and more grace and peace as you come to know our Lord more and more" (2 P 1:2). The epistle emphasizes knowledge of God and Christ as a means of salvation. This emphasis supplies a corrective to the teaching of false teachers. Christian knowledge is never merely speculative but springs from a personal relationship with and experience of God in Jesus, our Lord. It is not academic information nor is it invitation to a mysterious religious experience; it is personal acquaintance with Jesus as Lord.

This true knowledge is the divine power which enables one to live the godly life, and the source of this power is the risen Lord. This life was concretely demonstrated in his earthly ministry. His presence (glory and excellence) among men, as revealing the purpose of God, is the pattern of the offer for us to "become partakers of the divine nature" (2 P1:4). This unique expression in the Bible is surprising because of its impersonal character. It is a description of our new life in Christ, the full Christian life of faith; it is the communication by God of the life which is proper to himself. The Christian enjoys intimate union with Christ and his Father, and with the Holy Spirit.

The object of all God's promises and dispensations was to bring fallen man back to the image of God, which he has lost. Being renewed in the image of God, and having communion with him so as to dwell in God and God in us, this is the sum and substance of the religion of Christ. Those who receive the promises of the gospel partake of the divine nature. They are "renewed in the spirit of their mind, after the image of God, in knowledge, righteousness, and holiness" (Ep 4:24); their hearts are set for God and his service; they have a divine temper and disposition of soul.

There is emphasis on the word, *become*. Human nature does not partake of the divine in its own right. This only becomes possible through the promises of the gospel fulfilled, that is, through the gospel of the Incarnate Christ and its appropriation by the believer. But thus the participation is attainable. The passage most akin to this is Jn 1:23, "To them he gave the right to become children of God." We have here, then, one of the great texts of the New Testament. Led by it some of the greatest of the early Fathers did not shrink from statements like the well-known expression of St. Athanasius: "He was made man, that we might be made God."

The Christian response to sharing the life of God should be to aim at producing and being the finest and most attractive character for God. Faith should lead to Christian virtues: knowledge, self-control, steadfastness, godliness, brotherly affection, in one word, love which is the coping stone for the whole edifice of character, the crown of all Christian virtues (2P 1:5-8).

"Go on growing in the grace and knowledge of our Lord and Savior, Jesus Christ" (2 P 3:18). The final thought of the epistle, like that with which it opens, is the growth of the Christian life. The Christian life cannot be static. The Christian must tread single-mindedly the path of divine and Christ-like virtues. Grace, that magnificently complex word, refers to the underserved gift of God's love which can never be known or experienced save by the surrender of all trust in human skills and ability, and the surrender to Jesus, the Lord. Knowledge is instruction in the truth of the Christian tradition. Both grace and knowledge come from Christ and characterize the growing Christian experience and life. The only response to such a lofty conception of Christian living is a doxology here addressed directly to Christ: "To him be the glory both now and in the day of eternity. Amen."

9

THE CONVERSION OF ST. PAUL

The conversion of St. Paul (Ac 9:1-9), prompted by a personal appearance of the risen Christ, was his special call to apostolic ministry. Paul's discourse at Antioch (Ac 13:16-42) is the sort of synagogue sermon he was accustomed to preaching throughout the Empire. His preaching at Ephesus was the occasion for a riot of the silversmiths (Ac 19:12-41).

The conversion of St. Paul is perhaps the most important event in the whole history of the Christian Church. No single man has done more to make Christianity a world religion, and certainly no single man has had a greater influence on the Christian thought. No one, except perhaps St. John, has ever been closer to the mind of Jesus or has more clearly seen the significance of what our Lord said and did. The conversion and apostleship of St. Paul alone, duly considered, was of itself sufficient to prove Christianity to be a divine revelation. Luke realized the importance of St. Paul's conversion in the history of salvation for, despite his limited space, he relates it in some detail three times, once in the third person, and twice as narrated by Paul himself. Luke emphasizes Paul's vocational call by giving the story of his conversion and commission as part of the general history of the early Church (Ac 9:1-9); as Paul's testimony before the Jews (22:3-16); and as the main element in Paul's defense before Agrippa II (26:9-19). This triple repetition is Luke's way of underlining its importance, and of impressing it on te reader's mind.

St. Paul's conversion recalls the call of Isaiah and Ezechiel. His question and the answer he heard, "I am Jesus whom you are persecuting" (Ac 9:5) recall that of Moses (Ex 3:6). Because of this parallel to the Old Testament vocations, we may see here an indication of the divinity of Christ; only God so appears and calls. Christ's revelation of himself to Paul, however, is really without precedent. Like the calls of the Old Testament characters in the history of salvation, Paul's call had no story leading up to it, and came from God as a claim that could not be refused. But there is no Old Testament parallel to Paul's being called while an unbeliever and a persecutor. Paul was called to something greater and more glorious than any of the Old Testament prophets and servants were. Paul's Damascus experience was the first revelation of Christ outside Palestine and it abolished the monopoly of the gospel hitherto enjoyed by the people of Israel in Palestine.

As persecutor Paul was terrible, but once he had yielded obedience to Jesus, the Christ, his loyalty was absolute and his service unstinting. He entered Damascus a stricken, broken man, physically blind, mentally shattered, to become on his recovery the humblest of the Christian family, the slave of Christ, and at the same time, the most fearless and able protagonist of the faith he had tried to exterminate. His own testimony is that Jesus laid hold of him (Ph 3:12). He came face to face with the risen Savior, as the apostles had done after the Resurrection, and he knew in that moment that Jesus of Nazareth was indeed the Messiah. St. Paul always maintained that the appearance of the risen Christ to him, which brought about his conversion, was as objective and real as the appearances to the other apostles. He regarded it as the turning point of his life, and the beginning of his new vocation. It was an important intervention of the risen Jesus, giving Paul his mission: "To bring my name before the gentiles and kings and the sons of Israel" (Ac 9:15).

The manifestation of Jesus, classed by Paul as one of the Resurrection appearances (1 Cor 15:8), is described in terms appropriate to a theophany. The light signifies the glory of the exalted Lord. The answer "I am Jesus" was a revelation which meant that, in one tremendous moment of time, Saul had to identify the Lord Yahweh of the Old Testament, whom he zealously sought to serve, with Jesus of Nazareth whom he ferociously persecuted in the person of his saints. The shock of his innermost soul was tremendous, but once the identification was made, Saul had no doubts or reserves, and from that time forward he could truthfully say, "For me to live is Christ" (Ph 1:21). "I am," here as in other Old Testament passages, is a formula of revelation. The words of Jesus are related by Luke with no variation in all three accounts; they exerted a profound and lasting influence on the thought of Paul. Under the impulsion of this experience he gradually developed his understanding of justification by faith, and of the Christian community with Jesus Christ (Col 1:18). Whatever is done to the disciples for the sake of the name of Jesus is done to Jesus himself.

Damascus was the scene of Paul's first fellowship with Christians, and of his first service for the Lord, and Christological depth marked his earliest messages for he heralded Jesus as Christ and Son of God. Paul's conversion and baptism were immediately followed by his bold proclamation of Jesus as Son of God: "He began preaching in the synagogue, Jesus is the Son of God" (Ac 9:20). This title is the central theme of Paul's ministry and of his epistles. It is characteristic of Pauline Christology. The Acts show how Paul in his ministry preached without compromise the divinity of Christ, and proclaimed his universal Lordship, before the Jews, the pagans, and his judges, often at the peril of his life.

Israel as a nation was God's son. The Messiah as summing up Israel in himself was in a special sense God's son. But St. Paul's use of the term goes beyond this; he was divinely prompted to see that the visible and temporary human sonship was an expression in time of a relation that is eternal in the being of God. For Paul and Christians generally, the title, Son of God, soon became the one most expressive of Jesus' true dignity. In

Pauline theology Son of God undoubtedly means a preexistent divine being, consubstantial with the Father, and his agent in the creation and redemption of the world.

The point of the occurrence before Damascus was that Jesus appeared personally to Saul. He made himself known in light from heaven. The first and strongest impression was, Jesus lives. Paul receives direct and personal certainty that Jesus, the crucified, is alive. He receives also a profound impression of the glory of Christ in his exaltation. And the voice with which Jesus addresses him has in it something overwhelming; Paul immediately feels the preeminence of the person who appears, and is compelled to bow and submit. In short, Jesus not only lives, but lives exalted in heaven, lives and rules in divine glory.

In the synagogue of Antioch, in a long discourse (Ac 13:16-42) Paul proclaims the fulfillment in Jesus of the divine promises made to Israel. The main theme of this sermon is Jesus as the Son of David. The introduction reminds one of Stephen's apology, but whereas Stephen laid the main stress upon Moses, Paul lays it upon David. The description of our Lord's rejection by the rulers, and of his death and resurrection reminds us strongly of Peter's earlier discourse at Jerusalem, but Paul adds the further claim that Jesus is God's Son. (33). Luke gives the summary of Paul's address at some length, probably to show the sort of synagogue sermon Paul was accustomed to preach throughout the Roman Empire. Paul's regular practice was to work from the synagogue outward; he would find there a field ready prepared, not only Jews but also God-fearers.

Paul's sermon falls into three parts: first a historical introduction (Ac 13:16-25). This is a summary of the history of salvation with an appendix recalling John the Baptist's testimony. Paul narrates the deliverance wrought by God for the nation of Israel at the Exodus, and outlines their history from Moses to David. As did Peter and Stephen, Paul recounts the origins of the Jewish people as the necessary presupposition of understanding the Christian faith. Salvation history under the guidance of God leads Israel to the Church. In the second part (26-37) Paul passes from David to the promised Messiah of David's seed, and declares that this Messiah has appeared in the person of Jesus whose death and well-attested resurrection prove him to be the Messiah foretold in Hebrew scripture. Like Peter at Pentecost, he argues that the words of Ps 16:10, "You will not allow your holy one to experience corruption," could not apply to David himself, but to the descendant of David, who has in these last days, as a matter of evidence, risen from the dead. Jesus who died and has risen is the expected Messiah. This closely resembles Peter's discourses, but this discourse ends with a suggestion of the Pauline doctrine of justification by faith. Finally comes the practical appeal. The sermon ends with an application to the present situation of the warning of the prophet Hobakkuk (38-41).

A recurrent element of the Christian plea is the innocence and unjust condemnation of Jesus (Ac 13:28). Paul insists also on the resurrection (13:30-37). The Jews must recognize Jesus as Lord, believe in him and be converted. On this condition they will obtain the remission of their sins. There is strong emphasis on the resurrection as God's act which negated the leader's verdict and made possible the preaching of the gospel. The incredible is made credible by the reliable witness of the early apostles. By his resurrection Christ was enthroned as Messiah, and from then on his human nature enjoyed all the privileges of the Son of God (13:33). Paul preached Christ crucified but to Paul it was the resurrection that gave meaning to the cross and marked God's approval of the sacrifice. The result of Paul's discourse is significant: "Many Jews and devout converts to Judaism followed Paul and Barnabas, who spoke to them and urged them to continue in the grace of God" (13:43). The expressions fearing God or worshiping God are technical terms for admirers and followers of the Jewish religion who stop short of circumcision. It is the adorers of God whom Paul converts and brings to the adoration of Christ.

The same thing happened with the Thessalonians. "Paul argued with them from the scriptures explaining and proving that it was necessary for the Christ to suffer and to rise from the dead, saying, 'This Jesus whom I proclaim to you is the Christ.' And some of them were persuaded and joined Paul and Silas; as did a great many God-fearing people and Greeks and not a few of the leading women" (Ac 17:2-4). Thessalonica was the capital of the province of Macedonia and became an important Christian center. St. Paul's plan was first to evangelize the seats of government and the trade centers, knowing that if Christianity was once established in these places, it would spread through the Empire. Paul's preaching as usual centered round two truths: first that the Old Testament scriptures foretold a Messiah who should suffer and rise from the dead; and second that the Messiah is Jesus.

At Ephesus Paul was so successful that his preaching provoked the silversmiths' riot (Ac 19:23-41). This is one of the most exciting passages in Acts. The story is vivid and full of humor. The temple of Diana was the pride of the Ephesians, one of the seven wonders of the world, and a major tourist attraction. Its marble blocks, according to some reports, were cemented together with gold instead of mortar. Pilgrims came from far and near to pay homage at the shrine, not of the chaste huntress of early Roman days, but of a repulsive looking goddess of fertility. She was not really the Greek virgin goddess, but the Oriental Nature deity, the great Mother, and her image, supposed to have fallen down from the sky, was a rude bust of a woman covered with breasts as a sign of fertility. The craftsmen of the city, silversmiths and coppersmiths, did a thriving business in making small images of the goddess and of her temple, and selling them as souvenirs to pilgrims. Paul's campaign against superstition was so successful that it occasioned an economic slump. Christianity becomes unpopular when it touches men's pocketbooks.

A silversmith named Demetrius called a general meeting of the men of his trade. "You see and hear, he said, that not only at Ephesus but almost throughout all of Asia, this Paul has persuaded and turned away a considerable number of people, saying that gods made by hand are not gods. The danger grows not only that our trade will be discredited, but even that the temple of the great goddess Diana will count for nothing, and that she whom all Asia and the whole world worship may soon lose all her prestige" (Ac 19:24-27). Demetrius organizes the workmen in defense of their trade which is now endangered by

Paul's success in converting the pagans. Demetrius plays alternately on the theme of financial loss and on that of injury done to the goddess. The mob takes over and there is a rush to the great amphitheater. A riotous assembly, gathered in the great open-air theater of the city, for two hours kept up the cry, "Great is Diana of the Ephesians" (19:34).

The town clerk eventually succeeded in calming the crowd by reassuring them that nothing could damage the fame and prestige of the goddess of Ephesus. No one can deny that her statue fell down from heaven. "What man is there who does not know that the city of the Ephesians is temple keeper of the great Diana and of her statue that fell down from heaven . . . and in any case, these men are not guilty of any sacrilege or blasphemy against our goddess" (19:36-37). This points to Paul's method of doing mission work without maligning gentile gods, expressing his views gently and with moderation. His procedure was positive; the testimony of the true God and of his Christ, the publication of the gospel, is the power of God which illumines, edifies, and saves. Finally, the scene has apologetical motifs. It shows the impact of Christianity which threatened even so influential a cult as that of the great Diana; the respectability of Paul, who is a friend of such important officials as the Asiarchs, the dignitaries of the province of Asia; and the triumph of Christianity which remains unhurt while the demonstrators eventually disperse in cowed submission.

10

THE UNKNOWN GOD

Paul's discourse at Athens (Ac 17:22-31) is clearly anti-adolatry. After the three discourses which sum up the preaching of Paul to the Jews (Ch 13), to the pagans (Ch 17), and his last testament to the Ephesian elders (Ch 20), Acts records three apologies: before the Jewish people (Ch 22), before the procurator Felix (Ch 24), and before King Agrippa (Ch 26).

At Athens Paul's "spirit was provoked within him as he saw that the city was full of idols" (Ac 17:16). His speech before the Council of the Areopagus (Ac 17:22-31) is directed against idolatry. He tries to lead his audience to adoration of the risen Jesus. In the development of his discourse, Paul speaks about God (24-25), then about man in relation to God (26-28), then about the obligation this relation imposes (29), and concludes by stressing the urgency of this obligation in view of God's judgment of the world (30-31).

Even in Paul's day when its heyday was past, Athens must have been a place of dazzling loveliness. Paul, however, saw it as a city of souls groping in darkness for truth, an idol-ridden city. He shared the view of the satirist, that it was easier to find gods there than men. Not content with the usual approach through the synagogue, Paul frequented the market place (Ac 17:17) where he had discussions with anyone who would face him.

This is the only explicit mention of this kind of preaching in Acts. His presence came to the attention of the local philosophers, Epicureans and Stoics are mentioned (18), and he was invited to state his case formally and publicly before the light and learning of Athens, the councilors of the Areopagus, the guardians of religion and education. He met them on their own ground, even quoting from their own poets, but they laughed at him when he mentioned the resurrection (32). He convinced no more than one or two of his hearers (34).

After an introduction suited to the occasion (Ac 17:22-23), Paul proclaims the existence of the true God as opposed to current pagan conceptions. God created the universe; one cannot then suppose that he dwells in a temple or that he needs the cult rendered to him (24-25). God created man and surrounded him with gifts; it is absurd to identify him with material objects like statues (26-29). The speech ends with a call to repentance, in the perspective of judgment (30-31). The discourse is clearly anti-idolatry. Paul is inspired by the usual monotheistic approach of Hellenistic Judaism.

Paul's speech appeals to the Greek world's belief in divinity as responsible for the origin and existence of the universe. It contests idol worship, the common belief in the multiplicity of gods supposedly exerting their powers through their images. It acknowledges (17, 27) that mankind's attempt to understand God is one of the most anxious of all its endeavors. It declares further that the divine being is the judge of mankind, and concludes by hinting that the Apostle has information on the latter subject concerning a man whom God raised from the dead and who is to be the judge of all men. The speech reflects sympathy with pagan religiosity, handles the subject of idol worship gently, and appeals for a new examination of divinity, not from the standpoint of creation, but from the standpoint of judgment. It is possible that Luke intends to show in the whole incident, the difficulties of the learned men of the time in accepting the Christian message.

This is a confrontation between the gospel and the wisdom of the Greeks. The apostle is portrayed as the first Christian philosopher, using Stoic and Jewish arguments. Luke makes of this Pauline discourse one of the highlights of the apostle's missionary activity. It mirrors the reaction of a Christian missionary confronted with pagan culture, Greek intellectual life and piety, as Paul speaks from the depths of his faith. The significance of this discourse is seen in that the primitive proclamation of the Christians, that Jesus is the Son of God whom God has raised from the dead (Rm 10:9), has now been cast in a different form due to the needs of preaching to the gentiles. The form of the confession now becomes, "One God, one Lord" (1 Cor 8:6), who is author of creation and salvation.

"Men of Athens, I perceive that in every way you are very religious. For as I passed along, and observed the objects of your worship, I found also an altar with this inscription, 'To an unknown god.' What therefore you worship as unknown, this I proclaim to you. The God who made the world and everything in it, being the Lord of heaven and earth, does not live in shrines made by men, nor is he served by human hands, as though he needed anything, since he himself gives all men life and breath and everything else. And he made from one stock, every nation of men to live on all the face of the earth, having determined allotted periods and the boundaries of their regions, that they should seek God, and by groping for him succeed in finding him. In fact, he is not far from each one of us, for in him we live and move and have our being. As even some of your poets have said, 'For we are indeed his offspring.' Being then God's offspring we ought not to think that the Deity is like gold, or silver, or stone, that has been carved and designed by man. The times of ignorance God overlooked, but now he commands all men everywhere to repent, because he has fixed a day on which he will judge the world in righteousness by a man whom he has appointed, and of this he has given assurance to all men by raising him from the dead" (Ac 17:22-31).

Athens, although less important commercially and political-ly at this time than Corinth, remained the intellectual center of the ancient world, and an important city for ancient tourists. For Luke Athens was a symbol. This is evident from the fact that Paul's speech there, the only sample of his preaching to pagans, is the only one in which he argues philosophically. If Christianity could be planted here, the effect on the educated world in all lands would be tremendous. But Paul's appeal fell hopelessly flat. We hear of no Christian community in Athens, only of stray individuals.

Paul preaches to the Council on the knowledge of God, a theme very popular in the propaganda of contemporary Hellenistic Judaism. He accuses the pagans of not knowing God, the proof being that they worship idols. This ignorance is culpable since all men are capable of knowing God as creator and controller of the cosmos. The universalism of God's rule pervades the speech; note the frequency of the words all and every. It is God who is responsible for the spread of peoples and for all history. This universalism permits a polemic against all temples and sacrifices.

The pagans used to dedicate altars to the unknown gods lest they provoke the vengeance of gods whose names they did not know. Paul turns the practice to his own purpose, seeing here the biblical idea that pagans do not know God, and this parries the charge of preaching an outlandish God. He asserts the existence of God, the creator and providential ruler of the universe. And he argues that the Lord of the whole world has no need of temples to dwell in, even like the costly and beautiful buildings upon the hill of the Acropolis.

That the gods need nothing was a commonplace belief among Greek philosophers and religious thinkers. The biblical tradition relative to Adam rejoins the Stoic conception of the unity of the human race. The order of the world was a central notion of Stoicism. Paul argues that the order of the cosmos is enough to lead to a knowledge of God. The Platonic triad, life, movement, and being, corresponds to verse 25. To help his audience banish their ignorance, Paul finds in paganism analogies to his own message. His first quotation is sometimes attributed to Epimenides; the second is from Aratus, a poet of Cilician origin. They express God's necessary, intimate, and most efficacious presence, the continual and necessary dependence of all created things, in their existence and all their operations, on the first and almighty cause, which the truest philosophy as well as theology teaches.

Man being created in the image and likeness of God, it is absurd to worship lifeless idols. The pagans represented the gods after the image of man; from their own principles, the opposite approach is suggested (Ac 17:28-29). The argument probably is: since we are the offspring of God, in that our souls are immaterial and immortal, we ought to regard the author of our souls as an immortal and immaterial spirit and not like silver or gold or any material object. The ignorance of the Jews came from their misunderstanding of the prophecies; that of the pagans comes from their failure to discover God in creation. Paul suggests that this ignorance is culpable.

Paul carefully avoids the reference to scriptural evidence that he would use in the synagogue and starts from a visible example. Through the evidence of natural theology he sees man as God's ultimate creation, and with this conception the pagan poets themselves agree. Then he throws down the challenge to repentance before the world is judged by the man whom God has chosen. The proof of this choice is made clear to all by God "raising him from the dead." In this preaching addressed to pagans, Paul does not mention the life and death of Jesus. Jesus is presented as a man who will be judge of all men. His resurrection is mentioned as a guarantee of this mission of judge confided to him by God. Christ's resurrection justifies belief in his coming as judge and savior at the end of time. The stress on the resurrection and silence on the redemptive value of Christ's death are characteristic of the theology of Acts. The apostles set their appeal to the gentiles for repentance, against the background of God's judgment.

The audience listened interestedly enough until Paul spoke of resurrection. This they could not stomach. The immortality of the soul was a commonplace of several of their philosophical schools, but the resurrection of the body was to them as absurd as it was undesirable. It is still much a stumbling block to many as it was to the Athenians, but it is integral to the Christian faith.

Paul's farewell to the elders of Ephesus (Ac 20:17-38) at the end of his third missionary journey is his third great discourse in Acts. Addressed to Christian pastors its purpose is to present the goal of his entire mission. It serves at once as Paul's last will and testament, as an example of hortatory preaching, and as the conscious farewell to his missionary activity. We find in 20:20-21 a summary of Paul's apostolic ministry. "I have preached . . . urging both Jews and Greeks to turn to God and to believe in our Lord Jesus Christ." Conversion and faith go together. His gospel was a message of repentance and faith in Jesus as Lord and Messiah. This was what was chiefly signified by baptism. Paul emphasizes the substance of the gospel he had preached and that the elders must continue to preach. They must "feed the Church of God which he bought with the blood of his own Son" (28).

In Jerusalem a howling mob of fanatical Asian Jews set upon Paul in the Temple, and he barely escaped with his life by the intervention of the Roman garrison quartered in the Temple area (Ac 21:27-32). Despite Paul's effort to justify himself, in his speech to the crowd from the steps of the Antonia Tower, the scene of Jesus' trial before Pilate, his defense of his association with gentiles only served to infuriate the mob further (Ac Ch 22). After the three discourses which sum up the preaching of Paul to the Jews (Ch 13), to the pagans (Ch 17), and his last testament to the Ephesian elders (Ch 20), Acts records three apologies: before the Jewish people (Ch 22), before the procurator Felix (Ch 24), and before King Agrippa (Ch 26); each is cleverly adapted to the audience. Before the people, Paul defends his conduct as being a devout Jew. He recounts his conversion and again preaches the risen Christ.

At Caesarea Paul makes his profession of faith before Felix, the governor (Ac 24:14-21). "It is according to the way, which they call a sect, that I worship the God of our fathers, believing everything laid down by the law or written in the prophets" (24:14). Christianity is not a different religion, it is Judaism with its ancient hope fulfilled. If the Jews reject Christ, they reject their own religious tradition. Christianity is a way of righteousness within Judaism as rightly understood and interpreted. Christian faith is in full accord with the law and the prophets. Christians spoke of their movement as the way; for them it was the true fulfillment of Israel's faith and the one way of salvation. When men follow this way God is served as he wishes to be served. The way, that is, the true way of the Lord, was one of the earliest names for Christianity. The unqualified use of the word is peculiar to Acts. The term expresses the idea that Christian discipleship is the culmination of God's revelation to men and of men's relationship to God.

Before Festus, successor of Felix, and King Agrippa, Paul pleads his cause recalling his vocation to the ministry (Ac 26:1-23). He testifies to Jesus, risen from the dead and savior of all nations. "And now I stand here on trial for hope in the promise made by God to our fathers to which our twelve tribes hope to attain, as they earnestly worship night and day. And for this hope I am accused by Jews, O King! Why is it thought incredible by any of you that God raised the dead? . . . To this day I have had the help that comes from God, and so I stood firm testifying both to great and small, saying nothing but what the prophets and Moses said would come to pass: that the Christ must suffer and that as the first to rise from the dead, he was to proclaim that light both to our people and to the Gentiles" (Ac 26:6-8, 22-23). A flattering address (26:2-3) is followed by Paul's assertion that his Christian faith in bodily resurrection is shared by the Pharisees (4-8). He then describes the circumstances of his conversion (9-18) and ends with a summary of his preaching which presents the Christian faith simply as the fulfillment of the scriptures (19-23). The Messianic hope takes definite shape in the belief in the resurrection of the virtuous who are to have their place in the kingdom at the end of time. This hope has its initial fulfillment in the resurrection of Christ which is the ground of Christian hope. Paul appeals to the Temple cult and argues that it makes no sense unless it is related to the resurrection (7).

Right through his ministry Paul combatted untiringly idolatry and strove to bring Jews and pagans to recognize, receive, and adore the risen Lord, Jesus Christ. Transferred to Rome and imprisoned for two years, Paul manifests the same attitude. This is stated in the last verses of Acts. "He lived there for two years and welcomed all who came to him, preaching the kingdom of God and teaching about the Lord Jesus Christ quite openly and unhindered" (28:30-31). It was a time of uncessant activity, and placed the gospel in the very heart of the great gentile world.

During those two years Paul wrote his letters to the Colossians and Ephesians, as well as his note to Philemon. We owe the deep and ful Christology of these writings, the climax and crown of his special revelation, to his meditations and inspirations during this time when he could not travel, and was therefore freer to receive and express the truth of Christ and his Church, the center of God's plan throughout the ages. His epistles give us further details concerning his teaching. He constantly stresses the absolute dependency of every creature upon God and his Son, the necessity of acknowledging this by conversion, of proclaiming it by our attitude. He gave the example in his own frequent outburst of sentiments of deep and fervent adoration.

11

THE PAROUSIA

Paul's main concern in his two letters to the Thessalonians is the Parousia, a constant element in the faith of the early Church (Mk 14:62). The Parousia is the climax of salvation history. For Paul, Messianic eschatology includes a present and a future aspect. The Parousia may be considered in its ecclesial and sacramental dimension, and as an existential challenge, as the goal of human development.

Paul's two letters to the Thessalonians are the earliest in Paul's extant correspondence. His main concern was to reject false ideas about the Parousia, Christ's coming in glory at the end of time, as judge of all men. What Christ's coming again will mean and when it will happen, seems to have been almost an obsession among the Christians of Thessalonica. Paul's two letters to them are famous mostly for his remarks on the Parousia, which give evidence of the tenor of early Christian eschatology, that is, belief regarding the end of time. Eschatology is a very elastic word that includes all manner of concepts on the future; eschatology is a built-in aspect of all thinking about the life of man and the nature of history. Thus Christian eschatology concerns the kingdom of God; the Marxist eschatology concerns the classless society at the end of the historical dialectic; and nihilistic eschatology speaks of the extinction of life on our planet either by uncontrollable

technological war or by the disappearance of conditions
necessary for life. Christians regard the resurrection of Jesus as
the inauguration of end time.

The Parousia was a constant element in the faith of the early
Church. The speedy end of the present age with the return of
Christ, the last judgment, and the final establishment of the
Messianic rule, is taken for granted by St. Paul and every other
New Testament writer. If Philippians is Paul's swan song, his
expectation of the Parousia was as keen at the end of his days
(Ph 1:10 4-5), as it was in the full flush of his missionary activity.
In what he says, Paul is repeating the Old Testament apocalyptic
phrases, applying to Christ what had been said about the day of
Yahweh, with the descent of the Lord to earth in judgment. For
Jewish Christians conscious of living in the midst of supernatural events, the greatest being the resurrection of Jesus, it
was natural to think or hope that God would speedily bring the
old evil order to an end and would convince all mankind, that
Jesus is lord and King of all the nations. The Old Testament
language Paul uses with regard to the end of the world is as
much the language of symbol and poetry as the Old Testament
description of the world in Gn 1. Both the beginning and the end
of everything are beyond human understanding and can only be
suggested in symbolic form.

The hope of the early Church for an immediate Second
Advent was not unduly disturbed when Christ did not return as
speedily as might have been expected. The basic Christian
concern was not so much with the time factor, but with the
sense of the nearness of God in judgment, and the certainty of
Christ's victory. The original meaning of Parousia is presence,
and in its later use the word meant the visit of a king. The Church
believed that the King had come, that he was already present
with his people through the Holy Spirit, but one day, sooner or
later, the King must be acknowledged by the whole world; his
triumph over evil, sin, and death must be absolute. In this sense
the expectation of St. Paul and of the Thessalonians, underlying
the unfamiliar Old Testament imagery, is still the faith of our
twentieth century Church.

The day of the Lord, the end event of time and history, will come as the Lord himself said, suddenly and unexpectedly. But Christians who live in the light of the gospel have nothing to fear. If we are protected by the armor of God, faith, hope, and love, against the temptations of the world, the flesh, and the devil, it makes little difference when we are called on to give an account of our lives to our maker (1 Th 5:1-11). Jesus himself suggested that he would return gloriously at the end of time (Mk 14:62). He used the Old Testament apocalyptic ideas to emphasize his own identity and mission as standard bearer of the kingdom of God, and to give force to his teaching that the kingdom of God could come not by any human efforts but only by the direct and supernatural action of God. He definitely anticipated his personal return to inaugurate the kingdom of God, without specifying clearly the time or the manner. Actually he has already returned in that life of the Spirit which sprang up among believing men, best exemplified in the Church. He is still in process of returning according as men see more clearly and apply more consistently what he can mean to the world. He is yet to return in still greater power as men surrender more completely to his Spirit. Ultimately there will be a final consummation in the recognition of his universal Lordship, described by St. Paul as the time when "all things have been made subject to Christ." (1 Cor 15:27).

The Parousia is the coming of the glorified Christ as the climax of salvation history. The resurrection and ascension of Christ and the sending of the Holy Spirit are the beginning of a process in which the history of salvation, mankind's and the individual's, goes on and will come to an end in what Scripture calls the Parousia. The Parousia is the consummation of this process, and when it will happen is unknown because it is the free and incalculable act of God (Mk 13:32). It will reveal to all how they have achieved their God-given finality of their salvation or damnation. Christ's return is for judgment and will be the definitive crystallization and manifestation of the eternal results of history. It will make clear that history is the work of God, whose purpose is centered on Jesus Christ. Empowered by the example of Jesus, the Church anticipates and foreshadows in the celebration of the Eucharist, the communion of the saints

with the risen Lord of glory, which will be the ultimate result of
his Parousia.

The coming of Yahweh is a conception which appears in the
Old Testament, but the conception which lies at the root of the
New Testament idea of the Parousia is the coming of the Son of
Man in Dn 7:13, with very little elaboration. In Daniel the coming
of the Son of Man is the last act of world history, the erection of
the reign of God and the subjection of all hostile powers. Early
Christian tradition, basing itself upon the words of Jesus
himself, applied this image to Jesus as savior and judge. To the
first Christian generation the Parousia, which is the consummation of the work of Jesus and of history and of God's providence,
was not an event to be feared but to be eagerly desired.

A belief that history tends to a term in which judgment will
be final, God vindicated and evil definitely overcome, the
Parousia is basic to biblical and Christian faith and cannot be
renounced without reducing that faith to zero. Its imagery,
derived especially from Old Testament apocalyptic passages,
should be understood as such. Jesus, and his disciples after him,
not only asserted that the time of the Parousia is unknown but
also gave no concrete and detailed description of its external
features. That there must be an end to the present order goes
without saying. History is the working out of a divine purpose;
and a story which has no end can have no meaning, since it is
only in relation to the end to be attained that the details can be
understood. Moreover, since Christ is the fulfiller of the divine
purpose and the heir of all things, the end must come through
him; and it is wholly in accordance with the principle of the
Incarnation that his final manifestation should be one that all
can see.

For Paul the final age of salvation history is the Messianic
age which begins and ends with Christ. If the eschaton, the final
stage, has been inaugurated, the end has not yet come (1 Cor
15:24). Christ, the Pantocrator, the omnipotent Lord of the
universe, does not yet reign supreme; he has not yet handed the
kingdom over to the Father. His Parousia has not yet taken place.
Paul also calls the Parousia, the day of the Lord, the day of Christ,
his day, the day, that day, the day of the Son of Man, the day of

God, the day of visitation, the great day, the last day. It is the fulfillment, in the eschatological era ushered in by Christ, of the day of Yahweh foretold by the prophets (Am 5:18). The fulfillment of the day of Christ begins with his first coming (Lk 17:20-21) and the punishment of Jerusalem (Mt 24:1); its final manifestation will be Christ's glorious coming at the end of time as sovereign judge. In the pastoral Epistles, the term epiphany, that is, appearance, manifestation, is adopted in preference to Parousia or apocalypse, that is revelation, as the technical term both for the manifestation of Christ in his eschatological triumph, and also for his manifestation in the results of his action as savior. The title of the book of Revelation ("Revelation of Jesus Christ") summarizes in one word the contents and the message of the book: the eschatological Lordship of the risen Christ.

Messianic eschatology includes a present aspect and a future aspect. The future holds in store the Parousia, the resurrection of the dead, the final judgment, and the glory of the justified believer. But the eschaton has already begun, the first fruits and the pledge of salvation are already the possession of Christian believers. Christ has already transferred us to the heavenly realm (EEp 2:6). Paul does not only speak of Jesus as the absent Christ, but also of the unveiling or epiphany of Christ invisibly present even in this age. In Paul's view, Christians live in the eschaton, in the age of the Messiah. This is an age of dual polarity. It is an age that looks backward to the first Good Friday and Easter Sunday, but also forward to a final glorious consummation when "we shall always be with the Lord" (1 Th 4:17). It is an age that has initiated a status of union with God in faith, and destined to a final union in glory. This is the basis of Christian hope and patience.

The final scene of God's acts in history, the last judgment is dramatically presented by Paul (1 Th 1:7-10). He is not really describing the judgment but evoking its majesty and certainty to the minds of his readers. God's judgment will bring relief to the afflicted as well as punishment to the persecutors: a complete reversal of fortunes. The ultimate disaster or eternal ruin for mankind is to be cut off from the presence of the Lord and denied participation in the splendor of his might, which is the lot of the faithful. The expectation of Christ's revelation from heaven becomes a prayer (1 Th 1:11-12), a concise expression of the delicate coordination of grace, the divine initiative, with human effort in the progressive wor ɔf man's glorification: his name is glorified in us and we ourselves are glorified in him.

The meaning of the Parousia can be expressed in terms and categories of modern thought. Since the New Testament nowhere speaks of the Parousia as Christ's second coming, many interpreters like to think of one coming of Christ, and one presence, a lowly presence experienced only through faith from the Incarnation to the end of time, which emerges into a visible, triumphant presence at the Parousia. The Parousia may thus be considered in its ecclesial and sacramental dimension, then as an existential challenge, as the goal of human development.

First the Parousia can be seen as the final shape of the redeemed Christian community. The Eucharist is a proclamation both of Christ's death and of faith in his Parousia: "You proclaim the Lord's death until he comes" (1 Cor 11:26). The Eucharist is the Messianic banquet and a perpetual symbol and assurance of the Parousia. Every Mass is celebrated with Paul's hope, "Until he comes," that is, until the aim is achieved, his arrival. And this coming is not so much from the outside, as a development from the inside. Through the Eucharist, the whole Christian body gradually grows up to the measure of Christ, so that his likeness and vitality gradually appear (Ep 4:11-16). The Parousia is better understood as a conformation to Christ from within, than as a confrontation of the universe from without. Comparing human existence to a train racing through time, the Parousia can be pictured as the terminal station where all travelers must alight, the sheep on the right hand platform and the goats on the left. Perhaps it may more meaningfully be conceived in a dynamic fashion as the greatest speed which the human train can achieve. The Parousia would be a breakthrough into perpetual motion plunging us for all eternity into the depths of God. The Parousia is thus an ecclesial and sacramental development, rather than a universal dissolution.

It is noticeable that the conception of Parousia appears in

the Pauline epistles in almost inverse proportion to that of the Body of Christ. These two images can stand as theological equivalents for that eschatological reality to which the whole work of God is moving. Both represent his final "gathering of us to himself" (2 Th 2:1). Paul's later notions of Body and Pleroma balance his earlier apocalyptic leanings, with their universal cataclysm and disintegration. On the analogy of the boiling point which is the critical threshold marking passage from water into steam, the Parousia would be a critical threshold marking a sharp qualitative change in the community of the redeemed.

The Parousia can also be seen as an unremitting challenge, as the presence of a Christ who always comes. This is the view most deeply rooted in the parenesis or moral exhortation of the New Testament. The farewell discourses of our Lord, the crisis parables, the longing of Peter and Paul for the revelation of Jesus, are all punctuated by appeals to watch, struggle, be concerned, pray. This is the lesson of the thief in the night theme. Christ is continously coming to each culture as need and opportunity. He daily comes to each individual as the call of his inmost being to wholeness, and as the invitaton, mediated through circumstances and persons, to share and achieve. The Parousia is the future climax of the present developing Lordship of Christ, the final reason for taking Christ seriously here and now: "Put on the Lord Jesus Christ," (Rm 13:14); "You did it to me" (Mt 25:40). The Parousia is the judgment which marks the interim period as one of freedom, growth, and participation.

The Parousia is really a theology of hope. The historical Christ-event has not yet fulfilled all the promises of God. The teaching concerning the Parousia is not so much a prediction based on foreknowledge, as a promise suggested by past and present salvific experience. The present life of the Church growing towards the Parousia may be compared to the anticipation of courtship which will be climaxed in the intimacy of the marriage union, that is, the arrival of Christ. In a word, the Parousia passages of the New Testament are in contexts preparing believers for the future, and thus they shape rather than describe the future.

All the main doctrines found in the other Pauline epistles

are already in 1 and 2 Thessalonians: the redemptive work of Christ, his resurrection and the resurrection of all faithful believers into eternal life with him, sanctification through the Holy Spirit and grace. Thus, for example, the fundamental Pauline teaching on our union with God in Christ, the Son of God, and his full divinity and equality with God the Father is made clear in the first salutation of both epistles: "To the Church of the Thessalonians in God the Father and the Lord Jesus Christ"; "Grace to you and peace from God and the Lord Jesus Christ" (1 Th 1:1, 2 Th 1:2).

12

UNION WITH CHRIST, GOD'S WISDOM

The keynote of the epistles to the Corinthians is the union of the believer with Christ (1 Cor 1:9). In Paul's thinking Christ is the answer to any question. This is because he is divine wisdom incarnated and manifested in the paradox of the cross in which alone is found salvation (1 Cor 1:17-2:8).

The master-thought of the epistles to the Corinthians is the union of the believer with Christ. Paul prays that they may rise by grace to that higher level where Christ and his love dominate thought and conduct. What he experiences in his own life transpires throughout his letters and hopefully will be transfused into his readers. Christ and the Apostle are so united in mind and spirit that the very life of Christ, so to speak, pulsates in him. He has yielded himself so completely to Christ's influence, and drunk so deeply of his spirit, that he acts, speaks, thinks, and suffers in Christ. The sense of personal union with Christ sustains him in all his efforts, and he desires to realize Christ's presence abiding with him in increasing degree. From this controlling thought of the union of Christ with the Christian, the Apostle deduces his two dominant ideas: the necessity of union with one another, and the necessity of purity of life. What is insisted throughout is that the whole purpose of the death of Christ was to produce the life of the Spirit in the souls of men. It is mainly the dark side of the Church life which is disclosed in 1

Cor; but there was also a bright side. There was life in the Church; its members possessed the gifts of the spirit; they were growing in the knowledge of God, and the Apostle could give thanks, in spite of all the drawbacks, for the many aspirations and efforts and achievements which gave promise of better things to come.

The prologue to 1 Cor (1:1-9) shows that adoration of God and of Jesus Christ filled the soul of Paul and of his correspondents. The Lord showers the Corinthians with spiritual gifts, and Paul encourages his charges to remain irreproachable as they wait for the Parousia. "To the Church of God which is at Corinth, to those sanctified in Christ Jesus, called to be saints together with all those who in every place call on the name of our Lord Jesus Christ, both their Lord and ours: grace and peace from God our Father and the Lord Jesus Christ. I give thanks to God always for you because of the grace of God which was given you in Christ Jesus . . . so that you are not lacking in any spiritual gift, as you wait for the revealing of our Lord Jesus Christ, who will sustain you to the end, guiltless in the day of our Lord Jesus Christ. God is faithful, by whom you were called into the fellowship of his Son, Jesus Christ our Lord."

The Church of God is one of Paul's favorite expressions. The Church is of God. It is not merely an earthly assembly: it is the fellowship of those whom the risen Christ has summoned from a life of sin to a life of holiness. The holiness of the Church is constantly suggested in this epistle. Incorporated by baptism into Christ, whom God has made our wisdom and our justice, our holiness and our redemption, Christians are holy, just as Israel was a holy nation by divine election. Christians form a sacred assembly, the community of the Lord. In the words, sanctified in Christ Jesus, and called to be saints, we see the double thought involved in the idea of holiness, that of religious status and that of moral demand. The Christian is sanctified to God through faith in Christ, having Christ living in him and Christ's influence molding him. We are called to be saints because we are consecrated to Christ. We bear the name and should also show the nature of saints. Christians are saints, not in the sense that they have achieved perfection, but in the sense that they have been called to life with Christ.

The Christian is joined to all believers who acknowledge Jesus as Lord, that is as God. The expression, to call upon the name of the Lord, occurs frequently in the Old Testament with the meaning to adore God. In the New Testament it designates the faithful united by their adoration of Jesus as Lord. The expression clearly indicates faith in the divinity of Christ. A common adoration of Christ unites all the faithful. Prayer was offered to Christ by all Christians from the time of the Ascension, and this is one of the clearest proofs that he was regarded as truly divine. The Lord Jesus Christ, living in Palestine only twenty-five years before, is now wondrously resident in God's Church everywhere. He is also regarded as one with God as the source of blessing. The Lordship of Christ is mentioned six times in these opening verses.

In Christ Jesus, is an original and favorite Pauline formula to express the Christian's intimate and vital union with the risen Jesus. The phrase, in Christ, means as a member of the Church. Paul later refers to the Church as the Body of Christ. It is in some way a part of Christ's own personality. All the divine powers and all the qualities of character which belong to Jesus Christ himself are passed on the members of the Christian community, so that in a real sense they share in the life of the Son of God.

"Grace and peace," Paul's customary salutation, signify the gracious goodness of God and the gifts that are the effect of the divine liberality. In the New Testament grace is a soteriological term; it is the favor God shows and the gift he gives to men whom he saves in Christ. Grace is God's overwhelming kindness towards us, a kindness which we have done nothing whatsoever to deserve. It is shown to us by Jesus Christ. Augustine defined grace as "God's love at work in man's behalf." Grace is the God-given basis of all the Christian life; peace is the outcome of God's redemption in Christ. Peace is the fruit of the salvation God gives in Christ. It includes the forgiveness of sins and reconciliation with God as well as harmony among men. Perfect peace will be realized only at the Parousia, when Christ's redemptive work is completed.

God is faithful, a God upon whom one can depend. God's fidelity to his promises is a major Old Testament theme; it is realized by the call of men to communion with Christ, to share his divine filiation and his life. Communion finds it a basis in the realities held in common by several persons, material or spiritual realities. The communion among Christians, from which all others derive, is the sharing in strictly divine benefits. It unites us to the Father and to his Son, Jesus Christ. It gives us a share in the glory to come. Because Christ assumed our human nature, we share in the divine nature. The word communion became characteristic of the Christian community (Ac 2:42).

The fellowship of God's Son, that is, union with him, is the keynote of 1 and 2 Cor. Fellowship (koinonia), or better, communion, in its usual signification is the sharing together, the joint participation as common possessors of anything. Here it refers to the life, which by means of faith, is common to the believer and his Lord. The vital union of the faithful among themselves arises from their union with Christ. Reception of the Eucharist is the expression and the cause, the nourishment of this fellowship (1 Cor 10:16-17). The nine verses of Paul's introduction (1 Cor 1:1-9) record nine occurrences of the name of the Lord Jesus Christ. In all Paul's thinking, Christ is of cardinal importance and whether it be a problem of division, moral failure, or doctrinal error, Christ is the answer.

Paul establishes at some length the supremacy of divine wisdom, true wisdom, over the false wisdom of the world (1 Cor 1:17-21). This divine wisdom was incarnated in Jesus and crucified in him (1:22-31), but went unknown (2:8). This is the paradox of the cross: God saves through weakness and in spite of folly, revealing in Christ nailed to the Cross, his true power and wisdom. The life of those who believe in the gospel is transformed by the influence of Christ dwelling in them by his Spirit, and molding them to God's will. "The message of the cross is folly to those who are perishing, but to us who are being saved it is the power of God" (1 Cor 1:18). In all this passage Paul is rejecting not genuine human wisdom, a gift from God enabling one to know God, but a proud self-sufficient wisdom, vain philosophical speculation and tricks of rhetoric. Paul contrasts human wisdom, which leaves God out of account and is man-centered, with the wisdom of God. St. Thomas Aquinas remarks that men are accustomed to regard as foolishness whatever surpasses their understanding.

"Jews demand signs and Greeks seek wisdom, but we preach Christ crucified, a stumbling block to Jews and folly to Gentiles, but to those who are called, both Jews and Greeks, Christ the power of God and the wisdom of God. For the foolishness of God is wiser than men, and the weakness of God is stronger than men" (1 Cor 1:22-25). The supreme power and wisdom are to be found in Christ. The absoluteness of the Christian religion is the absoluteness of Christ. Christ crucified, the living, risen Christ who was crucified, is the power of God because he enables the sinner to overcome his sin; and the wisdom of God because he reveals the mind of God and the practicable way of salvation. It is on Calvary and nowhere else that souls are mastered and saved; it is on Calvary as nowhere else that they discover the truth about God and man and destiny.

Humanly, the cross appears contrary to expectation both for Jew and Greek, a failure, a defeat, instead of a glorious manifestation, a folly instead of wisdom. But to faith, the cross appears as divine power and wisdom, fulfilling and surpassing expectation. In men's eyes the gospel is both offensive and absurd. To the Jews the idea of a crucified Messiah is self-contradictory and blasphemous. To the Greeks the divine claims of one ignominiously executed cannot be taken seriously; for God to take human form and then be put to death was to them incomprehensible. The gospel message shocks Jewish nationalism and Greek intellectualism. The Jews looked for a Messiah who would inaugurate their nation's sovereignty over the Gentiles by a display of miraculous power. The Greeks studied philosophies that pretended to give a satisfactory explanation of man and the cosmos. The Jews were seeking human security: miracles guaranteeing the truth of the message (Jn 4:48); the Gentiles, wisdom or doctrine satisfying an intellect avid for knowledge. This quest is not in itself reprehensible, and paradoxically the cross of Christ will answer it. But if it is a preliminary requirement without which adhesion is refused, it is inadmissible. The gospel is not a new philosophy, but a message to be accepted and lived.

"God it is who has given you life in Christ Jesus. He made him our wisdom, our righteousness and sanctification and redemption" (1 Cor 1:30). Christian wisdom is found in Christ and it contains a total salvation: righteousness, sanctification, redemption. These three ideas are the basic themes of the epistle to the Romans. In Christ the Christian possesses all that the Jew and the Greek yearned for. Christ who is the yes to all the promises of God, embodies the divine righteousness, that is, God's faithfulness to his promises of salvation. As the embodiment of God's holiness and the dispenser of the spirit of holiness imparted at baptism, the risen Christ has become holiness for us. Finally, Christ has freed man from slavery to sin, the flesh, the law, and death.

In proposing Christ Jesus as wisdom, Paul points out Christ as the culmination of the three chief tendencies in the Old Testament search for God. The Mosaic code and cult strove to impart justice and sanctification. The prophets proclaimed Yahweh's definitive act of redemption. The sapiential literature strove to teach humano-divine wisdom. Thus Paul shows that the striving of pagan religion as of the Jewish faith finds its consummation in Christ Jesus.

Our real existence is an existence in union with Christ, and all that we need of wisdom is present in him. Righteousness, sanctification, and redemption fill out the meaning of wisdom. Righteousness refers primarily to forgiveness and justification. In sanctification the notion is of the new life of holiness as brought about in us by Christ. Redemption is an inclusive word describing the freeing of the Christian from the slavery of sin. Observe that the content of wisdom is given in terms which apply to the religious and moral, not the definitely intellectual side of life. Christianity is not an esoteric theosophy.

"I decided to know nothing among you except Jesus Christ and him crucified . . . that your faith might not rest in the wisdom of men but in the power of God . . . We impart a secret and hidden wisdom of God, which God decreed before the ages for our glorification. None of the rulers of this age understood this; for if they had they would not have crucified the Lord of glory" (1 Cor 2:2-8). Glory is the manifestation of Yahweh's power, it is the incommunicable attribute of God. The title, Lord of glory, implies the same dignity for Jesus as that of Yahweh himself.

The discourses of human wisdom are convincing of themselves; they generate a purely human adherence. Of this Paul will have no part. His word is a demonstration but it manifests the action of the Spirit and demands an adherence of another order, that of the Spirit. The basic theme of Paul's preaching was Christ crucified. Paul's invariable practice was to concentrate on the central truth: who Jesus is, that is, the Christ or promised Messiah; and that hope of salvation lies in what he did, his crucifixion. He refused to abate anything of the paradox of a crucified Messiah.

The Christian message is rightly termed a wisdom, but a God-given wisdom pertaining to man's ultimate destiny through God's power. It is not an enigmatic wisdom but one whose object is God's wise plan of salvation, not an afterthought but an eternal plan realized in Christ. The secret wisdom which Paul imparts is the plenitude of God's purpose of redemption in Christ, which includes, among other things, this incorporation of both Jews and Gentiles in the Church, and man's victory over death. Behind the evil designs of the earthly authorities, like Caiaphas and Pilate, were the demonic powers of darkness, using them as their tools. Not recognizing Christ for what he was, they crucified him; but his cross was the means of his victory over them. They brought their own destruction on themselves.

13

THE MIND OF CHRIST

The man with the Spirit has the mind of Christ (1 Cor 2:16). Christ belongs to God, we belong to Christ (1 Cor 3:23) by baptism in his Spirit (1 Cor 6:11). It is on an energetic recall of the first commandment that Paul (1 Cor 8:6) bases the course of conduct he suggests in solution for the problem of idol-meats. The problem of the resurrection of the dead is the occasion for Paul to celebrate the supremacy of the risen Christ (1 Cor 15:5-28).

The wisdom of God is not an attainment but an endowment, a gift of God which is mediated to man through the Spirit (1 Cor 2:12). The natural, unspiritual man may have all the intellectual qualities necessary to comprehend the wisdom of man, but he cannot understand the wisdom of God without the spiritual qualities that come only from acceptance of the gospel: humility, purity of heart, and submission to the influence of Christ. The man with the Spirit has the mind of Christ (1 Cor 2:16). The Spirit of the Lord dwells and acts in the spiritual man so that he thinks as Christ does and judges all things rightly from a supernatural viewpoint. God's truth is only revealed to those in sympathy with the spirit and character of Christ. There can be no revelation apart from Christ. The mind of Christ is at once the source of revelation and the test of its authenticity, the ultimate touchstone.

The Christian preacher has his place in the spreading of the gospel, yet the good done on earth is done by the Lord. "I planted, Apollos watered, but God gave the growth . . . We are all God's fellow workers; you are God's field, God's building" (1 Cor 3:6, 9). Such declarations as this bring God very near to his Church. The harp yields no sound till it is touched by the hand of the musician. The heart is never made good till God's love is poured into it. "No other foundation can any one lay than that which is laid, which is Jesus Christ" (1 Cor 3:11). Organization has its place, forms of worship have their place, but the Church is not founded upon a program or a platform; it is founded on a person, Christ. Faith in Christ as savior and willing submission to his influence are the foundation on which Christian character must be built.

"Do you not know that you are God's temple, and that God's Spirit dwells in you? . . . God's temple is holy, and you are that temple" (1 Cor 3:16-17). God's building becomes God's temple. The Christian community, the body of Christ is the true temple of the new covenant. The Spirit who dwells in it realizes what was prefigured in the old temple, the place where God's glory dwelt. Temple (naos) designates the innermost part of a sacred precinct, in which in the pagan temple areas, the statue of the god was found; the word applied to the Jewish temple indicates the Holy of Holies, the most sacred part of the temple, in which God had his special dwelling place. God's Spirit sanctifies the Christian community, making it holy, that is, set apart for God's use, and sanctified by his presence. God reigns in the hearts of his servants by the power of his grace; there is his kingdom. They serve him, giving him thanks and praise; that is his glory. Such is the religion and worship of God in this temple. Here the Corinthian community is the temple of God, because the divine Spirit dwells in it. Later (1 Cor 6:19) the metaphor will be applied to the body of the individual Christian, because the Spirit dwells in every one of the baptized. In Ep 2:19 the universal Church is God's temple.

"You belong to Christ and Christ belongs to God" (1 Cor 3:23). This impressive peroration is characteristic of Paul. He never stops until he has traced the streams of authority and power and glory back to their springs in the bosom of the Father. Christ is the gift of God's eternal love and mercy to mankind. Each believer belongs to and is responsible to Christ. Christ is God's. No subordination within the Godhead is intended. Christ's essential nature and equality (Ph 2:6) with God are not under discussion, but his mission for man's salvation. The Messiah and his people are viewed as one entity belonging to God. The incarnate Son voluntarily took a lowly place among men to bring about man's salvation. Christ has all because he is content to belong to the Father (Jn 14:28, 1 Cor 11:3); and we have all, while we are content to belong to him.

"You were washed, you were sanctified, you were justified in the name of the Lord Jesus Christ and in the Spirit of God" (1 Cor 6:11). The terms washed etc. are in reality synonymous, each presenting one aspect of the total effect of baptism. Baptism is given in the name of the Lord Jesus, that is, through spiritual union with him and continual submission to his influence. The Holy Spirit also is the instrument of our sanctification and justification, by virtue of our indwelling in him and he in us, making Christ's death to sin and his life in righteousness an accomplished fact in our hearts and lives. Purification from sin, sanctification, that is, holiness, a state of consecration to God, and justification are the consequences of baptismal incorporation in Christ. The Spirit is the agent of this spiritual regeneration, of this new creation which is God's gift to us in Christ. Christ is the meritorious cause of justification, the Holy Spirit, by appropriation, is its efficient cause; both operate in the sacramental rites, which create a state of interior and spiritual holiness by the grace of the Father. Note the unconscious Trinitarian formula.

At an early date the eating of idol-meats, that is meat offered in pagan sacrifices, was expressly forbidden in a decree of the Apostolic Council (Ac 15:28-29). The prohibition raised serious practical difficulties. In Gentile communities it was often inconvenient, if not impossible, to procure food that had not been offered to idols. The result was that the Christian could not always be certain that he was not eating food that had been offered to idols. In a long passage (1 Cor 8, 9, 10) Paul answers these specific difficulties. In principle, enlightened Christians are completely free to decide for themselves; but they must avoid leading astray other Christians who are not yet emancipated from their pre-conversion ideas.

Much of the meat sold in the market places had come from animals sacrificed in pagan temples. Many Christians had scruples about eating such meat. Others, however, felt superior to scruples, and contemptuous toward those troubled by them. These superior people with their knowledge, Paul rebukes for their lack of love. The true blessedness consists not in knowing but in being known by God, and it is in love that one is thus known. "Knowledge puffs up, but love builds up . . . If one loves God, one is known by him" (1 Cor 8:1, 3). Love must be allowed to settle the problem, not superior knowledge; the latter makes men conceited, the former strengthens the Church (Ep 4:16). Knowledge must be tempered by love. Knowledge easily breeds conceit, provides glib answers. What matters more is love. This promotes the good of others and means being known by God, that is, acknowledged by him as his. Love (agape), a noun rarely found in profane Greek before the Christian era, has become in the New Testament the technical term for what we call the virtue of charity. It is used to express God's gratuitous love for men exercised in Christ and passed on to believers that they may love one another.

"For us there is one God, the Father, from whom are all things and for whom we exist, and one Lord Jesus Christ, through whom are all things and through whom we exist" (1 Cor 8:6). It is on this energetic recall of the first commandment that Paul bases the course of conduct he suggests. The worship of idols is without foundation. There is only one God, the Father and creator of the universe who has made us for himself, and only one Lord Jesus Christ through whom we are brought to the Father. The prepositions are instructive: of God, from whom indicates the source of creation; for whom, the flow-back of redeemed creation, suggesting the direction of our lives. We live for him. There is in reality only one God, who has created the whole universe. It is this God toward whom we move. The eventual destiny of the whole human race, and each separate member of it, is life with God.

God the Father is the source of all things and the goal of each one of us; the Lord Jesus is the agent of all creation to whom we owe our being. It is distinctive of us Christians to acknowledge the one God as Father, and as the first and final cause of the universe; and with him to acknowledge Jesus Christ also as Lord, as God, and as the agent of all creation. Christ is called Lord because the Father has given him all sovereignty over heaven, earth, and the nether regions (Ph 2:9-11). Christ is presented as anterior to creation and as its author. The phrase "through whom we exist" expresses the mediatorial role of Christ. He is the way that leads us to the Father, the ultimate goal of our life. We depend on him at every moment of our existence as creatures and of our life as children of God.

The problem of the resurrection of the dead is the occasion for Paul to celebrate the supremacy of the risen Christ. He reaffirms the resurrection of Christ (1 Cor 15:5-20); it is by him that our resurrection will take place (21-28). "Christ has been raised from the dead, the first fruits of those who have fallen asleep . . . Christ, the first fruits, then at his coming those who belong to Christ" (1 Cor 15:20, 23). The first sheaf of the harvest brought to the temple on the first day following the Passover celebration, represented the entire harvest, given by God and consecrated to him. Just so the raising of Christ by God's power portends and pledges the resurrection of all Christians. First fruits implies community of nature with the harvest to follow; Christ's resurrection promises the ultimate home-gathering of all God's people. The full harvest was foreshadowed and consecrated by the first sheaf brought as an offering on the day following the sabbath after the Passover, that is, on Easter Day, the day of Christ's resurrection. Death with its sting gone is for Christians no more than falling asleep. The resurrection of Christ has changed our whole outlook; it has transformed all our "sunsets into dawns" (Clement). Now that Christ has been raised, the grave has become the Cape of Good Hope in the life of the Christian.

Paul summarizes briefly the final events of Christ's kingdom. "Then comes the end, when he delivers the kingdom to God the Father after destroying every rule and every authority and power. For he must reign until he has put all his enemies under his feet. The last enemy to be destroyed is death. For God has put all things in subjection under his feet" (1 Cor 15:24-27). Paul applies to Christ, the new Adam what is predicated of Adam and mankind in general in Ps 8:7. The Father has subjected all created things to his Incarnate Son who was sent to redeem the world and establish divine sovereignty. Since his glorious resurrection, Christ reigns in glory; he is Lord. At his Parousia, his royal majesty will be manifested to all. With the resurrection of the dead at the end of time, Christ's victory will be complete; everything, death included, has been placed under his feet.

The preaching of Jesus and his purpose was to establish God's reign, his sovereignty. This commission granted to the Son will then have been fulfilled and will be delivered to the Father. Christ's work as Messiah will then be completed. As Messiah he is the divinely appointed king, and his rule is in force in the period of time between his resurrection and his return. His function is to overcome and abolish all the forces of evil, all that is hostile to God. Death is here personified as one of these enemies, the supreme evil power. The preliminary defeat of death took place when Jesus was raised from the dead, but complete victory will not be achieved until the general resurrection occurs. When this happens it will show that all the forces of evil have been at last annihilated. The Messianic function of Christ will therefore come to an end.

"When all things are subjected to him, then the Son himself will also be subjected to him who put all things under him, that God may be everything to everyone" (1 Cor 15:28). When the whole cosmos has been subjected to him, Jesus will go to the Father and report that his task is complete. This is not, however, the ceasing of Christ's rule but the inauguration of God's eternal kingdom. The question here is one of function. His task completed, the redeemer, man's mediator, surrenders the kingdom to him who sent him. Their essential equality and unity remains. Paul contemplates the last majestic scene; earth's history ends as the Son delivers up the kingdom to the Father, and God is all in all.

With the completion of Christ's redemptive mission, God will be manifested as the first principle of all life and the final end of all creation and of salvation history. All in all, is an expression of unlimited comprehensiveness. Everything will answer to God's will and reflect his mind. The goal is that God may be everything to everyone. This does not mean loss of all distinction by absorption in God, but the perfectly acknowledged rule of the God of love over all his creatures. God's kingdom will be completely established and he will be the sole object of contemplation and adoration by all created beings. The resurrection of Christ is not only a pledge of the believer's personal resurrection; it is also an earnest of the ultimate triumph of the kingdom.

"Thanks be to God who gives us the victory through our Lord Jesus Christ" (1 Cor 15:57). God gives us the victory over sin now and hereafter over death. The thought is characteristic of Paul. It is in Christ and in him alone that the believer finds the antidote to sin; it is only as we live in him that we can share in his victory over death and sin.

14

THE GLORY OF CHRIST

In 2 Cor Paul continues to foster the spirit of adoration. Through Christ we share abundantly in the consolation offered by the God of all consolation (2 Cor 1:5). Christ is the yes of God (2 Cor 1:20). We are the aroma of Christ to God (2 Cor 2:15) and the reflection of Christ's glory, being transformed by the Spirit into a more and more perfect image of God in Christ (2 Cor 3:18). The controlling power in a Christian's life is the love of Christ (2 Cor 5:14). The Christian living in Christ is a new creation (2 Cor 5:17) and shares in the righteousness of God (2 Cor 5:21). The rich Christ became poor for our sake (2 Cor 8:9). Christ is God's inexpressible gift (2 Cor 9:15).

In 2 Cor Paul continues to foster the spirit of adoration. "Blessed be the God and Father of our Lord Jesus Christ, the Father of mercies and the God of all consolation, who comforts us in all our afflictions, so that we may be able to comfort those who are in any affliction, with the consolation with which we ourselves are comforted" (2 Cor 1:3-4). Consolation is announced by the prophets as characteristic of the Messianic era and was to be brought by the Messiah (Lk 2:25). It consists essentially in the end of trial and the beginning of an era of peace and joy. The Christian united to Christ is consoled in the midst of suffering itself. Its only source is God through Christ and the Holy Spirit;

and the Christian must communicate it. Among its causes the New Testament mentions: progress in the Christian life, conversion, the Scriptures. It is the source of Christian hope.

"For as we share abundantly in Christ's sufferings, so through Christ we share abundantly in comfort too" (2 Cor 1:5). Paul constantly insists on the presence of antagonistic, even contradictory realities in Christ and in the Christian: suffering and consolation, weakness and strength. This is the Paschal mystery, the presence of the risen Christ in the midst of a sinful world.

Paul's critics accused him of being vacillating. "As surely as God is faithful, our word to you has not been yes and no. For the Son of God, Jesus Christ whom we preached among you was not yes and no; but with him it was always yes" (2 Cor 1:18-19). The fidelity of God is above all his reliability. He is the rock of Israel; one can rest on him in all security. This solidity explains the constancy of his plans and the fidelity to his promises, and especially in the New Testament, God's fidelity to his plan of mercy and salvation in Christ. Christ is God's affirmation to man's highest hopes, the fulfillment of all God's promises.

"For all the promises of God find their yes in him. That is why we utter the Amen through him, to the glory of God" (2 Cor 1:20). God's fidelity to his promises was expressed in all fullness in Jesus Christ. Yes represents the Greek, and Amen the Hebrew form of affirmation. Paul characteristically brings together the two languages. Christ is God's yes; that is why it is in Christ's name that we say Amen at the end of our prayers. Amen means it is solid, true, sure, worthy of trust; it is man's answer of fidelity to God's fidelity in Jesus. It is given to Jesus as a proper name (Rv 1:2, 5), since he is the truthful witness of God's promises.

"Thanks be to God who is in Christ and always leads us in triumph and through us spreads the fragrance of the knowledge of him everywhere. For we are the aroma of Christ to God" (2 Cor 2:14-15). Like a victorious general making his solemn entry into Rome, God passes triumphantly through the world with his apostles in his train. The fragrance is the odor of incense in connection with such processions and with sacrifice. The gospel of Christ is depicted as the fragrance of the knowledge of God; the apostle as one who spreads the aroma of Christ. Through the apostles the fragrance of the knowledge of God is everywhere manifested. Then with a change in the metaphor, the Apostles themselves appear as an aroma, though it is Christ's, not their own. The apostles are the aroma of Christ, that is, a sacrifice pleasing to God. The term aroma is a technical term for a sacrifice acceptable to God. Those who preach the gospel please God by their work which is Christ's work. It is an offering made by Christ, since it is Christ who inspires and directs their preaching.

Paul describes the metamorphosis of the Christian. "We all, with unveiled face, reflecting the glory of the Lord, are being changed into his image, from one degree of glory to another; for this comes from the Lord who is the Spirit" (2 Cor 3:18). The glory of the Lord is that of Jesus Christ, since the glory of God shines on the face of Christ (2 Cor 4:6). The Christian is transformed by the Spirit into a more and more perfect image of God in Christ. Rm 8:29 states that it is God's intention that Christians should become true images of his Son. He who keeps the memory and the example of Christ ever before his mind's eye and tries to follow him in his life, will gradually come to show in his own character and life an increasing likeness to his Lord. We contemplate Christ and reflect like a mirror the glory of the Son of God. So we are being continually transformed into the image of Christ, who is the image of God. This divinization cannot fail, for it takes place under the action of the Spirit of the Lord Jesus, to whom such transforming efficiency is proper.

"The Lord who is the Spirit" is a summary statement which does not deny the distinction of Christ and the Spirit, but affirms their identity in the work of salvation of both testaments. In the same manner later theology will affirm that all the works of God are common to the three Persons. St. Paul is thinking here of the sphere of divine and creative revelation, he is not expressing a metaphysic of deity. There is a dynamic identification of two known magnitudes, since where the Lord is and works, there is also the Spirit. Paul uses interchangeably Christ and Spirit; both indwell believers and the Church. There is equivalence of function, the work of the Lord being undifferentiated from that of the Spirit. In the Christian experience Christ and his Spirit are one.

"The light of the gospel is the glory of Christ who is the image of God" (2 Cor 4:4). We behold the Lord's glory especially in the mirror of his word, as we fix the eye of our mind on his glory displayed in the gospel. Such is the value of persevering Christian contemplation. As speech is the organ of human society and the means of human civilization, so is prayer the instrument of divine fellowship and divine training. Christ is the image of God; in Jesus the likeness of God the Father is fully present. Christ is the visible representation, expression of the invisible God. Christ is the expression of God's character of love and holiness. The terms glory and image express the consubstantiality of Christ with the Father in his divinity.

"It is the God who said, 'Let light shine out of darkness' who has shone in our hearts, that we in turn might make known the glory of God shining on the face of Christ" (2 Cor 4:6). He who gave natural light gave also spiritual life. In the first creation God's fiat brought light. To live as a Christian is a totally new kind of life, a re-creation in which light comes personally. The knowledge in faith of Christ as Incarnate Son of God is the foundation of the Christian transformation, and it must be passed on to others. Paul associates light and glory to the possession of the Spirit in our hearts.

"The love of Christ impels us . . . He died for all, that those who live might live no longer for themselves but for him who for their sakes died and was raised" (2 Cor 5:14-15). In his dealings with people Paul is motivated by love for Christ. His life was subjected to a compelling influence, the self-giving love of Christ. The love that Christ had for Paul produced a resultant love for the Lord Jesus. By its nature, love is mutual; there must be a movement from within and from without; that is, of each of the lovers toward the other. The love that Christ has for us works on us by grace. The love of Christ is an abiding motive. It is neither a fancy, nor a sentiment, nor an evanescent emotion. It is a principle, calm, steady, undecaying. Of all principles, affection to the Savior is the steadiest and most secure. Other incentives to action are apt to alter or lose their influence altogether.

As God so loved the world as to give his Son for it, and as Christ so loved the world as to pour out his life for it, so we, moved by the very same love, desire to spend and be spent for the glory of God and the salvation of souls. The controlling power in Paul's as well as in a Christian's life, is the love of Christ; and of the death in which that love was revealed, Paul finds the meaning to be the death of all when one died for all, and the purpose to be an incentive to men to find the center of their lives not in themselves, but in him who died and was raised on their behalf. There is a new internal relation to Christ, and he who possesses it is a new creation; the old has passed away, has been transformed into the new. The whole process has its source in God.

"If anyone is in Christ, he is a new creation . . . It is all God's work" (2 Cor 5:17-18). God, who created all things through Christ, has restored his work, deformed by sin, by re-creating it in Christ. The central figure of this new creation is the new man created in Christ, to lead a new life of justice and holiness. The belief that Christ acted representatively on behalf of the whole human race is the key principle of Paul's theology. Because Christ died, the sinful human race whom he represented has in principle been destroyed so that there is the possibility of a fresh start, a new world, for those who are united to Christ and so share the life he now possesses. There is a new creation because there are changed methods of appreciation and values. A Christian looks at things from a different standpoint, tries them by a different standard, because he is united to Christ in such a way that he lives always under Christ's indwelling, purifying, and transforming influence. In Christ is Paul's favorite expression for a Christian and denotes the most intimate faith-union with Jesus in his death and resurrection. In the New Testament the death and resurrection of Jesus are always linked. Death without resurrection would evacuate Calvary of all its meaning. And as in the old creation, everything was created by God through his word, so in the new all is from God through Christ.

"For our sake he made him to be sin who knew no sin, so that in him we might become the righteousness of God" (2 Cor 5:21). By a kind of legal fiction, God identified Jesus with sin so that he might bear the curse incurred by sin. It could be that the word sin is taken here as sacrifice-victim for sin, since the same Hebrew word (hattat) can have both meanings. Paul does not say "made him a sinner;" the sinless Christ bore the burden of our sin that we might be acquitted before God. Christ, though not himself a sinner, identified with man in his sin, becoming so involved in it that he shared man's fate and dealt effectively with his predicament. Christ had to bear not the guilt but the burden of sin. He bore its penalty not as a punishment, but as the innocent suffers for the guilty; feeling all its shame and horror, but free from the sense of guilt and degradation. The spectacle of Christ thus bearing our penalty touches the heart and conscience, and makes us respond to the love wherewith he loved us. Christ, in paths beyond our ability to trace, became identified with a righteousness which is divine in character and origin, God's righteousness. Because Christ has identified himself with our sinful situation, we in turn may identify ourselves with his goodness which belongs to God himself and which Christ shares.

In 2 Cor 6:16 Paul reaffirms once again the fundamental opposition between Christ and idols. "What agreement has the temple of God with idols? For we are the temple of the living God." There can be no dealing with idols on the part of those who are themselves God's temple. He warned them against idolatry by referring to the Lord's Supper (1 Cor 10:14-16); he warns them now by the great truth that believers are the temple of God.

"You know the grace (generosity) of our Lord Jesus Christ, that though he was rich, yet for your sake he became poor, so that by his poverty you might become rich" (2 Cor 8:9). Christ voluntarily despoiled himself on earth of his glory and divine privileges because he wanted to share our sufferings and our death, to enrich us with the privileges he had renounced. The same theme is found in Ph 2:6-11 but it focuses here on Christ's saving work and not on his ultimate glorification by the Father as in Ph. Christ's preexistent glory and his incarnation are briefly stated in the two words, rich and poor. The impressiveness of this Christology is the greater for its almost casual appearance. The self-abasement of the incarnation is made here the basis of an appeal for charity, in the same way as in Philipians it is for humility. Paul's ethical teaching is rooted in doctrine.

In reflecting on the grace of generosity to be given by God to the Corinthians, Paul is led to think of Christ, God's inexpressibly generous gift. "Thanks be to God for his inexpressible gift" (2 Cor 9:15). Not only for the generosity he inspires but also and much more, for the gift of Christ himself, the embodiment of the self-giving of God, the source of all Christian giving.

2 Cor closes with the fullest form of Paul's usual benediction. "The grace of the Lord Jesus Christ and the love of God and the fellowship of the Holy Spirit be with you all" (2 Cor 13:13). It is in keeping with Paul's character for him to think first of the grace of Christ, or of the grace of God revealed through Christ, for thereby has God's love been apprehended, and there from the fellowship of the Holy Spirit has become a continuing reality. This benediction sweeps majestically from eternity to eternity. It contemplates the love of God rooted in an infinite past, realized in the historical Jesus, and perpetuating itself through all time by the Holy Spirit.

15

CHRIST LIVES IN ME

Gal 6:18 sums up the teaching of the epistle to the Galatians: salvation by grace and not by law, and the centrality of the Lord Jesus. Paul received his gospel through a revelation of Jesus Christ (Gal 1:12). The vital acts of the Christian become somehow the acts of Christ who lives in him (Gal 2:20). Our union with Christ is ratified by baptism (Gal 3:26-28, Rm 6:1-11). Paul glories only in the cross of our Lord Jesus Christ (Gal 6:14).

The epistles to the Corinthians contrast Christ as the wisdom of God, with vain human wisdom. The epistles to the Galatians and the Romans contrast Christ, the justice of God, with the justice men would pretend to achieve by their own efforts. Rm and Gal face the same problem and develop the same theme: the true function of the Mosaic law and its relation to God's grace manifested in Christ. Gal is a first reaction provoked by a concrete situation, the Judaizing teachers who were insisting on the obligation of keeping intact the Mosaic Law. Rm is a more complete exposition of the question expressing the full maturity of Paul's thought on the subject.

Gal is often called the Magna Carta of Christian liberty; man becomes right with God only by faith in Christ. The principles enunciated here made Christianity a world religion instead of a Jewish sect. Some important themes of Gal are, first, salvation by grace alone. This is the gospel of grace, the central issue of Christianity. No man can win acceptance with God on terms other than God's grace given freely. Anything less amounts to a denial of the completeness and finality of the cross of Christ. Another theme is justification by faith; faith on man's part is the only proper response to God's movement towards him in grace. Faith and grace are irreducible and crucial elements of the gospel, the hallmarks of Christianity. Another theme is the freedom of grace and faith, which is not an invitation to false security and to careless standards of living.

From the onset, Paul affirms the resurrection of Christ, redeemer for the sins of the world, and gives glory to God (Gal 1:1-5). He recalls his conversion, the ground of his apostolate (1:12-16). "Grace to you and peace from God the Father and our Lord Jesus Christ, who gave himself for our sins to deliver us from the present evil age, according to the will of our God and Father, to whom be glory for ever and ever. Amen" (1:3-5). The letter's dominant theme is sounded: salvation through Christ according to the Father's plan. We must not overlook the importance of this passage at this early stage of Christian teaching. The name of our Lord Jesus Christ is already coupled in equality with that of God the Father. Moreover, his self-giving is for our sins; the redemptive purpose of the death of Christ is already established as the basis of the gospel. These are the most essential elements of Christian preaching and belief.

Paul received his gospel "through a revelation of Jesus Christ" (Gal 1:12) and God who called him through his grace "was pleased to reveal his Son in me" (16). Christ is at the same time the author and object of the revelation Paul received at the time of his conversion. It is Christ who was revealed to Paul, which disclosure carried along with it the conviction of the truth of the Christian doctrine. The revelation included for him divinely prompted reinterpretation of the Christian facts, which he before held to be punishable blasphemy, and divinely given new insights on the Christian realities. Paul thus got a true understanding of who Jesus Christ is, and of what he came to do. Paul is not denying that his vision was real; he is stressing the inwardness of this real vision and relating this inwardness to his call as apostle of the Gentiles. Paul's highly personal testimony and confession of indebtedness to grace alone, in his conversion, is a powerful apologetic for the gratuitous and decisive character of the saving act of God in Christ.

The key terms found in Gal 2:15-21, such as justification, grace, cross, faith, and union with Christ, comprise the heart of the gospel and of Christian experience. "I have been crucified with Christ; it is no longer I who live, but Christ who lives in me; and the life I now live in the flesh, I live by faith in the Son of God, who loved me and gave himself for me" (Gal 2:20). This is a declaration of Paul's own living faith. Though still in the flesh, the life of the Christian is already spiritualized by faith. The vital acts of the Christian become somehow the acts of Christ. Life for a Christian is lived in a new dimension. Paul's mystical union with Christ does not destroy his own personality, but sustains and molds his Christian life. The perfection of the Christian life is not merely an existence dominated by a new psychological motivation, living for God. Faith reshapes man internally with a new principle of activity on the ontological level of his being. A symbiosis results of man with Christ, the glorified Kyrios, who has become as of the resurrection a vivifying Spirit (1 Cor 15:45), the vital principle of Christian activity. The Christian's life is reshaped by the transcendent influence of Christ's indwelling. This is a gem of personal testimony on the nature of salvation and of Christian living. By faith the Christian is identified with Christ in his death, a fact symbolized in baptism (Rm 6:3-4). Henceforth Christ lives within the believer in a supremely personal relation. Only by the interpretation of personal lives do men become personal. Through Christ's own presence in us we become true spiritual persons. Dead with Christ, the Christian lives in Christ and Christ in him. He lives by trust in Christ, just as he committed himself by faith to Christ initially.

Redemption comes not by a mere verbal protestation of love, but through Christ's love for us which brought him to self-sacrificing death. His death was not merely an act of human violence or an accident of history, but the self-giving of Christ on behalf of sinners. Notice that it is the crucified savior who lives in those who have shared his crucifixion. Only those whose former lives have come to an end upon the cross of Christ, have Christ living in them. For union with Christ implies union with his death (Rm 6:3). Through the power of Christ's cross, the Christian dies to his old life of sin, and yet he lives in a truer sense than before. He lives by faith in the Son of God who is the source and support of his life, the indwelling power of a new righteousness. He is so entirely under the influence of Christ that his thoughts and deeds are prompted by his savior. All that is, he owes to Christ who abides in him. The spiritual relation between Christ and the believer is so intimate that it can only be described as Christ living in him. Christ is the fountain of life in his inmost soul, from all his tempers, words, and actions flow.

"He loved me." Paul appropriates himself the love which belongs equally to the whole world. For Christ is indeed the personal friend of each man individually; and he is as much to him as if he had died for him alone. We have here the beginning of Paul's thought on identification with the body of Christ which later leads to the doctrine of the Church as the body of Christ. We should also think of the link with the death of Christ that is expressed and realized in the Lord's Supper.

Three essential aspects of the new life are expressed in this verse (Gal 2:20). First it is bestowed in the twofold event of Christ's crucifixion-resurrection. By participation in Christ's death one dies to his old self and is freed from the tyranny of sin. And by participation in Christ's resurrection, one lives to God and is freed for a life of responsible and grateful obedience. The Christian's life is so invested by the power and grace of God that Paul may say it is not the Christian himself who lives but Christ who lives in him. Secondly, the new life is lived in the flesh, in the world, but it is by faith. Faith is man's response to God's saving initiative taken on the cross, openness to the gift of grace, and obedience to the demands of love. Finally, Paul defines the object and content of his faith as "in the Son of God who loved me and gave himself for me." Here, as in Jn 3:16, it is the whole event of the incarnation, but especially the crucifixion, which is in the author's mind as the decisive act of self-giving love. And in each passage the benefits of Christ's passion are said to be received by faith which each writer understands as grateful

obedience to the commandment of love. Love is total, uncon-
ditional surrender to God's will, the complete giving of oneself to
others, as the instance of God's own sacrificial love on the cross
effectively reveals.

Our union with Christ is ratified by baptism. "In Christ Jesus
you are all sons of God, through faith. For as many of you as were
baptized into Christ, have put on Christ. There is neither Jew nor
Greek, there is neither slave nor free, there is neither male nor
female, for you are all one in Christ Jesus" (Gal 3:26-28). That
we are all sons of God is one of the most characteristic and at the
same time one of the most profound doctrines of Christianity. To
Paul this was the ultimate idea. It is by reason of the vital union
of believers with Christ, the only-begotten Son of God, that we
are sons of God.

Faith and baptism go together. In baptism we put on Christ.
The figure of changing garments attests to the inner spiritual
change. We strip off the clothes of the old life to be clothed with
the garments of Christ's righteousness through faith-baptism.
Baptism is the sign and seal of one's crucifixion and new life
with Christ. And since baptism unites all men with Christ, it
unites them with one another, for all are brethren for whom
Christ died, and all who believed, without distinction have one
Lord.

The effects of baptism are described at greater length in Rm
6:1-11. Here is the basis of the idea of the Church as the body of
Christ, and of believing existence as incorporation into Christ.
"All of us who have been baptized into Christ Jesus were
baptized into his death. We were buried with him by baptism into
death, so that as Christ was raised from the dead by the glory of
the Father, we too might walk in newness of life. . . Our old self
was crucified with him so that the sinful body might be destroyed
and we might no longer be enslaved to sin. . . If we have died with
Christ, we believe that we shall also live with him. . . You must
consider yourselves dead to sin and alive to God in Christ Jesus"
(Rm 6:3, 4, 6, 7, 11). The Christian life should be like Christ's
risen life; it should be lived in God's loving presence.

The phrase into Christ connotes the movement of man
toward Christ, the movement of incorporation by which one is

born to life in Christ. Faith and baptism introduce man *into* Christ, identifying him specifically *with* Christ in his passion, death, and resurrection. As a result the Christian in this life lives *in* union with the risen Christ, a union that finds its term when the Christian will one day be with Christ. What is true of Christ is true of the Christian. For a man to be in Christ implies that he was there at Golgotha and in the garden tomb.

Baptism goes with faith and gives it outward expression by the effective symbolism of the baptismal ceremonial. Paul ascribes to faith and to baptism the same effects. Entering the water is like Christ's entering the grave; coming up out of the water is like Christ's coming out of the tomb. The sinner is immersed in water and thus buried with Christ, with whom he emerges to resurrection, as a new creature, a new man, a member of one body, animated by one Spirit. The resurrection will not be complete until the end of time, but is already taking place in the form of a new life in the Spirit. The death-resurrection symbolism of baptism is particularly Pauline, but this initial rite of the Christian life is already spoken of in the New Testament as a cleansing bath, a new birth, an enlightenment.

In Gal 4:8-11 Paul underlines the inanity of idolatry. "Formerly when you did not know God, you were in bondage to beings that by nature are no gods; but now that you have come to know God, or rather to be known by God, how can you turn back again to the weak and elemental spirits whose slaves you want to be once more?" This last reference is to the elements that make up the physical universe.

The Galatians were converted by God who knew them before they knew him. Their knowledge of God did not merely spring from within them; it is the result of the divine predilection, of God's gratuitous election. There is special significance in Paul's preference for the phrase, "be known by God," as a description of the Christian life. The knowledge of God about which Paul speaks is love of him, a response to his love for us (1 Cor 8:2-3). The initiative was God's; they became the object of his gracious concern. We cannot know God unless he gives us the power to do so by taking knowledge of us and bestowing his gifts upon us.

In Gal 4:19, the apostle appeals to their personal loyalty to him through whom Christ was formed in them: "My little children, with whom I am again in travail until Christ be formed in you." The shaping of Christians after the form or model of Christ is the goal of Paul's missionary endeavors. They owe to him their life in Christ because he announced the gospel to them, and now suffers to maintain its truth.

There is a special poignancy in Paul's appeal, though the metaphors are mixed. Paul's mention of his travail suggests he is like a mother to them, even though finally he speaks of Christ's being formed in them. Formed suggests that Christians are destined to share the very nature of Christ. Paul usually speaks of Christians as being in Christ; here it is Christ who is in the Christian. Both forms of expression are consonant with Paul's conception of the Church as the body of Christ. The Christian at his conversion is in Christ and Christ is in the Christian as a pattern and power of his new life. Paul is concerned that his converts should become full-grown men and women in Christ, until maturity of Christian character and comprehension result from their initial turning to Christ.

"Far be it from me to glory except in the cross of our Lord Jesus Christ, by which the world has been crucified to me, and I to the world" (Gal 6:14). The only thing a Christian can be proud of is the cross of Christ, for by the cross the power of the world has been broken. To be in Christ is to be completely reoriented in terms of ultimate values and objectives. So total is this reorientation that it may be spoken of as a crucifixion of self or of the world. By using Christ's full title Paul intends to reaffirm not only the indispensable redemptive act, but the divine nature of Christ, hence of the act. Through the cross Paul's life has been revolutionized. That by it the world has been crucified to Paul, and he to the world, reaffirms his having died in the death Christ died, by which event he is reckoned dead to the world, that is, the world-system as life ordered in alienation from God.

Paul's concluding remarks are noteworthy. "I bear on my body the marks of Christ" (Gal 6:17). He alludes to the scars left by his sufferings for Christ as the brand-marks of his master's ownership. Devotees as well as slaves were tatooed or branded.

The marks of ill-treatment suffered for Christ, the scars of persecution for Paul are glory signs, evidences of the genuiness of his consecration to Christ. Jesus is my master, my protector. A list is given in 2 Cor 11:23-29.

"The grace of our Lord Jesus Christ be with your spirit, brethren. Amen" (Gal 6:18). This sums up the teaching of the epistle: salvation by grace and not by law, and the centrality of the Lord Jesus.

16

THE RIGHTEOUSNESS OF GOD

The obedience of faith (Rm 1:5) is man's answer to the righteousness God offers him (1:17). Paul describes the revelation of God's righteousness in Jesus Christ (3:21-26) and what faith does (27-31). Redemption is in Christ Jesus, whom God appointed as an expiation, by his blood, to be received by faith.

Romans, the longest of Paul's letters contains the fullest and most balanced statement of his theology. Written at the height of his career, it conveys the full richness of his experience of Christ, as well as the full maturity of his thought. In Romans, Paul pens what is in effect his credo, the distillation of over twenty years' reflection on the nature and meaning of the Christian faith. Neither Judaism nor paganism can bridge the separation between sinful man and the utter holiness and perfection of an eternally transcendent God. Only Jesus Christ can lift us up to the heights where God dwells. The unique Son of God makes it possible for all who are united to him by faith, to share his sonship and call God, Father.

In Romans, Paul contrasts the perfection people can achieve by purely human efforts with Christ who is the perfection of God. From the beginning of the epistle he proclaims his vocation: to preach the divine filiation of the risen Jesus, to bring the pagan nations also to "spiritual worship by preaching the good news of his Son" (1:9). It is a spirit of adoration which animates all his efforts in his apostolate, and which he tries to communicate to his correspondents. The apostolic ministry is an act of worship offered to God, like the Christian life itself, since both depend on love. Paul's preaching of the gospel is a priestly service in which he offers the Gentiles as a sacrifice to God. He offers worship in his spirit, that is, the highest element of a human being.

The obedience of faith is the obedience implicit in the virtue of faith. Faith, the answer to the gospel, pledges the whole man. That is why it is always obedience. It implies that man will submit himself freely to God who reveals himself as faithful and truthful, and who, by renewing man, enables him to obey the divine will. Faith and obedience go inextricably together. Only in obedience is there faith, for faith is not emotional feeling, or simple intellectual acceptance, but active response to a person, God; it is trust. A faith in a person creates the relationship in which it is easy to accept his guidance, and so obey him. Paul conceives of faith as a process that begins with hearing and ends with a personal commitment and trusting submission.

The theme of Romans is stated in 1:16-17: in Christ, God has acted powerfully to save men, offering righteousness and new life to be received in faith. "The gospel is the power of God saving all who have faith" (1:16). The gospel message contains a divine efficacy by means of which God can save men. Salvation is one of the most comprehensive terms used in the New Testament to describe the whole purpose of the Incarnation, or to cover the whole range of Christ's mission on earth. Faith is the response of a human being to God as truth and goodness, and so as the one source of salvation. We must believe the kerygma or proclamation of the good news. The kerygma proclaims that God raised Jesus from the dead, made him Kyrios, and through him offers life to all who believe in him. Only faith can effect true holiness, the saving holiness of God himself.

"For in it the righteousness of God is revealed through faith for faith, as it is written, the righteous shall live by faith" (1:17). Shall live implies the gaining of salvation, and is equivalent to the phrase in the gospels "inherit eternal life." Salvation is a matter of faith from start to finish; it starts from faith and ends in faith. Faith is its sole condition.

The righteousness or justice of God is not distributive (reward for deeds) but the saving justice of God who fulfills his promise to save by giving salvation as a free gift. It is the creative goodness of God in action, the Pauline counterpart of the kingdom of God in the teaching of Jesus. In both cases we have a divine intervention, which reveals God at work to deliver man from the powers of evil and to create that right relation between God and man which is man's true life. The righteousness of God is a state of pardon, or acceptance with God, which is not man's achievement, but God's gift, originating in God's own righteous nature.

Righteousness is preeminently in Scripture a divine attribute which sets a lofty standard for human behavior. Indeed, it is too lofty for man's unaided attainment. But the term equally describes God's activity in setting people in the right with himself: its outworking brings salvation. So it can be revealed, that is, brought by God within the sphere of human experience, and received by faith. As a third extension, righteousness becomes the quality of life expected of the believer in his personal relationships; and the standard, hitherto unattainable by a man's natural powers, becomes possible by the indwelling and energizing Holy Spirit. Righteousness is God's saving victory over sin, man's enemy, as well as a moral attribute of God and man, and man's acceptance by God. In the cross and resurrection of Jesus Christ, God has acted in moral and saving righteousness; he has offered to man the gift of righteousness of acceptance with the intent that man may go on to live a life of moral righteousness.

Paul now proceeds to describe the revelation of God's righteousness (3:21-26) and what faith does (27-31). There has now been revealed through Christ, a way of becoming righteous; it is the way of faith. This new way of acceptance with God declared in the Christian message is independent of law (21), a free gift from God through faith in Christ (22-24) and made possible because Christ's death was propitiatory (25-26). Paul's explanation of the relevance of Jesus' death to God's action (3:21-26) is one of the key-passages of this epistle, and indeed of the whole Pauline Corpus, for it contains one of the few approximations to a theological statement of the idea of atonement. Paul sketches, rather than defines, the outlines of the idea of atonement under three main aspects: as a redemption, as propitiatory, and as an object-lesson of God's own righteous character. He makes no effort, however, to construct anything like a dogmatic theory of the atonement, or to explain the modus operandi of the saving efficacy of Christ's death.

"It is the same justice of God that comes through faith to everyone who believes in Jesus Christ . . . since all have sinned and fall short of the glory of God" (3:22-23). This universal deficiency is one view of sin. Both in reality and consciousness, all are far removed from the blazing light of the divine perfection. Men sprung from Adam's stock, have failed to reach their God-intended destiny, and in that sense all fall short of the glory of God. But in face of this universal sinfulness, justification is provided by God in Christ.

The verb to justify and the substantive justice or righteousness appear frequently, especially in Romans. Paul develops this theme along four principal orientations. God is just, that is, he remains faithful to himself and to his plan for man's salvation; this justice is then less distributive than sovereign, royal, salvific; it is a constant feature in the historical action of God; it manifests what God is; it is revealed to man in Jesus Christ and communicated by the gospel (1:17). This justice in action is exercised in favor of sinful man. It results in a verdict of grace which requires from man simply a humble reception, the obedience of faith. All auto-justification is consequently excluded. Finally, God's gratuitous act, which justifies man, creates in him a new life, the life of the Spirit, sanctification. Man justified places himself in the service of justice, that is, lives a life approved by God and bears fruits to God's glory.

God's glory is God as present to human beings and communicating himself to them more and more, the gift par excellence of the Messianic era. It is the splendor which emanates from the perfect character of God. This is the Shakinah glory of the Old Testament and in the New Testament is expressed in the incarnate life of Jesus, the Word or expression of the Father. God's glory is the holiness and splendor of God as communicated to men. Jesus is the Lord of glory. God's glory is on his face since he is the image of God. All men because of their sins are deprived of this glory, but it is communicated to believers by Jesus Christ. We are already clothed with it, in anticipation, according to the measure of our transformation into the image of Christ, while awaiting the full glorification of the parousia. The glory of God is the reflection of God's radiant being in man, the moral and spiritual kinship to him, the image of God sadly disfigured in fallen man. It is only in Christ, the Second Adam and the greater image of God, that the work of restoring the image can begin, through faith in him.

Biblical faith is presented under two leading views: the first is that assent or persuasion, which naturally leads to the second, that of confidence and reliance. One is intellectual assent, the other a work of the heart, a motion of the soul towards God, to lay hold upon his covenant promises and to rest in them. Faith is such a belief in the gospel by the power of the Spirit of God, as leads us to come to Christ, to receive Christ, to trust in Christ, and to commit the keeping of our soul to him, in humble confidence of his ability and willingness to save. Christ is the concrete manifestation of divine uprightness and man appropriates to himself the effects of that uprightness by faith. Faith is man's trustful acceptance of God's gift, rising to absolute self-surrender, culminating in personal union with Christ, working within as a sprit of new life. The benefits of God's saving act are open to any who have faith. Faith is less an effort on man's part than a response, a reaching out of the hand to accept God's gracious offer. Faith is essentially a response to God's initiative. Man's business is to recognize his dependence on the gracious controller of his destiny, who is revealed in the self-sacrifice of Christ's death. Responding with gratitude he can face his moral obligations with what Paul calls the obedience of Faith.

"Both (Jew and pagan) are justified by his grace, as a gift, through the redemption which is in Christ Jesus, whom God appointed as an expiation (mercy-seat) by his blood, to be received by faith" (3:24-25). The true righteousness, now revealed in Christ, rests not upon obedience to law but on faith in God's act of redemption in Christ Jesus. Being justified is qualified in three directions: those of the mode (gift), the origin (grace), and the means (Jesus Christ). Justified means not so much made righteous in the sense of morally perfect, as pronounced righteous, that is acquitted. The gift is thus freedom to leave court rather than go to prison, freedom to resume life with all its obligations, in grace, in the power of Christ, in the Spirit.

Grace means the unmerited favor of God shown in forgiveness and salvation and in special gifts of calling to and fitness for Christian work. Grace is something given free and unearned. It describes the way God saves through Jesus; it is a work of spontaneous love to which no one has any claim. It is a gift which includes all divine favors; justification, salvation, and the right to inherit. It is God's love for us. For human beings to be agreeable to God depends primarily on God's initiative and secondarily on human response.

Redemption means emancipation, deliverance. Slaves of sin are set free through God's act in Christ. Redemption is God's gracious gift, and its availability for mankind is due to what Christ was and did. Jews would point to its exemplification in their deliverance from Egypt and from Babylon. Christians point to the new life in Christ as the great example, and to Gentiles, not Jews only, as the beneficiaries. The ransom was Christ's life, not considered as paid to any one, but as the price which it cost him to procure our deliverance, and to restore us to God. We receive it in Christ Jesus, that is, by union with him.

In the Old Testament there is frequent reference to God's deliverance of his people from the Egyptian servitude and the Babylonian captivity, and more deeply from sin (Ps 130:8). This Messianic deliverance was realized in Jesus Christ. It is the remission of sins (Col 1:14) and its purpose is to establish for God a new people (Ep 1:14). It is a gratuitous gift of God's sovereign freedom in Jesus Christ. The notion of ransom, of a price paid for the deliverance of a prisoner or the buying back of a slave, is not absent from Paul's thought, but the elements of this idea are not all equally valid. Paul frequently says that the Christian has been bought or bought back, but this expression means above all else that the Christian belongs to God and is delivered from the slavery and the captivity of sin and death. If the price of this ransom is mentioned, it is to insist on the burdensome character, the hardships of this redemption for which God did not hesitate to deliver his own Son. It is the blood of Christ, that is, his life delivered out of love that is the price of this ransom. The metaphor should not be pressed any further, for example, by asking to whom the ransom is paid.

To express the manner by which God works our redemption in Christ, Paul expresses it simultaneously with the help of juridical categories: "Sending his own Son in the likeness of sinful flesh, and as an offering for sin, he condemned sin in the flesh" (Rm 8:3); a sacrificial terminology; expiation, sacrifice for sin; and a vocabulary of participation: "If we have been united with him in a death like his, we shall certainly be united with him in a resurrection like his" (Rm 6:5). There is no choice to be made between these formulations but an evaluation of their import, with privileged consideration for the sacrificial aspect. By his sacrifice Christ identifies himself with sinful humanity and becomes the head of the new humanity which participates in his life, offering itself to God, and placing itself with love at the service of all men.

The death of Christ was an atoning sacrifice, analogous to the piacular sacrifices of the Old Testament, and fraught with an objective efficacy. This doctrine is diffused throughout the New Testament writings, and doubtless derives from our Lord's own words, in which, borrowing a phrase from Ex 24:8, he attributed a sacrificial significance to his coming passion: "This is my covenant-blood which is poured out for many" (Mk 14:24). Sin is expiated, that is, neutralized or canceled. God is always the same, always loving and compassionate towards his creatures: but sin interposes a barrier which prevents man from receiving the full benefits of God's love, a barrier which the perfect self-dedication of Christ, expressed through the shedding of his blood, has now swept away.

The suggestive term expiation implies the efficacy of sacrifice. The blood of sacrificial animals was believed to have potency for restoring a right relationship between men and God. Paul's affirmation is that Christ's blood, his self-sacrifice does have this efficacy. By his blood signifies the principle of life sacrificed. Jesus himself said that he came to give his life as a ransom for many (Mk 10:45). The cross of Christ stood on the borderline of the seen and unseen world; it looked both ways: up to God and the satisfying of his justice, and down to man and the security of his pardon.

Christ crucified takes the place of the mercy-seat in the Holy of Holies. The mercy-seat or propitiatory was the cover of the ark and place of propitiation (Heb 9:5). Christ is our mercy-seat and sacrificial victim. On the day of Atonement the propitiatory was spinkled with blood. The blood of Christ has performed what the ancient ritual could only symbolize: purification of sin. The mercy-seat was the place where reconciliation was effected, according to Jewish ritual. The mercy-seat for Christians is Calvary.

By faith, by the total act, interior and exterior of self-surrender to Christ expressed in conversion and baptism, man can so identify himself with and incorporate himself into the glorified Messiah, so as to be able to make his own the Messiah's attitude of perfect obedience to God. Faith is indispensable: the atonement only avails for the individual in so far as its fruits are consciously appropriated by him, let no man boast of his own righteousness, since it is God's free gift.

17

THE KNOWLEDGE OF GOD

*To know God is capable of many degrees of meaning
from the rational certainty of a supreme, personal
maker and Lord (Rm 1:18-32), up to the holy intimacy
of divinely given communion, the knowledge that
comes through personal encounter with God, whose
love is poured into our hearts through the Holy Spirit
(5:5).*

By way of antithesis, the subject of the good news being the
revelation of God's saving justice (Rm 1:16-17) is interrupted by
considering what the human race is like before it hears the good
news (Rm 1:18-32). Error benighted and moral depravity
corrupted paganism. Contrary to nature itself which provides
evidence of God's existence, power, and divinity through
creation, pagan society misread the evidence, fashioned its own
gods who could exert no moral restraint, and freely indulged its
perverse desires through every kind of wickedness. The pagans
might have had a knowledge of God (1:18-10) but have turned
away to idolatry (21-23), and are sunk in consequence, in moral
corruption (24-32).

"What can be known about God is perfectly plain to them
since God himself has made it plain" (1:19). Nature teaches a
knowledge of God, and man has the faculty of receiving the
teaching. Luther called the whole creation "a mask of God." To
know God is a phrase capable of many degrees of meaning, from

the rational certainty of a supreme personal maker and Lord, up to that holy intimacy of divinely-given communion with the Father and the Son to which the words of Jn 17:3 refer. Paul is speaking not of the full self-disclosure of the Father of our Lord Jesus Christ, but of what is called natural religion.

"Ever since God created the world, his everlasting power and deity, however invisible, have been there for the mind to see in the things he has made. That is why they are without excuse: they knew God and yet refused to honor him as God or give him thanks; instead they made nonsense out of logic, and their empty minds were darkened" (1:20-21). Confronted by facts which pointed to the creator of the world, men gave their reverence and gratitude not to him but to things created. The forces and mechanisms built into nature became for them the final truth about nature. The sun with its light and heat, the seasonal growth and decay, the mysterious reproductive power of living creatures, these and many other elements of creation were deified and allowed to usurp the place of the creator. Sinful men cannot claim the excuse of ignorance, for knowledge of God is available. They do not lack truth; they suppress it. Behind the visible world is an invisible creator. The universe points beyond itself to an author whom human observers, if they really think, will recognize and reverence.

The natural world is a window through which God shows part of himself to man. God's invisible perfections are manifested by his visible works, and may be apprehended by what he has made: their immensity showing his omnipotence; their vast variety, his omniscience; and their adaptation to the most beneficient purposes, his infinite goodness. His works prove his being. God's power and divinity are so clearly impressed upon the visible creation, that no one can plead ignorance. "To honor him as God and give him thanks" are two attitudes by which scripture sums up man's duties towards God. The first stage in the Gentile apostasy consists in neglect of God's worship. They did not give him that worship which his perfections required: they manifested no gratitude for the blessings they received from his providence. To know there is one personal God means to know that one must pray to him and adore him.

"Since they refused to see it was rational to acknowledge God, God has left them to their own irrational ideas and to their monstrous behavior" (1:28). Idolatry is the big lie that darkens the mind; it is the big sin that corrupts the will. Sexual excesses (1:24), homosexual perversions (26-27), and general moral degradation (28-31) follow idolatry. It is God's order that the first commandment is the cornerstone of all religious and moral life. Without it the other commandments are a building that has no foundation. Wrong behavior is the consequence of wrong worship. The price paid for rejecting God is to become moral rejects. Sin has within itself its sanctions and consequences. If a man will not worship God he is so left to himself that he throws away his very manhood. The traditional biblical phrase "God abandoned" or left them means that culpable religious error results in moral and social ills. Sin produces its own consequences and punishment. Those who forsake God forsake him who restrains evil and inspires good. Further, one sin leads to another. God gave them up because in turning from God they violated their true nature becoming involved in terrible and destructive perversions; God leaves the process of death work itself out.

Paul, of course, is not satisfied with this natural knowledge of God. He urges us to aim at the full development of this knowledge by our life of union with Christ. Rm 4:25 is probably a quotation from a confession of faith used in the worship of the Palestinian churches. Its background is Is 53 with a picture of Christ as the servant who atoned for his people's sins and who is the guarantee by his living presence of their acceptance with God. "Jesus was put to death for our sins, and raised to life to justify us" (Rm 4:25). Our Lord's passion and resurrection constitute one single redemptive act: they are two aspects of the same mystery. Paul never isolates the death of Jesus from his resurrection. Justice or righteousness is in effect the first sharing in the life of the risen Christ. Like Abraham we are justified by faith in God's promise; for us the promise is manifested and summarizes in Christ's resurrection. The atonement and the resurrection are not to be separated from Christ's death. On the cross our Lord gave himself up for us; through the resurrection he gives himself to us. The resurrection brings about our justification because it shows the divinity of Christ, and therefore the value of his death; through the resurrection, faith in the atonement became possible for it showed that the atonement was complete. Christ risen becomes the source of new life by our union with him.

For the Christian who has received justification, the love God has for him, and the Spirit bestowed on him are a pledge of salvation. Such is the theme of the second section of Rm (chs. 5-11). Faith guarantees salvation (5:1-11). It gives the security and happiness of the state of justification. Justification is for Paul not merely a doctrine to define and defend; he has found it a cup of blessing that runs over his whole life. Peace, hope, and assurance of eternal life are the fruits of justification. Acceptance of God's salvation brings about triumphant hope of glory, which is guaranteed by our assurance of the love of God. Paul, however, never contemplates the possibility of a justification which was not invariably followed by a sanctification; justification and sanctification are inseparably connected in fact. The one is the wicket-gate, introductory absolution; the other the long road to the heavenly Jerusalem. The hardships of this life should teach the Christian patience, and strengthen his hope which will not disappoint him because the Holy Spirit dwells in his heart and infuses into it God's love (5:1-5). Christ in his death has borne the consequences of our sin and thus reconciled us to God (5:6-11). Note that Paul never speaks of a reconciliation of God to us; it is we who were estranged.

"Now that we are justified by faith, we are at peace with God through our Lord Jesus Christ. Through him we have access by faith to his grace in which we stand, and we rejoice in our hope of sharing the glory of God" (5:1-2). The word peace expresses the new situation simply. It is synonymous with the more theological term, reconciliation (11). The basic human problem was involvement in a vitiated relationship towards God, a state of cold war. God himself takes the initiative and his revelation of righteousness through Christ makes a new relationship of peace possible. Our fellowship with God is restored, like that of the prodigal son, and we have the feeling of peace with him.

Justification is never alone; all the graces follow in clusters, privileges of the highest order. Paul mentions some of the blessed effects of justification. By it we have peace with God; we have access to God, we are introduced in the presence-chamber of the king. This presentation before the royal throne is effected by one near the monarch himself; it is Jesus who leads us to God. The active favor of the Father to believers is described as grace. The justified are ushered into a state of grace which brings security and confidence. A third blessed result is joy, based on hope and victorious over tribulation.

The peace the Christian experiences is derived from his introduction into the sphere of divine favor and grace by Christ. Jesus has reconciled him by leading him into the divine, gracious presence. Grace in St. Paul's usage stands for a disposition or attitude of God towards men, namely kindliness, favor, or good-will, and is usually employed with the implication that such divine favor is gratuitous and unmerited. It does not exactly correspond to sanctifying grace in the later theological terminology which derives from St. Augustine; grace in this context means not so much a kindly disposition of God, as that which is the external expression of such a disposition, namely, some kind of objective assistance and influence towards good infused by God into our soul. This Augustinian notion, however, follows closely from the first, the biblical meaning of grace, as its intended effect.

For a Christian to hope is to be confident that he will receive the eschatological gifts; the resurrection of the body, eternal life, glory, in short salvation. Glory is the radiant brightness of God's presence, the future and everlasting presence of God. Christians are already privileged to share the restoration of this radiant glow and its progressive growth, but the consummation of the process is yet to come. The basis of our hope is God himself, his love and fidelity in implementing his promises in Christ's person. Faith is its prop, its stay, and charity its food, and the Holy Spirit its source. Hope is built on justification through faith in Christ.

"More than that we rejoice in our sufferings, knowing that suffering produces endurance, and endurance character, and character produces hope, and hope does not disappoint because God's love has been poured into our hearts through the Holy Spirit who has been given to us" (5:3-5). This is the clearest affirmation in the New Testament of the link between love and the Holy Spirit. Christ has given believers access to God's presence and a new experience of God's grace, whiich means essentially God's willingness to have dealings with sinful humanity, and in this sense it is the same as his love. It is a product of our encounter with God which Paul describes by the vivid metaphor of the pouring of God's love, flooding our inmost heart. The souls of believers are flooded with God's love which is in fact the presence of the Paraclete. The justified become conscious of God's love towards them through the indwelling Spirit.

The promised Spirit, distinctive of the new covenant, is an inward principle of new life, a God-given principle, poured out into our hearts and dwelling in them. It is the spirit of Christ making a Christian a son of God. It becomes a principle of faith, of love, of sanctification, of moral conduct, of apostolic courage, of hope, and of prayer. It unites men with Christ and thus secures the unity of his body. The Holy Spirit is a pledge of God's love for us, and by his active presence in us he bears witness to it. Through him we stand before God as sons before their father; the love is mutual. Through sanctifying grace the Christian shares in the life of the Trinity.

"While we were still helpless, at the right time, Christ died for the ungodly. It is not easy to die even for a good man, though perhaps for a good man one might be prepared to die. God shows his love for us in that while we were still sinners, Christ died for us. . . We rejoice in God through our Lord Jesus Christ through whom we have now received our reconciliation" (1:6-8, 11). Christ's death on the cross was for us at the right time. This right season, the psychological moment of the world's clock is frequently mentioned by Paul. For us, in the fullness of time, Christ died, even though we had nothing to commend us, but in very truth had everything to condemn us. Behind this display of saving mercy stands God's love which is proved to us by the cross. God's love for us is the first proof for the certainty of our hope of final salvation. If when still sinners we received the grace of initial salvation from God's love, in view of Christ's death on the cross, how much more can we now, as his friends, that is, justified by responding in faith to his first love, expect to receive the grace of final salvation from his love in view of Christ's life in heaven?

Since God refers to the father, and it is his love that was poured out through the Spirit and is now demonstrated in the death of Christ, this triadic text is the starting point of the Trinitarian dogma. Note that there is no quid pro quo in the love manifested; divine love is demonstrated towards the sinner without a hint that it is repaying a love already made known.

Finally, to be reconciled is the same as to be justified. Paul's image implies always man's need to be reconciled to God, not God's need to be changed at all in his attitude towards man. Justification is not a judge's acquittal so much as a father's welcome, and reconciliation brings in the idea of reunion with the life of the family.

18

CHRISTIAN SPIRITUAL LIVING

The Christian life is lived in the Spirit and is destined for glory (Rm 8:1-11). In Gal 5:22-26, Paul spells out the characteristics of Christian living, which are the various manifestations of the indwelling Spirit.

Rm Ch 8 is the peak of the entire epistle. It describes the freedom which justification brings from the dominion of sin (Rm 8:1-11); the adoption as sons of God (12-17), the hope of deliverance from all earthly woes (18-27); and the assurance of God's eternal and unchangeable love in Christ Jesus (28-39). It describes the life of those who are members of Christ's body, a life of freedom under the guidance of the Holy Spirit. It shows Christ abiding in the Christian by the power of his Spirit. It underlines the blessings of the spiritual life; the Christian life is lived in the Spirit and is destined for glory. A general characteristic of the effects of justification is the life and power and triumph of the indwelling Holy Spirit. The saving work effected by Christ is realized in Christians by the interior activity of the Spirit making them sons of God.

The Christian is sanctified as well as justified. In Christ he receives the Spirit, who frees him from the power of sin and death (Rm 8:1-2). The object of the death of Christ was not only to win pardon for man but also to produce right character and conduct (3-4). This is essential and is brought about by the indwelling Spirit (5-9). The change means life, of the spirit now, and also of the body hereafter (10-11). Rm 8:1-11 is a reflection on the redemptive work of Christ. The Christian is freed from God's judgment of condemnation by reason of Christ's death for the sins of humanity, but he must now live according to the Spirit who dwells in him and leads to life and peace.

"The law of the Spirit of life in Christ Jesus has set us free from the law of sin and death" (Rm 8:1). This verse contains a complete picture of the Christian life as Paul understood it. The expression "the law of the Spirit" is a sort of summary of Jr 31:33 and Ezk 36:27, where the Spirit of God is described as the creator of a new people and of real inner holiness. The Spirit is the divine principle (law) of life in the new order which God has created through Christ. Renewed and transformed by the Spirit of God, given by Jesus, the believer obeys the will of God, which is no longer an external coercion but the interior law of his new life. An inward rule regulates the believer's life, its controlling principle and power being the Holy Spirit as its author. It enables the believer to live a new life in Christ. Those in spiritual union with Christ Jesus by faith and baptism, enjoy a union as close as that of the head and the members of the human body, the vine and the branches, the foundation and the building. In Christ Jesus: this is St. Paul's gospel.

The great phrase "In Christ Jesus" contains in three words the whole doctrine of the Church as the Mystical Body of Christ. To be in Christ is to belong to this new order and thus to know the Spirit, who is the actual presence of God in our midst and in our hearts. The Holy Spirit is the life-force or energy pervading the Mystical Body of Christ and operating the interior transformation of the believer. The basis of the Spirit's work is the cross. God took it upon himself to end in principle the constant mastery of sin over man. God's Son became man and conquered man's enemy, sin, on its own ground. On the cross Jesus absorbed the worst that sin could do and drained it of its power. In Christ man finds himself released and put under a new authority, that of the Spirit of life.

"God sent his own Son in the likeness of sinful flesh and in that body condemned sin" (8:3). By sharing our sinful nature and dying as a sacrifice for sin, Christ has diverted the expected condemnation and given us new life instead. God condemned sin in principle as something unnatural and abnormal by exhibiting in the person of his Incarnate Son the same flesh in substance, but free from sin; and God condemned sin in practice by exhibiting in the life lived by his Incarnate Son, a life lived without sin. Christ proved by his sinless human life, that sin is not necessary to human nature; he made expiation for sin on our behalf; and made it possible for us to die with him to newness of life, by union in love with him, and by the power of the Spirit. He came in our nature. He conquered where we had fallen before our foe. He was in all things like us except in sin. The flesh, the scene of sin's former triumph became now the scene of its defeat and expulsion.

The crucial moment in the battle against sin was the death of Jesus. For it is in his death that his lower nature is seen to have been completely real; the one event which is shared by all who have the lower nature is death, and Jesus was not a divine being who put on the disguise of a lower nature which he could drop at the terrifying moment of death, and evade it. Death was the moment of greatest temptation; a few hours before his death he prayed vehemently to escape it, but accepted it as God's will. Death was the most likely moment for him to sin and fail; but he did not fail. Thus it was that in dying he triumphed over the flesh and defeated sin completely. God sent his own Son in the likeness of sinful flesh, and in the capacity of a sin-offering. Thus he condemned sin, that is, caused it to be defeated within the very sphere of the flesh over which it had claimed exclusive authority. In the Old Testament sacrifice for sin, the death of the victim manifested God's judgment of condemnation against sin. Here the condemnation realized in the flesh of Christ is unique and definitive; it ends the domination of sin over the flesh of the believer, who unites himself to Christ's act of obedience and love. Christian existence is dominated by the Spirit, not by the flesh.

A special feature of this passage is the contrast between flesh and spirit. Flesh for St. Paul is especially the sphere in which the passions and sin operate. The great divide in human life is living according to the flesh or the spirit: living for physical satisfactions or living at the spiritual level, for spiritual ends, with the assurance of life and peace, living permeated by the spirit of Christ. If our life accords with the flesh, the carnal streak will run through our mental outlook. If the spiritual elements prevail, the analogous results will be seen in our spiritual alignments. John's synonym for the flesh in the Pauline sense is the world. It is life without God in it: one of egotism, self-indulgence, and disobedience to the light of conscience. To live according to the flesh is to be dominated by selfish passions; to live according to or in the Spirit is to belong to the new community of faith where God dwells as the Spirit.

"Life and peace can only come with concern for the spirit . . . People who are interested only in the flesh cannot be pleasing to God. Your interests are not in the flesh but in the spirit, since the Spirit of God really dwells in you. Any one who does not have the Spirit of Christ does not belong to him. If Christ is in you then your spirit is life itself because you have been justified" (Rm 8:6-10). The new existence in the Spirit leads to eternal life, thanks to the saving justice of God. The Spirit is a new and conspicuous feature of Rm Ch 8. The Holy Spirit, the Spirit of God and of Christ, is the author and giver of life. The Spirit suffuses man's being and directs his conduct. The motive power behind the spiritual life is the indwelling Spirit. By grace, through faith, the Spirit is in the believers, and they in the Spirit. Paul's characteristic preposition *in* is used to express union or communion with God in Christ through faith.

Spirit means divinely provided equipment and moral power in virtue of which the Christian is proof against the downdrag of fleshly existence. Already in the Old Testament the Spirit had been viewed as leading many of its great men to perform heroic deeds, and the Messiah, expected by the Jews, was to be specifically endowed with the Spirit's help (Is 11:1-2). Following on from this, the New Testament sees the activities of Christians in God's service as the result of the Spirit's work. Indeed the whole life of the believer and of the Church is a life directed, inspired, and empowered by the Spirit. This is especially clear in Acts, where the Spirit guides the Church in every important decision. The exact relation of the Spirit to God and Christ is not worked out by Paul. Later Christian theology formulated the doctrine of the Trinity. While the germ of this is present in Paul's writings, it is not explicit. The Spirit is certainly distinguished from God the Father by being called God's Spirit, and from God the Son by being called the Spirit of Christ; in neither case is the relationship like that of a man's spirit to himself. Rather the Spirit is the agent of God's activity in the world, and in this way the Spirit gradually came to be regarded as a Person because he does the kind of things a person does.

Note the similar, almost interchangeable, use of the Spirit of God, the Spirit of Christ, and Christ. Paul's language is fluid. The believer is united with Christ, he is in Christ, because he has the Spirit dwelling in him. Paul also speaks of Christ dwelling within the believer. The Spirit of God is the Spirit of Christ because he comes from the Son as well as from the Father. Also his presence is in effect the presence of Christ. The Spirit of God, the Spirit of Christ are used interchangeably, showing the equality and functions of the one Godhead. The Father is the source of all grace; the Son, the channel, the Spirit proceeding from both the Father and the Son, is the agent. The criterion of the Christian is the Spirit's indwelling, divine motive power, apart from which dynamic there can be no communion with God. The Spirit of Jesus is that of God himself whom he has appropriated perfectly here below into his personal life, so that he can communicate him to his own. It is in this form that the Holy Spirit henceforth acts in the Church. A fundamental Christian experience is that of the mutual interpenetration of the activities of the Son and the Spirit, an experience which finds its appropriate articulation in the doctrine of coinherence (perichoresis, circumincessio) of the three Persons of the Trinity, as formulated by subsequent Church theology.

"To belong to Christ" is no mere external identification with the cause of Christ, nor even a grateful recognition of what he once did for man. Rather, the Christian who belongs to Christ is the one who has been enabled to live for God (Rm 6:10) through the vitalizing power of the divine Spirit. The expression, "the Spirit of God dwells in you," is the complement of the others, to be in the Spirit, or in Christ. It denotes the closest possible contact and influence of spirit upon spirit. The supreme work of the Spirit is to acquaint the soul with Christ; hence the indwelling of the Spirit as the divine teacher results by holy necessity in the indwelling of Christ as the divine guest. God's union with man is not a shadow, a figure or a dream; it is a statement of a fact as literal as any law of nature. The Spirit's work of comfort and sanctification is a part of heaven's covenant blessings, a turf from the soil of the holy land, a twig from the tree of life, the key to the mansions in the skies.

"And if the Spirit of him who raised Jesus from the dead dwells in you, then he who raised Jesus from the dead will give life to your own mortal bodies, through his Spirit dwelling in you" (Rm 8:11). The indwelling Spirit is our promise of a resurrection like Christ's. The body is not something to be shed as a useless clog. The Lord has purpose for the body sanctified by his Incarnation; it is indwelt by his Spirit, and useful in his service, and at last to be raised in a manner patterned on his resurrection. The resurrection of the Christian is intimately dependent on that of Christ. It is by the same power and the same gift of the Spirit that the Father will raise us to life in our turn. This operation is already being prepared; a new life is making the Christians into sons in the likeness of the Son himself, and we are being incorporated into the risen Christ by faith and baptism. The possession of the Holy Spirit, the Spirit of the living God and of the risen Christ, is the pledge of the Christian resurrection and the present proof of its future realization. In the outpoured Spirit, the power and life of the full age to come are anticipated. He is the pledge and foretaste of the future, and puts within the Church's grasp a new potential of which we not only may but must avail ourselves.

In Gal 5:22-26, over against the works of the flesh (19-21), is placed the fruit of the Spirit. This fruit is the full harvest of righteousness (Ph 1:11) bestowed on those who live by faith. By God's grace, in the power of the Spirit, man's whole life is transformed, and these are the marks of that transformation. "The fruit of the Spirit is love, joy, peace, patience, kindness, goodness, faithfulness, gentleness, self-control" (Gal 5:12-22). Fruit is a collective noun designating crop or harvest, and suggests the many-sided character of virtuous Christian living. It is not clear whether these virtues fall into classes, but they include inner personal qualities that govern social relations, and principles of conduct. The fruit of the Spirit is unique, namely love. Love is the first to be mentioned as the sine qua non of all the other virtues. Joy and peace are the signs of the reign of love; patience, kindness, goodness are the manifestations of Christian love; faithfulness, gentleness, and self-control are the conditions of its birth and growth. Faith is the root of love (Gal 5:6); gentleness is the attitude of the humble who are devoted to their heavenly Father, and it is also a characteristic of Christ (Mt 11:29). These splendid characteristics ought to be the hallmark of any Christian who takes his faith seriously; they are the various manifestations of the indwelling Spirit.

"And those who belong to Christ have crucified the flesh with its passions and desires. If we live by the Spirit, let us also walk by the Spirit" (Gal 5:24-25). The inner life should rule the outer life. This recalls the fundamental condition of Christian liberty: the Spirit effects it by crucifying us with Christ. Just as love is the proper content of freedom (Gal 5:2-15) so the Spirit is its proper context, that by which love is empowered and guided; the Christian walks by the Spirit. To be led by the Spirit emphasizes God's gift by which one lives; the exhortation to walk by the Spirit stresses the attendant moral demands.

19

ABBA, FATHER

The Christian, by reason of the Spirit's presence within him, enjoys not only a new life but also a new relationship with God, that of adopted son and heir through Christ (Rm 8:14-17, Gal 4:4-7). God has called us to share his glory (Rm 8:28-30).

The Christian, by reason of the Spirit's presence within him, enjoys not only a new life but also a new relationship with God, that of adopted son and heir through Christ, whose sufferings and glory he shares. "Everyone moved by the Spirit of God is a son of God. For you did not receive the spirit of slavery to fall back into fear, but you have received the spirit of sonship which makes us cry, Abba, Father" (Rm 8:14-15). Spirit-moved and God-adopted are names for people whose lives are spent in the service, not of an owner whom they fear, but of a father whom they love. In the highest sense Jesus Christ is the Son of God; in the widest sense all men are the offspring of God (Ac 17:28); in a special sense believers, begotten and moved by the Spirit of God are true sons of God. This is the highest conception of the Christian's glory and privilege.

The Spirit speaks the gospel in our hearts. He reveals God's fatherly love, manifested in the death and resurrection of Christ. He enlightens our understanding, guides our inclinations, and directs our actions. The Spirit is much more than one who inwardly admonishes; he is the principle of a life truly divine. The

Spirit establishes the believer in a new relationship with God, a new high level of privilege. Practical God-likeness which comes from a willing response to the control of his Spirit, is proof of being sons of God. Like father, like son, is the thought. Sonship with God is the goal of grace, its glorious end and triumph. It is the Spirit who imparts the assurance of sonship and enables believers to call God their Father. This sonship is no mere official recognition of a filial tie, a title only. It is an actual fact. We are sons with a right to say, Father, as sharing the sonship of the eternal Son.

Sin makes us slaves; the Spirit makes us God's sons. Thus we call God, Father, notably in the Lord's prayer. The presence of the Holy Spirit in our hearts represents an entirely new attitude towards God; we come to him as children to a father. For Paul the hallmark of Christianity is to call God, Father, and Jesus Christ, Lord, and mean it. The Spirit of sonship is sanctifying grace. The gift of the Spirit constitutes our adoption, and in adopting us God gives us a participation in the sonship of Christ. The Spirit of sonship is "the Spirit of the Son" (Gal 4, 6) transferred to the Christian. The Holy Spirit enables us to look at God with Christ's eyes, and makes in us the Son's own filial response to the Father, Abba. The cry passed bilingually into the worshiping vocabulary of the Church. The Hebrew and Greek words joined together (Abba, Pater) might be seen as expressing the joint cry of the Jews and Gentiles.

Abba is the familiar word a child would use for his own father; that Jesus used it makes us realize how close to God he felt. It may be a reference to the Lord's prayer which begins with it, but it is a whole prayer in itself, a kerygmatic ejaculation, a short sharp cry by the Christian under great emotion, moved by the Spirit of God; it is both a prayer to God and a joyful affirmation of what the Christian believes about God. Abba is the word meaning Father which Jesus used in his prayer at Gethsemane (Mk 14:36) and which passed in the liturgy of the early Church. It is the expression of filial intimacy, full of familiarity and tenderness, of Jesus for his Father. It indicates trust, affection and liberty. Our adoptive sonship lets us share in all this.

In referring to sonship, Paul is not alluding only to the Hellenistic custom of adoption, but no doubt has Old Testament parallels in mind. Son or sons was a title of the Old Testament people of God; it passed to Christ who summed up their destiny in himself and thus passed it to the Church in him. Paul's theology is basically one of personal relationships, new relationships which have become possible between God and ourselves and others because of Christ. What Christ has done is not to make a book entry in a divine ledger, which balances up what we have failed to do with what he has done on our behalf. The result of what Christ has done is essentially not simply to give us a new status but a new attitude to God. We are dealing with one who is still the author and creator of all that is, but whom we can now call our dear Father. The word Abba brings us very close to Jesus. It is the word for Father which he used himself in his prayers. It is what a Jewish boy affectionately calls his own father. Jesus taught us to think of God in just this way, and it is his Spirit within us who enables us to speak to God in these terms in our prayers.

"The Spirit himself and our spirit bear united witness that we are children of God" (Rm 8:16). The Spirit concurs with man as he acknowledges in prayer his special relation to the Father. The Christian's own belief of sonship is supported by the Spirit's evoking this cry in the worship of the Church. The Christian can speak to God in the very terms used by Christ. Uttered under the influence of the Spirit, the prayer of the believer is a proof that God loves him as he loves his own Son, and that the Father is the center and the end of the Christian's prayer and of his life.

"And if we are children we are heirs as well: heirs of God and coheirs with Christ, provided we suffer with him in order that we may also be glorified with him" (Rm 8:17). The advent of the indwelling Spirit is the earnest or guarantee, of the believer's inheritance. Paul uses the image of children sharing in what their father bequeaths. God, of course, does not die (the metaphor fails at this point) but his children still inherit. This is an image used in the Old Testament where the inheritance is the possession of the promised land. In the New Testament the promised land becomes the ensemble of the divine benefits: the kingdom of God, eternal life. Believers receive them through God's Son risen from the dead. The Christian, as an adopted son, is not only admited into God's family, but by reason of the same gratuitous gift receives the right to become the master of his adoptive Father's estate. God's true heir is his only Son Jesus. Once made a son, the Christian becomes a fellow-heir with Jesus, our brother (Rm 8:29).

Christ is heir to all God's promises, and we also, as we are found in him and share his suffering. Christ is the way; the main features of his life must be reproduced in the lives of his people. Just as, in the divine order of salvation, it was necessary that Christ should suffer, and through suffering enter into his glory, so also does the same divine order require that his followers must suffer with him in order that he and they may be glorified together. The Christian life is a reproduction of the life of Christ. To suffer with him implies the communion of cross-bearing or self-sacrifice; not that our experiences are redemptive in themselves, but we complete what is lacking in Christ's sufferings (Col 1:24). Identification with the crucified by faith is no substitute for identification on the level of practical life-experience.

Writing previously to the Galatians (4:4-7) Paul had broached the same subject of our adoptive sonship. This earlier passage contains a few noteworthy details. The Holy Spirit has recreated us as God's sons, and enabled us to live our lives according to the sense and spirit of this new relationship. "When the fullness of time came, God sent forth his Son, born of woman, born under the law, to redeem those who were under the law, so that they might receive adoption as sons. And because we are sons, God has sent the Spirit of his Son into our hearts crying, Abba, Father. So through God you are no longer a slave but a son, and if a son then an heir." The phrase "God sent forth his Son" points to Christ's preexistence, deity, incarnation, mission, that is, to his whole saving mission. "The fullness of time" indicates that the Messianic age fills a need felt for centuries. God in salvation history was preparing our redemption which is realized with the coming of Christ. The possibility of our new relation as sons, rests on God's purpose, the Incarnation, the atonement, and the Holy Spirit.

"Receive adoption as sons" says that those who are not natural heirs, acquire the status of sonship by sheer grace and gift. Sonship is vouchsafed to us through the indwelling Spirit who makes Christ a reality in our lives. Paul speaks of Christians as adopted because, unlike the heir in his will analogy, they are not in fact sons of the Father, until the Father makes them so by incorporating them in his Son. There are two aspects of redemption, negative and positive: the slave attains freedom by becoming a son. First and foremost, the adoption to sonship is not simply a legal right to inherit, but the real gift of the divine life. The gift of the Spirit of the Son is the constitutive element of Christian sonship. The Spirit is sent like the Son, and grounds our new life, in the very depth of our being. Like the Son, the Spirit also is the object of a personal mission from the Father; elsewhere he is a gift of the risen Kyrios. The vivifying Spirit of the risen Son is the dynamic principle of adoptive sonship. It empowers the Christians inmost conviction as he exclaims of God, Father. The Christian prays to the Father with the same formula that was used by Christ; but without the Spirit, a Christian would never be able to utter this cry. Adoption is the gift of the Spirit by which one is enabled to place his full confidence in, and pledge his total commitment to God the Father.

God has called us to share his glory (Rm 8:28-30). "We know that in everything God works for good with those who love him, who are called according to his purpose" (Rm 8:28). God cooperates with those who love him and this is the realization of his loving plan of salvation. "Those who love God" is an Old Testament expression for God's followers who throw themselves wholeheartedly into his service and identify themselves with his aims. God cooperates with them in everything to bring about a good end, conformity with his Son.

God's eternal purpose embraces all stages of salvation from first to last: first in foreordination, then in vocation, then in justification, and at last in glorification (Rm 8:29-30). The history of the individual Christian is here conceived as a line stretching from eternity through time and back to eternity. In this line five crucial points stand out: God's prevision, his predestination, his call, his justification, and his glorification. This is the outline of the Christian vocation as it is designed by God. In terms of God's initiative, the call consists in the exercise of the divine foreknowledge, God's predetermination, God's gift of the call, his sanctification and glorification of the Christian. Thus all that happens to one who loves God is directed by God toward the achievement of that good which is the likeness to God's Son through grace and glory.

Quite apart from human understanding or merit, there stands the divine plan in which Paul distinguishes: foreknowledge as the original conception; likeness to Christ as the object or pattern; the actual constituting of this new Christlike brotherhood as the purpose taking shape in history; the divine activity within us, conferring the new status of justification; and finally glorification. The thought of divine predestination is an encouragement, not a solemn threat. It need not imply the negative of ultimate reprobation, which is not in the Pauline view here. These verses are the basis of Christian confidence, whatever difficulties life in this world may bring.

"For those he foreknew, he also predestined to be conformed to the image of his Son, in order that he might be the first-born among many brothers" (Rm 8:29). First-born implies not mere priority but preeminence within the host of redeemed brethren. To be conformed to the Son is to share the resurrected life of Christ, to be a fellow heir, to be glorified. All spiritual growth is an increase of likeness to Christ. Christ is the perfect image of the Father. The Father reproduces the image of his Son in all who participate in the Son's filiation. This conformity to the image of the Son is accomplished by an interior transformation which is progressive and will be complete only at the Parousia.

Christ, the image of God in the first creation, has now come by a new creation to restore to fallen man the splendor of that image which has been darkened by sin. He does this by forming man in the still more splendid image of a son of God; thus sound moral judgment is restored to the new man, and also his claim to glory which he had sacrificed by sin. This glory, which Christ as image of God possesses by right, is progressively communicated to the Christian until his body is itself clothed in the image of the heavenly man. Man was originally made in God's image and likeness, but lost that likeness as he also forfeited glory (Rm 3:23) by sin. As a member of the new humanity in the fully restored new age, he will regain both the likeness and the splendor which Jesus already possesses.

Paul's vocabulary stresses the divine anteriority in the process of salvation, which comes from God's gracious bounty. Foreknew means that he chose in advance. Foreknowledge implies favor or grace as the eternal beginning of all other processes of salvation. God knew us: not just in the sense of knowing what would happen to us or of knowing who we are, but rather as one person knows another as a friend. God chose us and cares for us. Predestined means that God determined in advance the form our lives should take: we were to be Christlike. The pattern to which we are to be conformed is decribed in Ph 2:7. It is the form of an obedient servant. Christ's task is to bring men into the sonship and service of God, to be the senior member of a new human family in which all are brothers and sisters. The formation of these men and women begins with God's call to them. As they respond they come into their right relation to God; and that means that something of the divine glory becomes theirs. All these things are already within Christian experience.

Rm 8:29 speaks of God's purpose and intention; 8:30 tells how it is achieved. Men are called by God through preaching (Rm 10:14-15), they respond in faith and are justified, and so are given God's glory. "And those he predestined he also called; and those whom he called he also justified; and those whom he justified he also glorified" (Rm 8:30). Paul is not indicating a chronological succession between these stages some of which coincide. He is describing the providential care with which God accompanies the course of his chosen. He is indicating a motion to a goal: the glory with which Christ is already invested and which he will communicate to us. We already have the certitude of this glory since we possess its first-fruits. The divine decree passes over into time and is manifested as calling, justification by faith, and finally glorification. This miraculous consummation, planned in eternity, is worked out in our earthly experience. It holds promise of an issue in our creatural praise in the state of sanctification here below and of glory especially hereafter. "He also glorified," by inward holiness, changing us from glory to glory, in progressive religion, and by all the endowment of the rich and hallowed gifts of the Holy Spirit.

20

OUR INTERCESSORS WITH THE FATHER

We have two official intercessors before God in our behalf: the Holy Spirit within us (Rm 8:26-27) and our savior, the risen Christ at God's right hand (Rm 8:34, Heb 7:25, 9:24, 1 Jn 2:1-2).

.

It is the Holy Spirit who inspires the prayer of the Christian, and Paul prefers to emphasize this rather than repeat the traditional wisdom themes, namely, the necessary conditions for prayer. For Paul the efficacy of prayer is guaranteed by the presence of the Spirit of Christ within the Christian (Rm 8:26-27), enabling him to pray as a son to his father, while Christ himself intercedes at the right hand of God (Rm 8:34). The Father's response is therefore most generous.

"The Spirit helps us in our weakness; for we do not know how to pray as we ought, but the Spirit himself intercedes for us with sighs too deep for words" (Rm 8:26). Human weakness is sustained by the Spirit's intercession. Sighs probably means nothing audible, but an inward Spirit-motion which is intelligible to God alone. Even our best prayers are hopelessly inadequate. There is always too much of ourselves in our prayers; we pray for the wrong things; we really do not want what God wants. We need the help of the Spirit to offer God real prayer. The Spirit, not merely beside us but dwelling within us, strengthens us by energizing and inspiring the prayerful aspirations and longings of our soul, our faltering efforts in our infirmities and the problems and confusions of life. Inarticulate feelings of inadequacy, and vaguely conceived yearnings may at times be the nearest one can get to expressing oneself before God, for example, because we cannot tell what is really best for us, or the needs we do express in prayer are lesser needs. The Spirit gives meaning to all this by directing it to God's good purposes. When the Christian's prayers are too deep and too intense for words, when they are rather a sigh heaved from the heart than any formal utterance, then we may know that they are prompted by the Spirit himself. It is he who is praying God in and for us.

"And he who searches the hearts of men, knows what is the mind of the Spirit, because the Spirit intercedes for the saints according to the will of God" (Rm 8:27). Fluency in prayer is not essential to praying; a man may pray most powerfully, in the estimation of God, and still not be able to utter even one word. Although the yearnings of the Spirit within us cannot find adequate expression in words, they are effective with God. For he knows the secrets of the heart and hears the groanings of his Spirit there.

Rm 8:31-39 is a hymn to God's love, proclaiming the assurance of God's eternal and unchangeable love in Christ. Paul lifts up his heart in a lyrical assertion of security and triumph. The experience of God's goodness is the ground of unshakeable confidence. Nothing can touch the one thing that really matters, God's loving care for the younger brothers and sisters of his Son. The blessings of the spiritual life are summed up in the assurance of God's love for us in Christ. No matter what happens, the love of Christ for us remains unaffected, as the sun remains unaffected by the clouds that may hide it for a while. However dark the earth may turn, God's love for us in Christ remains undisturbed and continues its reign in our hearts.

"If God is for us, who can be against us? He who did not spare his own Son, but gave him up for us all, will he not also give us all things in him? . . . He not only died for us, he rose from the dead and is at God's right hand and pleads for us. . . Nothing will ever be able to separate us from the love of God in Christ Jesus our Lord" (Rm 8:31-39). If God be in our destiny nothing else matters. To us who are of the faith-family, he gave his own

Son, and with this greatest gift, all else is certainly included. Because of what God has done in the death and resurrection of Jesus, the believer has nothing to fear either in the present condition of the world from evil men and evil spiritual forces, or in the world to come when God judges men. His security rests on God's love made known in Jesus.

Paul in his ecstatic confidence defies every conceivable antagonism against which the gospel of God's love and care in Christ comes as a great deliverance. None of the dangers and troubles of life can make the true Christian forget the love of Christ. These are so many veils or clouds between us and the outward manifestation of God's love: things that might tempt the believer to think that his Lord has forsaken him. Paul assures us that this cannot be really so. Whether we live or die we shall not be separated from Christ; no supernatural beings or supposed astrological powers can separate us from Christ or defeat God's purpose for us. The loving Lord guards and guides us through all the unknown contingencies of the present and future. The love of God is the unshakeable foundation of Christian life and hope.

As Abraham did not spare his own son, Isaac, but was ready to sacrifice him at God's command, so God did not spare Jesus. But Jesus rose from the dead and now sits triumphant at God's right hand, as his people's king (Ps 110:1). The exalted Servant there continues his work of intercession. The right was the traditional place of honor beside the king, giving the occupant direct access to him. The phrase "Who is at the right hand of God" draws upon the oft-quoted testimony of Ps 110:1, used in the New Testament of the enthronement and consequent supremacy of Christ over all the Church's foes, and the guarantee of God's supply for every need (Ep 1:20-23). Paul ascribes to the risen Christ an activity that continues the objective aspect of man's redemption. Christ presents his supplication to the Father on behalf of Christians. He presents there his obedience, his sufferings, his prayers, and our prayers sanctified through him. In Heb 7:25 and 9:24 this intercession is linked with Christ's priesthood.

Christ, the eternal Priest, exercises in heaven his office of mediator and intercessor. His prayer is analogous to that of the

Holy Spirit who intervenes before God in favor of the saints (Rm 8:27). "He is always able to save those who draw near to God through him, since he always lives to make intercession for them" (Heb 7:25). As it was for men's salvation that he lived on earth, so also it is for this that he still ever lives in heaven. He is always living as man's representative. The sacrifice of Jesus cannot be limited to his death; his exaltation is an essential part, being the Father's acceptance of it. The intercession of the exalted Christ should then not be regarded as the sequel to his sacrifice but as its eternal continuance in heaven. This is no longer the humble supplication of "the days of his flesh" (Heb 5:7). This is the intercession of a fully authorized personage who shares God's glory. To plead on our behalf is one aspect of Christ's priesthood. Men need someone to approach God for them, because they are prevented by awe and by consciousness of their sins. A priest can approach God in virtue of his office, and so represent those who cannot. This idea is embodied particularly in the Day of Atonement service; our writer sees it perfectly embodied in Christ. When Aaron entered in the holy place, he bore the names of the children of Israel upon his heart, to bring them to continual remembrance before the Lord (Ex 28:29). In the same way Jesus, our High Priest, carries us in his heart.

To intercede for a person has a considerable latitude of meaning. It signifies to pray for, or intreat in behalf of another, to defend or vindicate a person, to commend, to furnish any kind of assistance or help. Christ's intercession includes every kind of mediation; all are included in it, and it cannot be limited by any or even all of them. The role of our mediator before God is ontological, because of his nature as the intermediary between the finite and the infinite; it is cosmic because of the order he preserves in the world; psychological because of the insights and good intentions he inspires into our hearts. The nature of his intercession may be indicated by Lk 22:32; Jesus, that is to say, is doing for his people now what he did for Peter in the hour of temptation, procuring for us the necessary spiritual strength to keep our faith from failing.

Christ's intercession is not to be confounded with his

earthly offering of himself. This he did once for all and without repetition; his intercession is continual representation on the ground of the completed offering. Neither is his intercession merely his appearance before the face of God for us, even if this is no small benefit. God having him ever in his sight is held in unbroken remembrance of Christ's work for us, and has in him the official type and representative of his people on earth. Christ's intercession can be regarded especially as a direct representation to God on the part of the Son. Immediately connected with it seems to be that we draw near unto God through Christ, and that through him we offer the sacrifice of praise unto God continually. That which enables him to make it pointed in our behalf is his fellow-feeling with us; that which gives it power with God is his personal offering and the fact that he is the Son of God; and that which gives the effect of it, is grace to help us in time of need. To define it completely in itself may be impossible. He has left us an example, in Jn Ch 17 his priestly prayer, of how he interceded in human speech to God in the days of his flesh, and translating this into the modes of heavenly communion, so far as we can imagine them, we may form some conception of it.

"Christ has entered into heaven itself that he might appear before God now in our behalf" (Heb 9:24). Through his death Christ has won an entrance in our behalf as our High Priest, into the immediate presence of God. There he is now openly manifested before the very face of God as our representative, guaranteeing that we shall be accepted and our prayer answered when we come. It is because he is there to support our cause that full salvation is assured to all who come unto God by him. Jesus' voluntary self-oblation has entitled him to enter the true sanctuary above and represent his people before God. Christ has opened heaven to all believers, entitling us to enter and enjoy eternal blessedness. He appears before God in our behalf, not that he alone might enjoy the beatific vision, but that we also may partake in the same blessing. So shall the covenant fellowship be finally and forever realized. There and thus he presents his offering for us and intercedes for us.

In the Old Testament to appear before God means to go into

the temple to worship. The earthly copy of this act of Christ is that of the high priest who once a year presented himself before God in the Holy of Holies on behalf of the people. To appear before God is to perform the function of Aaron, the high priest. God remained invisible to the high priest; he shows himself without veil in heaven, and Christ is admitted before him. Jesus Christ entered heaven for us and to introduce us in our turn. The best that the high priest could do in the Jerusalem temple was to burn incense and send fragrant smoke up to heaven; Jesus can himself come directly before God to intercede in favor of believers. Under the old covenant the presence of God was manifested above the mercy-seat on which the victim's blood was offered, here the priest who is also the victim offers himself upon the heavenly mercy-seat, that is, in heaven itself before God himself. Christ's sphere of service is the true Holy of Holies, and he enters it by virtue of the one final sacrifice made by him in history, the sacrifice of himself.

Christ meets the Father face to face; and as his appearing is for us, so in and through it man and God meet face to face, that is, the covenant fellowship is realized. And this is not merely at some past moment for a brief space of time, as the Jewish priest stayed in the Holy of Holies for a few minutes each year, but continually. Christ, our priest, his work now finished, is now at God's right in the plenitude of divine glory and the exercise of omnipotence. His resurrection is God's acceptance of his sacrifice of his oblation and adoration of God's will. His priesthood is an essential feature of his character, and his intercession and his ministry before God express simply in cultic language, that his Father has given him all power in heaven and on earth (Mt 28:18) in recompense for his sacrifice here below.

John, like the author of Hebrews, links the heavenly intercession of Christ to his atoning death. "We have an advocate with the Father, Jesus Christ, the righteous; and he is the expiation for our sins" (1 Jn 2:1-2). The death of Christ is an adequate expiation for all sin, and his righteousness enables him to act as the effectual friend and helper of men in the Father's presence. Not only was the blood of Christ offered willingly; he was also, as offerer, perfectly righteous. Only one who is perfect in virtue can remain in active communion with God, and assist men to attain the righteousness which is his.

Advocate means one who is called to one's side to give needed counsel, to help or plead a cause. The Holy Spirit is called another paraclete in Jn 14:15. Here the meaning is clear. Jesus, righteous himself, and the answer to the sins of those who trust him, stands before the Father fully accepted by God. His perfection and especially his perfect self-offering of himself avail to wipe away the sins of those who are united with him in faith and trust. We have an advocate, not a mean person, but him of whom it was said, "This is my beloved Son;" not a guilty person, who stands in need of pardon for himself, but Jesus Christ, the righteous; not a mere petitioner who relies purely upon liberality, but one who has merited, fully merited, whatever he asks. It is as a victim of expiation that he intercedes for us before his Father. The purpose of the Incarnation was to provide an adequate expiation for sin, but whereas the Old Testament laid the emphasis on appeasing the anger of a righteous God, the Johannine writings lay emphasis on the love of God which is to be seen at its acme in the voluntary sacrifice of Christ.

Instructed by the Father and the Son, the Holy Spirit is God's advocate within our hearts; the Lord Jesus is our advocate, representing our interests and pleading our cause before God. Christ is the intercessor for us above, and in his absence the Holy Spirit is the other intercessor in us. Christ's advocacy is inseparable from the Holy Spirit's comforting us and assisting our prayers.

21

GOD FOR EVER BLESSED

The long development in Rm Ch 9-11 begins and closes with an act of spontaneous adoration (Rm 9:5 and 11:33-36). The Christian apostolate is a liturgical function (Rm 15:16). The final doxology (Rm 16:25-27), like the blessing in Rm 15:13, sums up the central themes of the epistle.

Paul's theme of justification by faith led him to speak of the righteousness of Abraham (Rm Ch 4). Similarly the theme of salvation lovingly bestowed by God through the Spirit, makes it necessary to speak about the case of Israel (Ch 9-11), a people which remains unbelieving though it had received the promise of salvation. Paul deals with the tragic fact that the chosen people, whose whole history was a preparation for Christ, and to whom the gospel was first offered by Christ and his Apostles, for the most part rejected Christ and persist in their rejection. This rejection is not a frustration of God's declared purpose in the Old Testament; it was foreseen and provided for in the divine plan. This long development begins and closes with an act of spontaneous adoration (Rm 9:5 and 11:33-36).

"They are Israelites, and to them belong the sonship, the glory, the covenants, the giving of the law, the worship, and the promises. They are descended from the patriarchs, and of their race according to the flesh is the Christ, who is above all, God for ever blessed. Amen" (Rm 9:4-5). Paul lists the privileges that the

Jews enjoyed as God's people. He is proud of these benefits and recounts them with a certain flourish, the greatest of all being that Christ sprang from the Jewish stock. Israel was the special name given to Jacob by God. Israelite describes the Jews as the inheritors of God's promises. This is the most dignified name for the chosen people, suggesting all the theocratic privileges that are now enumerated. The sonship refers to Israel's place as Yahweh's people (Ex 4:22). This adoption is different from that of Rm 8:15; it applies to Israel as chosen by God as first-born son among other nations. The glory, the Old Testament Shekinah, denotes God's radiant presence with his people in their pilgrimage and at worship. The covenants are the agreements that God made with Abraham, Isaac, and Jacob, and then with Israel as a whole at the Exodus, that he was their God and that they were his people, and that therefore they should serve him. The giving of the law which embodies God's will was another great benefit. Another ancestral heritage was the worship of the one true God, the God of their fathers. The promises are the prefigurations of what God intended for his people, especially the promises concerning the Messiah and his kingdom. To this summary of Israel's prerogatives the climax is added, namely, physical relationship with Christ, the descendant par excellence of their race. The Messiah, however, their greatest title to glory, was unfortunately not recognized as such.

The doxology, "Christ, who is above all, God for ever blessed, Amen," represents the highest point to which St. Paul's Christology had hitherto risen, inasmuch as these words describe Christ simply as God without any reservation or qualification. This phrase expressive of adoring reverence is in place in this somber context. It balances a statement about the human side of Christ, his natural descent, with one about his divine side as in Rm 1:3-4, and gives a truly fitting climax to the list of the privileges which Israel has had, the divine Messiah. "God over all" balances "according to the flesh," that is, as regards his human descent. Paul completes this with the statement: as regards his eternal being, he is God over all. He is the self-existent, independent Being who was, is, and is to come. He is over all, the Supreme as being God who rules over and disposes all things according to his will. No words can express more clearly his divine, supreme majesty, and his gracious sovereignty.

Both the context and the internal development imply that this doxology is addressed to Christ. Paul rarely gives Jesus the title God (Tt 2:13) or addresses a doxology to him (Heb 13:21) but this is because he ususally keeps this title for the Father, and considers the divine persons not so much with an abstract appreciation of their nature as with a concrete appreciation of their function in the process of salvation. Moreover he always has in mind the historical Christ in his concrete reality as God made man. For Paul, Jesus is essentially the Son of God, his own Son, the Son of his love who belongs to the sphere of the divine by right, the sphere from which he came. The title Son of God became his in a new way with the resurrection, but it was not then that he received it since he preexisted not only as prefigured in the Old Testament, but ontologically. He is the wisdom and the image by which and in which all things were created and have been recreated, because into his own person is gathered the fullness of the Godhead and of the universe. In him God has devised the whole plan of salvation, and he no less than the Father is its intended end. The Father raises to life and judges and so does the Son. In short, he is one of the three persons enumerated in the Trinitarian formulae.

Rm 11:33-36 is a hymn to God's mercy and wisdom. Paul has reached the end of his argument and he breaks out into praise of God for his wonderful mercy in contriving a way to save both Jew and Gentile despite their disobedience. Paul's discussion dissolves into worship, for theology is doxology or it is nothing at all. The interpreter of God's purposes to man breaks out in spontaneous praise to God, the source, guide, and goal of all that is. It is the very heart of religion that God is in charge of the universe, planning and controlling all that happens, and that Jesus is the center of God's planning. It is equally of the heart of religion that man is responsible, and consciously responsible, for what he does. There is no easy solution to this paradox. Paul is very much aware of it and knows that he cannot surrender either side. That is why he finishes by confessing that God's ways are far beyond man's understanding. In the history of Christianity one or the other side has often been given up, and this has led to a caricature of the Christian faith.

The eternal decrees of God are beyond man's understanding, but they are both wise and good. The divine acts are all-mysterious. If God condemns, who shall question or annul the decree? We behold his works in redemption but the how of them utterly baffles; for, after all, he is God unsearchable, inscrutable. All things originate from him, continue through him, and find their consummation in or for him, for his glory. "O the depth of the riches and wisdom and knowledge of God! How unsearchable are his judgments and how inscrutable his ways! For who has known the mind of the Lord, or has been his counselor? Or who has ever given him a gift that he might be repaid? For from him and through him and to him are all things. To him be glory for ever. Amen" (Rm 11:33-36). This final reflection celebrates the wisdom of God's plan of salvation, which has now become open and comprehensible to the whole human race. Paul expresses admiration and gratitude at the boundless wonder of God's providence in arranging the mutual assistance of Jew and Gentile in attaining their salvation. God is no one's debtor either for his plans or for his gifts to men. All proceeds from his own gracious bounty, and he needs neither consultants nor research assistants nor commissions of inquiry.

Rm 11:36 is a doxology to God the Father as the creator, sustainer, and goal of the universe; it expresses the absolute dependence of all creation on him. It ascribes praise to God as the all-wise governor of human history and the ineffable source and ground of all being. Throughout the history of the world from its creation to the final consummation, in all the vicissitudes of history, it is he who brings men and things into existence, guides and controls them, and finally brings them to their predestined goal. There is no room on man's part for anything but awe and wonder, nothing that he can contribute but his adoration and thanksgiving. God is the efficient, sustaining, and final cause of all. All things in universal nature, through the whole compass of time and eternity, are from him, as the original designer and author; by him, as the prime and efficient cause; to him, as the ultimate end for the manifestation of his eternal glory and goodness. The story of mankind began with God, is shaped by God, and will reach the end which God has designed for it.

The glory of God, the reflection of his perfections in all that exists, that glory, now veiled in so many respects in the universe, must shine forth magnificently and perfectly for ever and ever. The highest end for which all things can exist and be ordered, is to display the character of God. This goal of history is, as it were, anticipated by the wish and prayer of the apostle: "To him be glory." Amen is the translation of a Hebrew word which was used in response to a prayer or an oath; it means truly or surely. Paul thus gives his assent to the words he has quoted. He may not fully understand God's plan, no man possibly could, but he himself is prepared to accept it and praise God for it. Even if we cannot fully understand, yet we can praise and adore. The blessing in Rm 15:13 sums up the central themes of the doctrinal section of the epistle: faith as source of justification, and hope of salvation as source of peace and fruit of the Spirit. "May the God of hope fill you with joy and peace in believing so that by the power of the Holy Spirit you may abound in hope." Three titles are given to God in this chapter: the God of patience (5), the God of hope (13), and the God of peace (33). The concluding benediction appropriately emphasizes the hope which arises out of the joy and peace that faith produces and that the Holy Spirit inspires and causes to abound. The God of hope means the God on whom we may rest our hopes. Trust in him brings joy and peace; and the Holy Spirit at work in the Christian's heart intensifies Christian hope. The Christian life is a joyful adventure on which we embark knowing that the issues are safely in the hand of God. Paul's prayer is for right perspectives. May spiritual qualities be exalted in the Christian community instead of discord over material and human matters. If hope, joy, peace, a continual attitude of faith, and the power of the Holy Spirit fill the vision of God's people and direct their judgment, then secondary matters will fall into their proper perspective and be viewed aright.

The apostolate, even more than the ordinary Christian life (Rm 12:1), is a liturgical function; the apostle, or rather through him in Christ (15:18), makes an offering of men to God. "God has given me the grace to be a minister of Christ Jesus among the Gentiles with the priestly duty of preaching the gospel of God, so that the Gentiles may be offered as a pleasing sacrifice, sanctified by the Holy Spirit" (Rm 16:16). The passage is remarkable because of its liturgical, sacrificial language in three terms: priest, sacrifice, offering. In his apostolic work Paul serves under Christ in the preaching of the gospel. His object is to bring a consecrated offering that God can accept, namely, his Gentile converts; to make them fit for the presence of God. He offers the sacrifice of the Gentiles made righteous to God and consecrated by the Holy Spirit. He offers God not slaughtered animals, but repentant men. He thus achieves what was symbolized in the sacrifice, the return of men to God. He is God's agent to the Gentile world, God's priest to offer him a sacrifice consisting of Gentile converts won to the gospel and nurtured in the faith. This is a specific application of the priesthood of all believers, whereby all Christian work is viewed as a sacrifice.

Paul began his letter with the expression of sentiments of adoration which are reechoed in the final doxology (Rm 16:25-27). He finishes, not as is his custom with good wishes but with an elaborate doxology. Nearly all the main points of the whole letter are gathered here in a powerful finale: the power of God unto salvation; the revelation of God's plan of salvation in the Gospel; salvation by faith in Jesus Christ; the Christian salvation offered to all; the new way as the real consummation of the old. "Now to him who is able to strengthen you according to my gospel and the teaching of Jesus Christ, according to the revelation of the mystery which was kept secret for long ages, but is now disclosed, and through the prophetic writings is made known to all nations, according to the command of the eternal God, to bring about the obedience of faith, to the only wise God be glory for evermore through Jesus Christ. Amen" (Rm 16:25-27). To declare that the only wise God commanded his saving purpose, which had been a mystery, to be revealed in Christ is the root of Pauline and Christian orthodoxy.

The idea of a mystery of wisdom long hidden in God and now revealed, is borrowed by Paul from Jewish apocalypse but he enriches the content of the term by applying it to the climax of the history of salvation: the saving cross of Christ, the call of the pagans to this salvation preached by Paul, and finally the restoration of all things in Christ as their one head. The whole burden of this liturgical formula lies in the words "now disclosed." The Church looking at the past rejoices to be living at a time when the revealed name of Jesus Christ is henceforth the key of general history and of the destiny of every man. The Old Testament scriptures are now unlocked by the key of Jesus Christ and seen to be the manifesto of the wise God's plan.

"Only wise" is another phase of the divine character which evokes the adoration of the apostle. The wisdom of God in the Pauline thought is not mere speculation, or philosophy, beyond the ken of human understanding. It is rather an attribute wherein Paul sees the mercies of God toward sinful men, practically designed and achieved through Jesus Christ. Such wisdom is the sole prerogative and property of God. Hence eternal glory be to God.

This lengthy doxology forms a worthy conclusion to this great epistle. It gathers up the main ideas of the whole epistle into one harmonious burst of wonder, love, and praise.

22

CHRIST, HEAD OF ALL CREATION

The principal aim of Colossians is to assert the preeminence of Christ. Paul begins with thanksgiving and prayer (Col 1:3-14). In Col 1:15-17, Paul presents Christ as head of all creation; he describes Christ's supremacy in the universe.

Just as Romans had systematized the ideas outlined in Galatians so now, at about the same time as Colossians, Paul wrote another letter, Ephesians, in which he presented the same teaching from another angle. The principal aim of Colossians is to assert the preeminence of Christ. Paul begins with thanksgiving and prayer (Col 1:3-14). The prayers of St. Paul are a rewarding study, and one more than this one, which provides a valuable pattern for the prayer-life of the believer. This liturgically cadenced petition is for a sensitiveness to God's will, consisting in a grasp of what is spiritually valuable; for the overflow of this knowledge into external activity; and for the strength to do this.

"We pray for you asking that you may be filled with the knowledge of his will in all spiritual wisdom and understanding, to lead a life worthy of the Lord, fully pleasing to him, bearing fruit in every good work, and increasing in the knowledge of God. May you be strengthened with all power, according to his glorious might, for all endurance and patience with joy, giving thanks to the Father who has qualified us to share in the inheritance of the saints in light. He has delivered us from the dominion of darkness and transferred us to the kingdom of his beloved Son, in whom we have redemption, the forgiveness of sins" (Col 1:9-14). In the Old Testament the heritage of God's people was Palestine. Here the heritage is the realm of light, that is, a share in Christ's kingdom. As Israel was delivered in the Exodus from Egypt, so too Christians have been rescued. The words redemption, heritage, and rescued draw upon the Exodus tradition to interpret Christian experience as release from the domain of darkness, that is, of evil and evil powers. Redemption releases from the power of sin; forgiveness from its guilt.

We need a fuller grasp of the working out of God's eternal purpose, and an effort to live in accordance with it. The more this knowledge deepens, the more will we manifest it in our lives. The strength for this will come from God himself, who will enable us to bear with gladness any trial. The knowledge for which Paul prays is that insight into truth granted by the powerful working of God to those who are open to spiritual wisdom. This wisdom expresses itself concretely in the life of the believer who increases in knowledge, as his life bears fruit in active goodness of every kind. The source of this growth, the strength for endurance and patience in obedience, and the ground for joy is God's own power. Knowledge is one of the key words of this letter. This is first of all a knowledge of God's will to save men in Christ, not merely a conceptual knowledge but a personal knowledge of God himself, and an experience of his loving design to save all men in Christ, through their being conformed to the image of his Son. The wisdom theme is also prominent in Colossians, for Paul draws heavily on the Old Testament wisdom to prove that Christ has a central place in the universe.

The phrase "a life worthy of the Lord" brings out the noble ideal of Christian living. The Christian life is a progressive activity not a static concept. Knowledge of God's will is a means of attaining more knowledge of God himself. Doctrine and practice cannot be dissociated; the continued effort to know more of God is a way to help towards Christian living. Right conduct is both the aim and the hallmark of right knowledge. In the divine therapy, a mental transformation is the means to achieve an ethical renewal. The expression "his glorious might" suggests that the omnipotence of God is an aspect of his glory. Men can see the evidences of God's power and can share it. But the outworking is not in spectacular wonders but in endurance under trial. "The inheritance of the saints" is the spiritual counterpart of the promised land which was the material goal of the Exodus of God's people in the Old Testament. The words "Son of his love" lead Paul to unfold the Christology which is his answer to the false teachers at Colossae. To realize that Jesus is the redeemer in time, leads to the thought of his Person in eternity.

Paul describes the primacy, the supremacy of Christ in two ways: in the universe and in the Church. Christ is the agent of creation and of redemption. In the order of the natural creation, he is the head of all creation (Col 1:15-17); and in the order of supernatural recreation, which is our redemption, he is the head of the Church (Col 1:18-20). The subject of this poem is the pre-existent Christ, but always considered in the unique and historical person of the Son of God made man. It is this concrete human being who is the image of God, insofar as he reflects in his visible human nature the image of the invisible God. It is he who as part of creation can be called the first-born of creation, by a primacy of excellence and of causality as well as of time. Though God is invisible, yet the Son is his eternal image who reproduces him, and in both position and time stands before all created things (Col 1:15). For everything created, whether earthly or heavenly, is founded on him; he is alike the agent and the goal of all (16). He stands as absolute head, he binds and sustains all that is (17).

Nowhere in the Pauline epistles is there a richer and more exalted estimate of the position of Christ than in this hymn (Col 1:15-20). Its exalted Christology synthesizes the growing awareness, in New Testament time, of Christ as man, Son of God, king and judge of the world, endowed with divine redemptive power, and containing in himself the fullness of the effective presence of God among men. His work is related not only to the rescue of mankind from sin but also, perhaps with special reference with false teaching, to the creation of the universe. The aim of this great exposition of the nature and work of the Son is to accord to him the supreme position in the world and in the Church, and sweep away the false teaching which assigned to angelic mediators the position and functions of the Son.

Christ is associated both with the creation of the universe and with God's new creation, the Church. A parallel is drawn between the work of Jesus in creation, and his part in reclaiming God's world, and it is because of the first of these activities that Jesus can perform the second. The first strophe centers on creation (1:15-17), the second on the resurrection (18-20), but there is interpenetration since the second thought illumines the first. All the affirmations of the hymn are grounded on the historical event of the cross; like the rest of the New Testament, it unites creation and redemption, the confession of Jesus as Lord to that of Jesus as Savior.

The kernel of Colossians is found in 1:15-20, which represents a high point of Pauline Christology. The hymn evokes a number of themes which made their appearance in previous letters: Christ is the image of God. God created the world through him; the Church is his Body. But it also contains new elements: all has been created in and for Christ; he is the head of the Body; the fullness dwells in him. The key insight which gives the hymn harmony and unity is the identification of Christ with the wisdom of God. The poem contains the central argument of the whole epistle. Paul delineates Christ's role in the universe in terms taken from the Old Testament descriptions of the wisdom of God. He recalls the role of the personified wisdom in creation and in the harmonious direction of the universe. Wisdom's role is continued in Christ himself in whom all God's wisdom and knowledge are hidden.

This hymn to Christ was probably taken over and modified from an earlier poem. Hence many currents of thought, even pagan, are suggested as lying behind the hymn. The dominant source of its themes, however, is apparently the Old Testament wisdom literature. Israel's developed portrait of divine wisdom is the forerunner of Christ as creator and redeemer. Like wisdom,

Christ in the image of God, preexists before creation, takes an active part in creation, and leads men to God. The hymn probably formed part of a baptismal liturgy, which Paul evokes in order to recall the Colossians to the original profession of faith which they were now in danger of abandoning. In its actual state it apparently was meant to counteract the errors propagated at Colossae.

The wisdom Christology of Col 1:15-20 is paralleled in the New Testament by two other hymns that celebrate the universal role of Christ; St. John's prologue (1:1-18) and the prologue of the epistle to the Hebrews (1:1-4). It is also in line with our Lord's own teaching in John's gospel. It proclaims the preeminent Son of God, alike in his eternal relation to the Father through all eternity, and his relation in time to all created things. In earlier epistles the center of the Apostle's teaching is redemption; now, owing to the heresy he is combating, it is headship. The picture of Christ on the cross is succeeded by that of Christ upon the throne. In Ephesians the same thought appears, but is applied to the relation of Christians to their Lord and head (Ep 1:22, 2:4); here we find, in answer to Colossian errors, a doctrinal statement which perhaps contains the special message of this epistle for the twentieth century. For the emphasis of today falls in undue proportion upon the life and death of the Jesus of history, the human Jesus, to the detriment of the divine Son of God.

"He is the image of the invisible God, the first-born of all creation; for in him all things were created, in heaven and on earth, visible and invisible, whether thrones or dominations or principalities or powers, all things were created through him and for him. He is before all things, and in him all things hold together" (Col 1:15-17). The nature of the Godhead has always been a favorite theme for study and speculation. Against the notion of God as unknowable, Paul places Christ as God's image; not merely a manifestation but a complete representation. For the biblical writers an image is not merely a faithful copy, but a visible reproduction, a radiant impression in which the being of the original is exteriorized. Whereas man is patterned after the image of God, being given a certain likeness to him, Christ is the actual likeness of God. Through faith, the remote reality of the Deity is rendered discernibly present in him and comprehensible to men. He is the image of the invisible God, in the sense that as a person he is supreme in every way over all creation. It is because man bore God's image that it was possible for God to become man. In this way what otherwise would be invisible becomes visible to man.

The image says more than resemblance, adding to the idea of likeness, the suggestion of a derivation from an archetype. The image is not necessarily a perfect representation of its archetype, the perfection is to be judged by the context. For example, in Gn 1:26 the image of God in man though striking is not perfect. Here, however, the image is so perfect that it equals its model. Christ is the revealer of God (Jn 1:18). He is the image that perfectly resembles and reveals the original, the invisible God. Jesus is the Word or Wisdom of God, the one and only way to God. Perfect revelation can be made only by one who is what he reveals. Image must be understood in the sense of personal relationship. The creature "views the unbegotten beauty in the begotten" (St. Basil), whom the Father has given to the world.

The word first-born is to be connected with the Old Testament meaning of the word and suggests the heir by virtue of primogeniture. The Son is first in position in his relation to the universe. He is also first in time in virtue of his eternal existence. The context makes it clear that Christ is the agent of creation, which at once places him above it. The word first-born must then be understood in the sense of supreme. It means a position of authority and power over all creation. Christ holds supremacy over all creation, as the first-born is supreme over the rest of the family. First-born expresses priority, preeminence, and consecration. It was in his Son that God contemplated the plan of the universe.

Christ stands in the same relation to the created universe as to the Church. In him expresses that relation in both cases. The conditioning cause of creation, as of conservation, resides in him. He is creation's principle of existence, its center of unity, harmony, and cohesion, which gives it meaning, value, and reality. Christ is also the efficient cause, the agent of creation (through), and the final cause, its goal (for). He is the goal of the universe, as he was its starting point. In him the purpose of the universe is found, in him is its principle of coherence, and it is he who impresses upon creation that unity and solidarity which make it a cosmos instead of chaos. In addition to being the result of the positive agency of Christ, creation is for him: for his glory, a sphere for revelation, for the display of redeeming love. Since all was created through him and for him, he is superior to all, as the source and end of their being. Christ's supremacy required not only that nothing appear in creation except in relation to him, but also that he himself share in the creation of all things.

In view of the Colossian speculations, Paul affirms the Paschal victory of Christ over all invisible powers which were imagined to participate in the government of the physical universe and even of the religious world. No beings whether visible or invisible are outside the supremacy of Christ. Whatever unseen powers exist, to borrow the language of the time, Christ is their creator and Lord. In the religious currents of the time, it was believed that many divine beings existed; and some thought they were represented as angels. Paul categorically subordinates such spiritual beings to Christ, for they are created things. Finally, in Christ all Christians have the freedom of the universe. The modern equivalent of this is the freedom which Christ can bring to those who are obsessed by a no less real fear of fate or destiny, or who feel themselves caught up in the inexorable forces of materialism or of the social and economic order.

Such is Christ's supremacy that he existed before creation came into being. This is not merely a statement of his priority but also of his eternal existence; he exists as the I am. "He is" expresses immutability of existence, eternity. The statement indicates both anteriority and supremacy. Christ's authority is primordial, his reign universal, and his power absolute. It is to him that creation owes all that it has been, is and will be.

Three divine attributes are implied in the phrase "hold together:" the power of conservation which is a perpetual creation; providence which presides over the relations of all creatures; and immensity which contains and surpasses all.

Through Jesus Christ, his Word, God is continually at work in the world; it is not a case that he created it and then left it to its own devices. The Son is the center of unity for the universe; he is the cement as well as the support of the universe. Christ is the unifying and cohering factor in creation. He is the conserver of creation, the keystone, as it were, of the universe as he is of the Church.

23

CHRIST, HEAD OF THE CHURCH

*Jesus is not only the agent of creation, he is also the
one who creates order out of the disorder that has
crept into it. He is the head of the body, the Church
(Col 1:18-20). A Christian is an active member of
Christ's mystical body, completing in his flesh what is
lacking to Christ's sufferings (Col 1:22-24). Christ is
the mystery of God (Col 1:25-27).*

Jesus is not only the agent of creation, he is also the one who
creates order out of the disorder that has crept into it. Not only
does he hold the position of absolute priority and sovereignty
over the universe, the natural creation; he stands also in the
same relation to the Church, the new spiritual creation. Thus in
all things, in the Church as in the world, he is found to have the
preeminence. For Paul the only loyalty that matters is that to
Jesus, who alone can bring men into a living relationship with
God.

"He is the head of the body, the Church; he is the beginning,
the first-born from the dead, that in everything he might be preeminent. It pleased God to make all fullness dwell in him, and
through him to reconcile to himself all things, whether on earth
or in heaven, making peace by the blood of his Cross (Col 1:18-
20).

Paul has used the body metaphor earlier, to stress that all
Christians have a part to play in the life and work of the Church.

Now, however, he wishes to underline the Lordship of Jesus, and so he varies the method of expression. In his earlier epistles Christ and the Christians form one body; in Col and Ep, a distinction is made between the body (the Church) and its head (Christ). Also distinctive is the fact that here Church means the entire Christian community, not simply a local Church as in the earlier Pauline usage. In 1 Cor 2:21 the head indicates simply one of the members of the body. Now head is used with two connotations: dignity and authority, and source of vitality. The figure aptly illustrates how close is the relationship and vital link between Christ and his Church. The Church exists only by his indwelling Spirit, operates by his power, and functions as his representative.

Head of the body is an expression which brings out the supreme importance of Christ in his Church. No member of the body can exist, and certainly none can function without the head. To us the head suggests the brains of an organism. Here it means rather the chief, the leader, the one who is supreme over the body. Only in Col and Ep is Christ the head of the Church; in the earlier epistles he is the body itself. In either case this organic conception is distinctively Christian. Occasionally earlier non-Christian writers had already compared a state or a group of people to a body; but the distinctive thing is that the Church is not the body of Christians, but the body of Christ, part of an already existing personality. The most probable explanation of this striking usage is to be found in the discovery, common to all Christians, that Jesus, vivid historical individual though he was, was also in some mysterious way more than an individual: he was and is, an inclusive personality; he is his people. To persecute Christians is to persecute Christ; to do something to the least of his brethren is to do it to him; and to be baptized into Christ is to become a member of his body.

Of the four figures used in the New Testament to describe the Church, namely, the branch, the bride, the building, and the body, the latter stresses the interchange of relations. The body depends upon the head for its existence and coordination; and the head expresses itself in thought, purpose, and activity through the body. Christ began the Church as he did the natural universe: he is the beginning. Nor did his death lower his estate. He is the first-born of the dead, not only in the sense that he rose first, but especially that he stands as the cause of our resurrection, the ground of that vast spiritual harvest whose full realization is yet to come.

Christ is the head of the Church by his priority in time, since he was the first to rise from the dead, and by his role as principle, or beginning, in the order of salvation. As head Christ is the principle, the source of the life that flows in the members, the supernatural life of grace and glory. The word beginning suggests supremacy in rank, precedence in time or creative initiative. Christ forms the nucleus of a redeemed humanity in his complement, the Church, in which he makes a new beginning, a new creation. Christ is the author of all supernatural life, especially of the glorious life. He is the first to be raised to a glorious and immortal life, first not only in time, but especially because he is the cause of the resurrection of all those who will follow. His resurrection from the dead is his title to the headship of the Church; for the power of the resurrection (Ph 3:10) is the life of the Church, spiritual and eternal life.

"First-born of the dead" alludes both to the physical resurrection of Christ and to the spiritual resurrection effected in baptism (Col 2:13) of which it is the type and cause. It is a characteristic of Pauline theology that Christ's resurrection marked a new beginning not only for humanity but also for Christ himself. Through his resurrection he was "constituted Son of God in power" (Rm 1:14) and "became a life-giving spirit" (1 Cor 15:45). Jesus is the only one in the world's history who has convincingly shown that death did not put an end to his career, and so he is alone supreme, the center of human hopes and aspirations. All the prerogatives enumerated show that Christ holds the first rank in all things: in the metaphysical order by his divinity; in the natural order, as creator; in the supernatural order, as redeemer; in the moral and mystical order, as head of a body in which he infuses spiritual life; and lastly in the eschatological order which he already began by his glorious resurrection.

The fullness that dwells in Christ is not here directly, as in

Col 2:9, the fullness of Godhead, but the fullness of being and of grace possessed by the Son in his incarnate state. This fullness is the guarantee of an inexhaustible source of grace, blessing, and power. It was this fullness which qualified Jesus to become the mediator. The fullness here probably refers primarily to the cosmos as being filled with the creative presence of God. For Paul the incarnation, crowned by the resurrection, makes the human nature of Christ not only head of the human race, but also of the entire created cosmos, which somehow is involved in salvation, as it was in the fall. This reechoes the Old Testament theme of the close bond linking the creator with his creation; for example, "Do I not fill heaven and earth?" (Jr 23:24); "The Spirit of the Lord fills the whole world" (Ws 1:7). In this perspective the pleroma (fullness) is the plenitude of being and englobes both the divinity and the material world.

The reconciliation of the whole universe, including angels as well as human beings, does not mean the salvation of each individual, but the collective salvation of the world by its return to the order and peace of perfect submission to God. Any individual who has not entered by grace into this new order will be forced to join it at his own peril. The whole universe is understood as having been estranged from God and rebellious; this estrangement has been overcome by the reconciliation effected by the death of Christ. Redemption in a certain sense extends to lifeless things. Paul explains this idea in Rm 8:20-22. After man's sin all the material creation is subject to slavery and corruption since it was created for man, to glorify God by man's intermediary, a purpose which can no longer be realized if humanity remains sinful. Once redeemed, man tends once more to Christ, his last end, and brings back creation to Christ. Creation will regain its full harmony when the union of all the just is consummated in Christ. There can be no denying that Paul is thinking of the work of Christ in sacrificial terms. Jesus of Nazareth, who had been done to death as an insurrectionary some thirty years before, occupies a position uniquely close to God in his creative and redemptive work; and this is inseparably associated precisely with that death on the Cross.

A Christian participates in the work of salvation. He is an

active member of Christ's mystical body, completing in his flesh what is lacking to Christ's sufferings (Col 1:21-24). "Christ has now reconciled you in his body of flesh in order to present you to God, holy and blameless and irreproachable" (Col 1:22). His body of flesh stresses that God's act or reconciliation was done not by remote control but right in the midst of human life. The human body of Christ is the locus where the reconciliation takes place. Into his body the entire human race, of which Christ has assumed the sin, is virtually, effectively gathered. Great stress is put in the Christian gospel on the real incarnation and real death of Christ. It is a real, physical body surrendered actually to death, by which God reconciles estranged men and women to himself. The idea behind the verb "present" is the presentation of sacrifice. The whole phase draws on Old Testament sacrificial requirements. To present us before God as a perfect sacrifice is the purpose and effect of the reconciliation (Ep 5:27).

"In my flesh I complete what is lacking in Christ's afflictions for the sake of his body, that is, the Church" (Col 1:24). As Paschal put it: "Christ will be in agony until the end of time." The Christian, united to Christ by baptism and the Eucharist, belongs to him in his very body, so that his life, his sufferings and his death become mystically those of Christ living in him and receiving glory from him. The sufferings of Christ would be first of all the apostolic sufferings endured as the gospel is preached. Jesus suffered in order to establish the kingdom of God, and those who continue his work must share his sufferings. Nothing can be added to the strictly redemptive value of the cross to which nothing is lacking. Yet Paul, by his sufferings as a missionary, shares in those that Jesus underwent in his own mission. These are the sufferings predicted for the Messianic era and are all part of the way in which God had always intended the Church to develop.

The apostle's sufferings can be spoken of as Christ's afflictions because of the communion which a Christian, incorporated in Christ, holds with the Lord; also because it is the destiny of the corporate Christ, the Church, to fulfill a certain tale of afflictions; thus the apostle's hardships and privations, incurred in his calling, are a contribution made for the sake of the whole body, towards the discharge of this quota. It is clear that the faith of the New Testament is that Christ suffered once and for all, and that his self-surrender was complete and unique, the fountain-head of reconciliation, a free gift that cannot be earned; yet also that those who are in Christ are caught up into this activity, and though never able on their own merit to win their own salvation, and still less that of others, are, by their very acceptance of this free gift, brought into the same stream of creative sufferings.

Until the end of time, the Church will be imperfect in the sense that it must continually develop both intensively and extensively. In virtue of their baptism all Christians are called to contribute to filling up this gap between the actual and the potential, the real and the ideal. This they do by living as authentic Christians which inescapably involves suffering. These sufferings are termed the sufferings of Christ because the suffering of any member is the suffering of the whole body, and of the head especially, which supplies strength, spirit, sense, and motion to all; also because they are for his sake, for the testimony of his truth. This idea is rich in doctrine. It constitutes a theology of suffering, describing its nature and value; a theology of work: Paul's suffering included all his missionary activity, so also all in a Christian's life should be sanctified by consecration to God. It underlines a beautiful aspect of Christian love, work for the mystical body; it establishes the fact of the communion of the saints, and consequently of the spiritual treasury of the Church, since the works and merits of the just are useful to the other members of the Church.

"I am a minister of the Church to make the word of God fully known, the mystery . . . How great among the Gentiles are the riches of the glory of this mystery, which is Christ in you, the hope of glory" (Col 1:25-27). For Paul a mystery is not something that must be kept secret, but rather a concealed truth which God is pleased to reveal when the time is ripe. The mystery or secret of God is that the pagans too are called to be saved through union with Christ, and so to reach eternal glory. The word mystery suggests the secret cults which were the most living part of religion in the heathen world of that day. The language of this whole passage seems to be suggested by them, and intended to show how different the Christian faith is from them and from the exclusive cult which false teachers at Colossae were propagating.

The word mystery stands in the religion of the Bible for God's purpose as divulged to his people, God's open secret. In the pagan world mystery could mean a secret religious rite, or an object or teaching connected with such a rite; and it was accordingly adopted by Greek speaking Judaism for a divine secret, hitherto concealed but now divulged, or concealed from others but revealed to God's chosen. More than ever, therefore, when Christians had recognized in Jesus God's unique act of salvation, the very focal point of all the beams of his light, the hinge of his plan, it was natural to speak of the incarnation as the long-concealed and at last revealed mystery. The word aptly conveys the paradox of revelation, that it is offered to all and yet it is only a few who prove capable of receiving it; that it is a secret, yet an open secret.

The mystery is first identified with the word of God and then with "Christ in you, the hope of glory." "In you" could simply be taken collectively so that the mystery would be Christ as found among the Gentiles, the Messiah in an unheard of position. It probably also has its usual theological meaning: that God's secret is the indwelling Christ, the character of Jesus reproduced in the believer's life through the Holy Spirit. In any case, this is an aspect of the gospel of the incarnation; and it carries in it the hope or guarantee of the revealing of God's presence, for that is what the Bible generally means by glory, God's splendor seen by men. Glory in the New Testament is a word which is inseparably bound up with the nature and activity of God. For Paul this is a treasure of inestimable wealth. In Col there is only one mention of the Holy Spirit (1:8). The risen Christ himself performs the functions attributed to the Spirit in other epistles. His inner presence in the community of believers all over the world is already a guarantee of a future community in glory. Christ is the center, but it is Christ in relation to man: "Christ in you." In

Christ is the correlative. This double relation is fostered and deepened by each Christian act, especially of sacramental union, by which the Christian dwells in Christ and he in us.

Here is the mystery of God contained hidden—the infinite wisdom of God: "To make known the knowledge of Christ in whom are hid all the treasures of wisdom and knowledge" (Col 2:2-3). The object of the mystery is Christ, himself the wisdom of God, mysterious and difficult to understand. The wealth of full understanding consists in the knowledge of the mystery of God, no other than Christ himself, since in him God's eternal purpose is revealed and realized. Christ is the entire storehouse of God's wisdom and knowledge. This notion is possibly derived from Pr 2:3-5 which likens wisdom to hidden treasure. Christ combines in himself all the wealth of wisdom and knowledge: knowledge of divine truth, and wisdom to apply the truth to relations with God and situations in life. The treasures of Christ are not hidden in any exclusive or forbidding sense. They are like a rich deposit in a storehouse, on which believers can draw throughout the ages. The world will never exhaust the meaning and power of the atonement.

NEW LIFE IN CHRIST

A Christian must live according to the true faith in Christ (Col 2:6-10). In Col 3:1-4 Paul gives the theological basis for a transformed life, namely, a radically new orientation respecting motives and goals. The demand and qualities of life in Christ are presented in Col 3:5-17. The duty of adoration is part of Christian living (Rm 14:8-11).

A Christian must live according to the true faith in Christ, who alone is the true head of men and angels (Col 2:6-10). "As you received Christ Jesus the Lord, so live in him rooted and built up in him and established in faith. . . In him the whole fullness of the deity dwells bodily" (Col 2:6-9). The sense of the word pleroma (fullness) is precised by the adverb bodily and the genitive deity. In the risen Christ is assembled all the divine world to which he belongs because of his preexistence and his present risen glory; and all the created world which he has assumed directly (his humanity) and indirectly (the cosmos) by his incarnation and his resurrection. Briefly, his is the plenitude of being, the fullness of all possible categories of being.

The word deity occurs only here in the New Testament and denotes the divine essence, all the inexhaustible perfections of the essential being of God. Every attribute, power, and moral excellence of God was revealed in his incarnate Son. The present tense (dwells) need present no difficulty in its application to Christ's glorified body. It points to the continuing effect of the incarnation as an act of revelation. It is a terse way of saying dwelt and still dwells. The adverb bodily stresses the incarnation of deity in the historical Jesus. Bodily, that is, assuming a bodily form. It is because the fullness took on some visible form in Christ that it became knowable to man. Bodily suggests the revelation of God in the life, death, resurrection, and present lordship of Jesus in bodily fashion. It refers to the person of the risen Christ and to the Church. The divine life is concentrated in Christ and from him is communicated to believers.

"And you have come to fullness of life in him, who is the head of all sovereignty and power" (Col 2:10). The fullness of Christ is transferred to the fullness of the salvation he brings. The Christian shares this fullness of Christ as member of his body, which also is his pleroma. Believers find in him every grace and blessing. Christ is filled with God and we are filled with Christ. The fullness of Christ overflows his Church. From the fullness of the Godhead which dwells in the exalted Christ, flows the being filled of the Christian, which has its basis in no other than Christ, and in nothing else than in fellowship with him. They who are in Christ, insofar as they are in him, find in him their needs supplied and their goal attained.

In Col 3:1-4 Paul gives the theological basis for a transformed life, namely, a radically new orientation respecting motives and goals. Christians are exhorted to exemplify in their lives the characteristics appropriate to new life in Christ. Paul presents the positive side of religion: life-giving union with the glorified Christ. The world we live in is a wonderful world in many ways, with natural beauties and pure enjoyments. But when it comes to setting the affections on these things, we discover a capacity which the world cannot fill. The mind may range from the most infinitesimal particle of matter to the most remote star and return unsatisfied. It is a high-grade life with an upward trend that is urged upon the Christian. The believer is ushered into the presence of the glorified Son of God.

"If then you have been raised with Christ, seek the things that are above where Christ is seated at the right hand of God.

Set your mind on the things that are above, not on the things that are on earth. For you have died and your life is hid with Christ in God" (Col 3:1-3). God set the seal of approval on Jesus by raising him from the dead. He therefore showed that the viewpoint of Jesus on human life was correct, that trust in the loving God and obedience to his will are the stuff of life. To be raised to life with Christ is to accept and share in this higher plane of life, which Jesus, now enthroned as king, embodies and represents. Paul conceives the Christian life as a constant quest, with the glory and triumph of Christ himself as the goal. The expression "seated at God's right hand" is from Ps 110:1 and implies Christ's position of Lordship and complete victory. Christians can share here and now the risen life of Christ. "The things that are above" refer to all that belongs to the will and purposes of God, the opposite of all that is sinful, trivial or selfish. This is not, however, a depreciation of earthly realities and true values.

The true Christian life is a new life, secure in God, hidden with Christ from the world. This reference to the life hid with Christ in God corresponds with the author's view of a hope (Col 1:5) or inheritance (1:12) presently laid up in heaven, thus already accomplished, but not yet actualized in its fullest sense for the believer. Christians now have a new life center. We must abandon our former way of life, and our whole existence is to be God-orientated. The hiddenness is as far as the world is concerned, which cannot fail to cause misunderstanding on its part. The hiddden life is one whose sources are unseen. Hid may also include the idea of security. Our new life is shrouded in the depths of inward experience and the mystery of its union with the life of Christ. This profound saying intimates that the believer even now shares the life of the eternal Son in the bosom of the Father.

"When Christ who is our life appears, then you also will appear with him in glory" (Col 3:4). Through union with Christ in baptism the Christian really shares already in eternal life, even if his life remains spiritual and hidden; it will be manifest and glorious at the Parousia. Whatever the present experiences, the future holds out nothing less than a share in the glory of Christ himself. Although Paul emphasizes the present sharing in

Christ's risen life, he nevertheless continues to look forward to the Parousia. At present the real dignity of the sons of God is hidden from the eyes of men, and, indeed, from their own eyes, as Christ is hidden from mortal sight. On that day Christ in his essential grandeur will appear, and with him will appear the grandeur with which he adorns his brothers and sisters.

Some general principles of Christian behavior are presented in Col 3:5-17, the demands and qualities of life in Christ. "Put to death what is earthly in you . . . You have put off the old man with his practices and have put on the new man who is being renewed in knowledge after the image of his Creator" (Col 3:5, 10-11). At the mystical level of union with Christ, participation in his death and resurrection through baptism is instantaneous and total, but at the practical level of life on earth this union takes place slowly and gradually. Already dead in theory, the Christian must experience death and rebirth daily, constantly by killing his old, sinful self. Paradoxically, those who are in Christ have died (3:3), yet they must put to death, give up completely, what is earthly in themselves. Much effort is needed to deal the death blow to evil habits.

Man, created in the image of God, lost his way by seeking the knowledge of good and evil apart from God's will, and became the slave of sin and sinful urges. The new man, reborn in Christ who is the true image of God, recovers his original rectitude and arrives at true moral knowledge. The Old Testament announced the renewal of man under the influence of the Spirit who gives man a new heart capable of knowing God (Ezk 36:26-27). By a new creation realized in Christ, the second Adam and the image of God, man is led to his true humanity. He is recreated after the likeness of God in true righteousness and holiness (Ep 4:24), and advances through obedience towards true knowledge. This new man constitutes a new humanity beyond the old distinctions of race, religion, culture, or social class. Christ is the perfect image of God, the perfect pattern of life for the baptized. Our aim should be a continual interior renovation to the model of Christ the new man.

The new man is the character and quality of life seen in Christ Jesus. Knowledge is set out as the target of the renewal process, in which case it denotes full understanding of Christian obligations as the end-product. It is psychologically true that the secret of advance consists not only in weeding out vices, but also in planting in virtues. The gospel does work a change of nature. It is the agent for daily renewal. As a child grows up into the parental likeness, so also the new-born in Christ grow up after the image of him who is the author of their spiritual life. The new nature put on by Christians is Christ himself. He is the image of God, the perfect, the last Adam; and consequently once incorporated in the body of Christ, believers are progressively renewed so as to become like the image. The theme old man-new man refers primarily to the condition of the individual, but it also carries corporate associations inasmuch as it forms part of Paul's presentation of the gospel in terms of the earthly man, Adam, and the heavenly man, Christ.

"There is only Christ who is all in all" (Col 3:11). This description of Christ expresses his preeminence. Paul uses the phrase of God himself (1 Cor 15:28). The expression points to the complete adequacy of Christ as supreme unifying agent. In Christ, head of a new humanity, the great social barriers of race, culture, and state of life are broken down. The new order will not be divided into races and religions and cultures and social classes; the whole world will be reunited in Christ.

"Above all put on love which is the bond of perfection. And let the peace of Christ rule in your hearts, to which you were called in one body" (Col 3:14-15). "In your hearts" designates the depth and sincerity of commitment to Christ's rule which is to characterize the Christian's new life. Love is above all the mark of the new Christian life. It is the bond wherein life has meaning, vitality, and integrity. It is that without which any attempt at virtue goes to pieces. Without this common bond any virtue may fall away from the Christian's character. Elsewhere Paul arrays the Christian in armor for conflict. Here he clothes him in garments of love and peace for daily walk and conversation. Note that Christ is both the principle of cohesiveness (Col 1:17) and the embodiment of love: in him the goodness and loving-kindness of God has appeared (Tt 3:4). In 1 Cor 13 Paul presents love as the source of all virtues.

"Let the word of Christ dwell in you richly, as you teach and admonish one another in all wisdom, as you sing psalms and hymns and spiritual songs with thankfulness in your hearts to God" (Col 3:16). The Christian life ought not to be regarded as a drudgery or its responsibilities grudgingly borne. The Christian surrenders himself to God, not as a conquered enemy capitulates to the victor; rather his surrender is to take the form of a joyful, grateful presentation of himself to God. Thanksgiving is thus a further characteristic of the new life and is to express itself both in public worship (Col 3:16) and in one's daily life (17).

Paul urges their participation in the liturgical hymns and prayers that center upon God's plan of salvation in Christ. Primitive worship emphasized the universal priesthood of believers. They taught and admonished each other. The gospel, the word uttered by Christ in his life and through his person, is to make its home in them; they are to be constantly with it, and it with them. The word of Christ is a source of strength and comfort; it supplies wisdom, the full apprehension of God's will and the wise application of it. The full implication of all that Jesus said and did has to be continually plumbed because of its rich contents. The word of Christ must have a permanent place in the Church, on the lips and in the thoughts of its members, thus making them truly rich.

"And whatever you do, in word or deed, do everything in the name of the Lord Jesus, giving thanks to God the Father through him" (Col 3:17). Do everything for Jesus' sake, that it may be as though he were doing it. This is a general summary of the Christian philosophy of living: the recognition of the Lordship of Christ in everything. Christians must recognize Jesus as Lord both in word and in action. In words they will show their recognition best when they call upon him in prayer as Lord. In deeds they will recognize him as Lord by personal engagement to him, by conforming their life to the pattern he has left.

In Rm 14:8-11 Paul stresses the duty of adoration as part of Christian living. "If we live, we live for the Lord, and if we die, we die for the Lord; so then whether we live or whether we die, we are the Lord's. For to this end Christ died and lived again, that he might be Lord both of the dead and of the living" (Rm 14:8-9).

Our whole life is to be devoted to our Lord as a living sacrifice. Whatever a Christian does is to be his personal act of worship to Christ and of thanksgiving to God. Christ confronts the Christian at every turn, in life and also in death; we are his for good and for all. Whatever we do and whatever may happen to us, the basic fact is that we belong to and acknowledge one Lord. That is the fact that must control both inward motive and outward act. It was to win this Lordship that Christ fought the decisive battle of Calvary. We live to glorify him in all our actions and affairs of life; we die to glorify him and to be glorified by him. Christ is the center in which all the lines of life and death do meet. This is true Christianity, which makes Christ all in all.

25

CHRIST'S CHURCH

The theme of Ephesians is God's eternal purpose in establishing and completing the universal Church of Jesus Christ. Paul's introduction (Ep 1:1-2) contains in germ the message of the whole epistle. Ep 1:3 introduces the description of God's blessings found in 1:4-14.

Ephesians is regarded by many as the most sublime of the apostle Paul's writings, as the crown of Paulinism. The theme of this brief letter is God's eternal purpose in establishing and completing the universal Church of Jesus Christ. It is primarily because of the original and systematic development of the idea of Church that Ep has a place of special prominence in the New Testament, and that its influence in the subsequent history of Christian doctrine has been considerable. Though drawn from various backgrounds and nationalities, the members of the Church community have been called by God the Father, redeemed and forgiven through the Son, and incorporated into a fellowship that is sealed and directed by the divine indwelling Spirit. In developing such luminous figures of the Church as the body of Christ (Ep 1:23, 3:16), the building or temple of God (2:20-22), and the bride of Christ (5:23-32), the author suggests the glorious privilege and destiny of believers as well as their duties.

The central theme of Ephesians is the plan, the mystery of

God decided in all eternity, veiled during many centuries, executed in Christ Jesus, revealed to the apostle, unfolded and realized in the Church. The Church is celebrated as a universal reality, at once earthly and heavenly, or better as the actual realization of God's action, that of the new creation. Its expansion, starting from Christ, the head, to the full dimensions foreseen by God, constitutes the vast perspective that is placed before the eyes of the believer. This dynamism is expressed by the overlapping images of the growth of the body and the building up of God's house. Integrated by their baptism in this body, which joins the pagan nations to Israel, Christians become new creatures by their praise, knowledge, and obedience, in one word, their adoration.

Ephesians has the originality of expounding the mystery of Christ in extra-temporal and cosmic terms. This mystery is essentially Trinitarian, as the author underlines in several passages. The Father has revealed his redemptive love for men through Christ, and this redemption is appropriated by Christians in the Spirit. The author's Christology is essentially triumphant. It is the glorious Christ enthroned as Lord of the universe and filling the whole creation by his influence, who is constantly in the background of the author's thought. By baptism and the life of faith, the Christian already shares in Christ's kingdom. This kingdom is expressed in vivid images: the vital head-body relationship, the cultic stone-temple relationship, and the loving wife-husband relationship. The eschatology of Ephesians is also remarkable; Christ's kingdom is already here, but it has yet to be fully realized. The present Christian condition is seen as a fundamental response to God's initiative through Christ in the Spirit, culminating in prayer. Finally, Ephesians is the epistle of unity, which is to be attained by ever deepening penetration in the Spirit into the mystery of Christ.

In Colossians the fundamental question at issue is the dignity of Christ and his lordship in the cosmic hierarchy. In Ephesians the question is the catholicity and divine origin of the Church. The glory of the head is now transferred to his body. While Colossians sets forth Christ's glory as head of the Church and of the universe, Ephesians sets forth the glory of the Church itself and draws practical conclusions from it. The main idea is the unity of Christians as forming one body with Christ as its unseen head. All men are one in the Church, which is the holy temple of God and the spotless bride of Christ. The existing Church has many imperfections but the full measure of perfection will at last be realized (Ep 4:13). And each Christian must labor for this, especially through purified family life (5:1-6:9); for the life of the family is a symbol of the life of the Church. Each individual member must have this ideal before him: the perfecting of the unity of the whole body. Unless this unity is realized, perfection is impossible. Paul gives his teaching a new center, the existence of the Church. Around this revolves the teaching of this epistle.

In Ephesians the reign of Christ and the status of the Church as existing in God's purpose from the beginning of creation are definitive and inseparable concepts. The significance of Christ's person and the nature of the Church are closely identified. For Ephesians the Church is the fullness of Christ and was always in God's purpose. It is the place where Christ actually reigns, where God is praised, where the Spirit dwells, where the mystery of God's will is revealed, where the gifts of God's grace are received and expressed in the transformed lives of the members of one body. The Church reveals an eternal plan of God's mind and is to endure eternally. It holds a place in the life of the world far beyond any human estimate and altogether different from its seeming weakness as an influence upon history. God's central and ultimate purposes are to be fulfilled through it. Its development is a revelation of God's triumph. The Church is eternal and universal in essence and meaning.

Christ is the head and the Church is his body; this relationship is another characteristic theme of Ephesians. The essential place of the Church in the divine scheme of redemption, as the Israel of God continuous with the old Israel, is never absent from the mind of St. Paul, but nowhere else does he treat the theme as full as in Ephesians, or make it so abundantly clear that redemption implies not merely a personal and individual reconciliation with God, but also membership in a corporate society of divine origin, the Church of Christ.

Ephesians presents the Church as one, holy, catholic, and apostolic, as divinely planned for the redemption of humanity in Christ, in virtue of his reconciliation. With this central idea of the unification of all men in one holy Church, Paul provides us with the principles of a true social gospel. It is in the Church alone that divided humanity is genuinely welded. Ephesians stands in a certain contrast to Romans. The latter provides the principles of individual salvation, and calls upon men for a life of love and morality, on the ground of God's mercy to them as individuals in Christ (Rm 12:1-2). Ephesians on the other hand appeals for a life of holy love on the ground of men's fellowship in the Church's holy unity (Ep 4:1-3). It has a social message.

The Church is a visible society consisting of all those who through Christ have access in one Spirit unto the Father. But it is more than a mere society, just as its origin is more than human. It is an organic unity, answering to and manifesting the unity of God, Father, Son, and Holy Spirit (4:3-6). It is a building fitly framed together, of which Jesus Christ himself is the chief cornerstone; it is a habitation of God in the Spirit (2:20-22); it is the sphere of God's glorious working (3:20) wherein his wisdom is proclaimed to the angelic powers (3:10); it is the training ground of all the elect (4:11-16); it is the bride of Christ which he loved and cleansed that it might be glorious and holy and without blemish (5:24-27). But the most frequent and characteristic of Paul's metaphors in this connection is that which presents the Church as the body of Christ; the Church is Christ's outward and visible manifestation, the organ of his self-expression, the instrument whereby he works. Moreover, it is an essential part of himself, just as his natural body was in the days of his flesh; without it he would be incomplete, not of course in his perfect deity, but as the incarnate savior of mankind. This is the force of the daring expression in 1:23 where St. Paul calls the Church, the fullness of Christ who all in all is being fulfilled; that is, it is the Church which gives him completeness. As the Church grows in holiness, Paul conceives Christ himself as being progressively fulfilled thereby.

Ephesians is not a letter in the strict sense. It nowhere deals with local problems; it is rich with the rhetoric of worship and doctrine, and it deals in a sustained way with a single theme, the Church. It shows that the world has been radically changed by the death and resurrection of Christ. It should be read less as a circumstantial letter than as a lyrical and didactic exposition of the Christian faith. Its language is quite constantly in the form of exalted praise and prayer.

In the main section of Ep (Ch 1-3), Paul describes the mystery of salvation and the unity of the Church. God's eternal purpose for man is now working and manifested in the Church. Paul presents the Church as the result of God's work in a style that is characteristic of the liturgy and of catechesis. The section opens with a blessing in the manner of Jewish worship. This praise of God's boundless grace (1:13-14) is the most clearly defined passage. A prayer for illumination introduces the exaltation of Christ, the Lord of the universe and the head of the Church (1:15-23). Chapter 2 evokes the great turning point brought about by Christ: what was dead now lives (2:1-10) and what was divided and alienated is now reconciled (11-22). Salvation in Christ is a free gift which reconciles Jew and Gentile to each other and to God. Paul is a servant of this mystery (plan) of God (3:1-13). This first part of the epistle ends with a prayer of adoration which sings the immeasurable love of Christ (3:14-19) and with a doxology (20-21).

Ephesians begins in a typically Pauline way, with an address and a salutation. "Paul, an apostle of Christ Jesus by the will of God, to the saints who are faithful to Christ Jesus: grace to you and peace from God our Father and the Lord Jesus Christ" (Ep 1:1-2). This introduction contains in germ the message of the whole epistle. Christ Jesus, that dearest name to Paul (mentioned three times here), apostleship, faith, grace, and peace were the controlling realities in Paul's life, which surface naturally whenever he writes. The will of God is a dominant theme in Ephesians: God's eternal will and plan to create a community of all men in Christ. Ephesians emphasizes also the continuity of God's holy people in the Old Testament. Saint is a technical name for all Christians who by baptism have received the dignity and privilege of God's chosen, consecrated people. The meaning of sainthood is dedication to God and usefulness in his service. Saints describe Christians as people called by God and set aside for his service. They are also faithful, that is believers in Christ Jesus, and it is one of the author's concerns throughout this whole treatise to specify what true belief in Christ, the head of the Church requires.

In Christ Jesus (more than 30 times in Ep) is the key to the whole epistle, a watermark of Paul's style. It implies not only personal identification with him but in some contexts it indicates relationship in the corporate Christ. Peace is another basic theme of the epistle: the possibility of unity and harmony among all men through Christ. Peace is ours only because of God's undeserved loving-kindness to us. "Jesus is Lord" is one of the earliest ways in which faith in Jesus was openly confessed by the candidate at his baptism and by the Christian congregation at worship (Rm 10:9).

The beginning of Ep (1:3-14) brings to mind the Johannine prologue. It is a hymn to the divine transcendence which in its wisdom, decided the redemptive incarnation for man's salvation. Paul launches himself into an elaborate eulogy or doxology, extolling the heavenly status of those who are in Christ. The greeting is followed not by the usual thanksgiving, but by a long prayer of praise to God for what he has done in Christ. Such praise is frequent in the Old Testament and in Jewish prayer.

This prayer reflects upon the divine plan of salvation, centering in Christ and revealed to Christians as fully at work in themselves. It celebrates God's grace using the literary type of blessing or benediction. God is the subject and his action is rhymed by the prose "in Christ" and punctuated with doxological formulas (1:6, 12, 14). God's blessings are considered under different but inseparable aspects: election (4-5), redemption (6-7), recapitulation (8-10), promised inheritance (11-12), and gift of the Spirit (13-14). These terms belong to the covenant vocabulary of the Old Testament. Ephesians presents a remarkable fusion of the biblical perspective of the people of God and of the new idea of the Church, the body of Christ. This introductory prayer reads like a baptismal hymn, with its stress on the high calling of God's adoptive sons, on the gift of the remission of sins, and on the seal of the Spirit, which impose on the believer the demand that he shall realize in his life a beginning of the world to come. The whole section (Ep 1:3-23) takes the form of a liturgical blessing of God's name. Both blessing (3-14) and thanksgiving (15-23) are used, and the whole section is rich in the language of Jewish and Christian worship. These opening verses sing of God's electing purpose accomplished through Christ, his gracious gifts of redemption and forgiveness, his call to praise, and his bestowal of the Holy Spirit as a guarantee of a future inheritance.

We may see here a Trinitairan pattern corresponding to the purposes and activities of the Godhead: of the Father who chooses his people (3-5), the Son who redeems at the cost of his own sacrificial death (7), and the Holy Spirit who applies the work of Christ to the Church and so makes real, in human experience, the eternal purpose of the Trinity (13-14). These Trinitarian implications of St. Paul's language are worth noting. The work of the Father, Son, and Holy Spirit in accomplishing man's salvation is mentioned in order; and each strophe ends with substantially the same refrain, "to the praise of his glory" (6, 12, 14).

Let us look at the words, "Blessed be the God and Father of our Lord Jesus Christ who has blessed us in Christ with every spiritual blessing in the heavenly places" (Ep 1:3). Paul places himself immediately on the heavenly level which is that of the whole epistle. This is where the blessings described (4-14) come from and where they will be fully realized at the end of time. The remarkable phrase "in the heavenly realms" occurs only in this epistle and refers to the unseen spiritual world which lies beyond the world of sense. Apocalyptic literature speaks of a series of heavens, frequently seven, with the throne of God in the highest heaven. God's blessings to us make us even now, through union with Christ (2:6), citizens of this spiritual world.

The hymn starts with the traditional Semitic form of recognition or thanksgiving to God, that of pronouncing a blessing and then following it with a list of God's favors or mighty deeds. Blessed picks up the Hebrew term (berakah) which plays an important part in Jewish worship. "Blessed be God" is a perpetual strain of the Old Testament, from

Melchizedek down to Daniel, of David in his triumph and Job in his misery. Paul plays on the word bless which basically means to speak well of. We bless God by declaring him to be blessed; he blesses us by actual enrichment. A blessing is essentially an explicit recognition given to God of a blessing, a benefit received from him, hence the description of God's blessings (1:4-14) which gives a resume of the whole epistle. The idea of blessing characterizes the author's entire attitude, not only in the prayer section of the epistle but also in the paranetic section where he emphasizes that the Christian life is essentially a response to God's initiative. Paul achieves an admirable synthesis of prayer and morality: the summit of the Christian life is the explicit and conscious recognition of God as he who blesses, while the leading of the Christian life is itself a most eloquent response to that blessing.

The phrase "in Christ" keeps recurring. It is Paul's way of underlining the importance of Jesus for the understanding of God and his purposes. It emphasizes the unity of men in Christ through their incorporation into a visible community under his leadership. The formula here means both through Christ and in union with him. It is because Christ by his resurrection and ascension is himself in the heavenly places, that Christians, by baptism in Christ, are themselves blessed in those heavenly places. The image of the heavenly enthroned Christ forms the main background to Paul's thought. Every spiritual blessing, all spiritual good is placed at the disposal of the Church which exists in, and draws its life from Christ its head. These benefits are spiritual in their nature, origin, and tendency, and shall be completed in heaven. The word spiritual may also contain an illusion to the Holy Spirit who resumes in himself all God's blessings.

26

BLESSINGS IN CHRIST JESUS

In Christ God has bestowed on us all spiritual blessing (Ep 1:3): election to holiness (4), predestination to sonship (5), bounteous grace (6), redemption and remission of sins (7-8), and knowledge of his will (9), to sum up, all things in Christ (10).

The praise of God's boundless grace (Ep 1:3-14) is hardly patient of an analysis; it is an exuberant lyric inspired by meditation on the will of God as disclosed to us and as blessing us in Christ. In him God has bestowed upon us all spiritual blessing (3): election to holiness (4), predestination to sonship (5), bounteous grace (6), redemption and remission of sins (7), and knowledge of his will (9), which is, to sum up, all things in Christ (10); in him Christians have the heritage promised of old (11-12) and are sealed by the Holy Spirit, whose bestowal fulfills the hopes of the Old Testament dispensation, and is the first installment of our full privilege as the redeemed people of God (13-14). Throughout the hymn there is emphasis on the sovereign freedom of God, the eternality of his redemptive purpose, and Christ's role as the revealer and mediator of God's grace, Christ the one in whom God's purposes have been set forth and realized. Words are crowded one on the other in an attempt to express the superlative blessings of God.

God chose us and destined us to be his sons, in accord with his eternal purpose in Christ, to unite heaven and earth in him

(Ep 1:4-10). "Even as he chose us in him before the foundation of the world, that we should be holy and blameless before him in love" (1:4). Here we confront the mystery of divine election which the New Testament consistently proclaims not as a conundrum to tease our minds, but as a wonder to evoke our praise; not as an element in God's character to be minimized but as an assurance that our lives are in his powerful hand, not in the grip of fate; and never as an excuse for carelessness in spiritual matters, but always as a reminder that Christians have a responsibility "to confirm your call and election" (1 P 1:10). God's first blessing is the call to faith and holiness. Chose emphasizes the freedom of God's initiative. God's election antedates creation, and the selection was made in Christ. God's choosing of his people, the Church, is traced back beyond creation, from all eternity: to show that the choice is not accidental, but part of God's plan from the beginning. The Incarnation took place in time, but its purpose and significance are eternal. God's eternal purpose of love is one of the main themes of Ephesians.

The phrase "without blemish" was used by the Jews to describe the perfect condition required in the animal offered to God in sacrifice. It is now applied to the living offering of the Christian uniting himself to Christ, the priest. It describes the perfect obedience to God that is required of Christians. This obedience is expressed in a self-giving love. The Church, as Israel before, is called to be holy and blameless, but not by means of the cult considered as an external performance of certain rites. Rather the source of the Church's holiness is in the existential quality of love which according to the prophets of the Old Testament, was the soul of true worship (Ho 6:6). Love here is primarily the love God has for us and that leads him to choose us and call us to be holy, but it includes our love for God which results from, and is a response to his own love for us. Love is the source of all God does and the essence of that holiness he intends to bring about in us; love is to be our response to the goodness of God.

"He destined us to be his sons through Jesus Christ, according to the purpose of his will, to the praise of his glorious grace which he freely bestowed on us in the beloved" (Ep 1:5-6). This is a second blessing: Jesus Christ, the only Son of God, is both the source and the model of the way God has chosen for us to become holy, that is, by adopting us as his sons. The words chose, destined, will, stress that to be right with God is not attained by human merit, but is something due to his sheer goodness. They underline the absolute initiative of God's grace; their object is our adoptive sonship. God's elective purpose has as its design the fulfillment of his intention that there should be many children in his family, all sharing the likeness of their elder brother.

In one sense God, as Creator, is the Father of all men, but the special sonship to him is a specifically Christian privilege bestowed by the Holy Spirit in the Church, through Christ, by sharing his Sonship. Through his obedience Jesus showed himself the true Son of God. He thus assured us of entrance in God's family with the dignified status of sons. Paul believes there is no wonder greater, for such beings as we are, than that Jesus has given us the right to call God, Father. It is in baptism that we are made the children of God, being established in a unique spiritual relationship with God the Father through Christ. The full meaning of our sonship lies ahead (Rm 8:23, 29), but the earnest is already given.

The word grace designates more than the interior gift that makes a human being holy; it is first of all the gratuitousness of God's favor and manifests his glory. Grace and glory are two themes that run through this account of God's blessings; their source is God's liberality, and their purpose is to make his glory appreciated by creatures. Everything comes from him and everything should lead to him. Our predestination is no arbitrary act of God's will, but something he knows to be good, in which he can have pleasure, and which will in the end give praise and glory to his grace. The recognition and praise of the divine grace is the ultimate aim of redemption. God's glory, his splendor and greatness, is shown in his coming down to our level in Jesus, an act which is a gracious gift, the result of his freely given love. The refrain "to the praise of his glory" is thrice repeated, referring to the Father (6), the Son (8), and the Holy Spirit (14). It punctuates the benediction and makes the glory of God the purpose of his action, just as his free will was its source. It introduces a recurrent theme in Ephesians: that men, understanding God's plan, should praise him and give him thanks.

Beloved was used in the Old Testament to describe the nation of Israel and the special part it had to play in God's revealing of himself (Is 5:1). It now describes Jesus as the one specially chosen to make God better known. Christians are, as it were, living showrooms displaying God's gracious gift, his offer of friendship in Jesus Christ; they are therefore centers of praise. A good illustration of this verse is found in the saying of Jesus in Mt 5:16: "And you, like a lamp, must shed light among your fellows, so that when they see the good you do, they may give praise to your Father in heaven." Beloved is a Messianic title which emphasizes God's love. It is through his beloved Son, who conveyed the grace of God in his life and death, that the Father's grand intention is realized. The Son, lovable in himself, is essentially the beloved; we are accepted because of and in the beloved; and if we are called beloved in our turn it is because God sees us in his Son. Beloved as a title for Messiah, carries a strong baptismal reference. The voice of the Father at Jesus' baptism (Mk 1:11) must have helped Paul to learn this title, "Beloved," and to recognize the wonder of divine sonship, and also the divine pleasure God takes in his children. The closest Old Testament background reference is the sacrifice of Isaac (Gn 22:1-8) which Paul has in mind in Rm 8:32.

Mention of God's grace leads on to a larger treatment of this theme. Sonship and membership of the divine family are made possible on the ground of redemption, through the blood of Christ. We are children by adoption, but it is nevertheless a blood relationship. "In him we have redemption through his blood, the forgiveness of our sins, according to the riches of his grace, which he lavished upon us imparting us full wisdom and insight (Ep 1:7-8). A third blessing is our redemption by an event in time, the death of Jesus. The redemption of Israel by God is a familiar theme in the Old Testament; the deliverance from Egypt is perhaps the most typical instance, and the sprinkled blood of the paschal lamb, typical of Jewish sacrifices in general, throws light on St. Paul's meaning here. Our redemption was wrought by the blood of Christ, his voluntary offering of his life on our behalf. Redemption is a word used of the freeing of slaves from bondage. People are free when they do the will of God, and so carry out the purpose for which they were made. Sins are not just the breaking of a law, but are acts of disloyalty to a personal God. They are a sign of human slavery.

The Old Testament shows that a close relation was seen between blood and life, and consequently between blood and the covenant relationship with God. Jesus saw his death as establishing a new and closer relationship with God: "This is the new covenant in my blood" (1 Cor 11:25). Paul sees it as demonstrating God's love and kindness shown without thought of human merit or desert. The climax of God's redemptive love lies less in the fact of Christ's death than in the revelation of its meaning. After all, this death would have been of small value had its meaning as an expression of God's grace not been revealed. The fruits of God's grace in us are insight into his counsels and consequent wise conduct. The notion that growing wisdom implies declining spirituality, and that a cool head cannot exist with a warm heart is quite alien to St. Paul's teaching.

A fourth blessing is the revelation of God's mystery, his plan of salvation in Christ. "He has made known to us the mystery of his will according to his purpose which he set forth in Christ, as a plan for the fullness of time, to unite all things under Christ's headship, things in heaven and things on earth" (Ep 1:9-10). The whole epistle develops the idea that Christ regenerates and regroups under his authority, the whole world corrupted and divided by sin, the human and the angelic world. In contrast with our modern use of the word mystery as something unintelligible, the chief stress in the New Testament is not on the concealment of God's purpose but on its present revelation in Christ. The mystery here is God's purpose that all men should be members of one body, gathered into one Church, under one Lord for the common praise of God and a united witness to his word. It is a plan for the whole course of human history, the manner in which God leads history to its fulfillment, culminating in a cosmic unification of all things under the sovereign rule of Christ. It finds its realization in the Church: in the call of the Gentiles to salvation, the conjugal union of Christ with his Church, but also the submission of the universe to Christ.

In Col 1:25-27 the mystery refers to the hidden presence and working of Christ; here in Ephesians it means the hidden plan of God to create a universal community of men in Christ. The Church was from the beginning in God's mind, and has appeared in the fullness of time, the time of the Church. The secret of the divine purpose is in Christ and is accessible to all who believe in him. It is a mystery in the sense that no human intelligence could have guessed what God intended to do in Christ, but it is now made known to Christians. This word in the New Testament always implies something only to be learned by revelation. It still remains something which surpasses all the knowledge even of true believers. No man understands the mystery of the redemption through Christ's blood. When revealed to him man realizes increasingly the deep wisdom and practical prudence, which God made to abound toward him.

In Jesus, God has provided a meeting point where the world is summoned to find a new unity. Though incarnate as man, as God's creative wisdom Christ is head of all angelic powers, and so in him all things find their apex or head, their coherence, and their principle of unity. He is the linchpin of the great chain of being, trancendent over it and at the same time immanent within the whole. This immanent power of God which providentially guides the universe is identified with Christ. Paul uses a special sesquipedalian word (anakephalaiosthai, translated "under the headship") to characterize Christ's redemptive work. The verb contains two ideas: to sum up, reunite, gather up into one, and to place under the sovereignty. In Christ alone can we make sense of the universe; all things seen and unseen find in him their principle of unity. The thought is expanded in Col 1:16-20.

Although the main theme of Ephesians is the Church, the universe is viewed as included in the unity destined to be achieved in Christ. The cosmic dimension of Christ is one of the epistle's most striking characteristics. Christ is thus presented as the summit of the whole creation. Paul is apparently interpreting the accounts of Gn 1-2 in the light of Christ, the whole creation being thus considered as receiving its full meaning and consistency in him. God's purpose was to give new hope to a world divided by barriers of race, color, culture, or political divisions, and make possible a unity among men through Christ. But in biblical thought man is closely related to the universe. God's plan has as its great objective the summing up of all things in Christ. In him the entire universe finds its full explanation and rationale. Christ gives meaning to the cosmos; he is not only the source and sustainer of all that is, but also the goal towards which the whole creation is moving.

What St. Paul looks forward to is the organization of the universe upon a Christian basis, in Christ. Christ is the rallying point of the forces of peace and blessing: the principle, the organizing head, the creative nucleus of the new creation. The potent germ of life eternal has been introduced into the world's chaos, and its victory over the elements of disorder and death is assured. Love is the all-embracing command which integrates, and gives coherence to all other commands. Christ's love performs this role on a cosmic scale by gathering the fragmented parts of human life as a whole, so forming a uni-verse.

27

THE PRAISE OF GOD'S GLORY

Christians have the promise of a share in God's heritage (Ep 1:11-12) and are sealed by the Holy Spirit to the praise of God's glory (13-14). The prayer (Ep 1:5-12) summarizes what has been said previously. It is a prayer that we may understand the glories of membership in the Church of which Christ is the head.

After contemplating the vast canvas of God's universal plan of salvation (Ep 1:3-10), the author delays on its references to the two ethnic groups within the Church: the Jews (11-12) and the Gentiles (13-14). Now in Christ these ethnic and religious connotations have lost their meaning, inasmuch as both Jews and Gentiles are members of the same body (3:6); but they did come from different cultures. "In him, according to the purpose of him who accomplishes all things according to the counsel of his will, we who first hoped in Christ, have been chosen (as God's portion) and predestined to live for the praise of his glory" (Ep 1:11-12). A fifth blessing is the election of Israel, God's chosen portion, as witness in the world of the Messianic expectation: the gift of faith in the Messiah bestowed upon the Jews.

It was the Jews who first hoped in Christ, waiting through the ages for his coming, and claimed as God's own people, were given a share in his heritage. The idea of inheritance is a constant one in the Old Testament, and is used here in a double sense concerning the children of Israel, both that they have an inheritance in God, and that they are God's inheritance. The two meanings are correlative and are richly true, both of the Old Testament saints and of the New Testament children of God. The Christians' heritage is their new status of being right with God. This status is secure because it is based on the purpose of God, who not only plans, but can carry out what he plans. Paul has a firm faith in the power of God. Christians have staked their all on the fact that Jesus offers the key to life. Therefore they are a kind of display center advertising, for all the world to see, the claims of God on his world; they are in this way to cause his glory to be praised.

The final blessing is the call of the pagans to share the salvation that had till then been reserved for Israel. They are assured of this by the gift of the Spirit. "In him you also, who have heard the word of truth, the gospel of your salvation, and have believed in him, were sealed with the promised Spirit, who is the guarantee of our inheritance, for the redemption of a people God has made his own, to the praise of his glory" (Ep 1:13-14).

The way to Christ is outlined in these verses. Hearing the word of truth, the gospel, is the first step, to be followed by a trustful acceptance of him of whom it speaks. The third step is the sealing of the Holy Spirit who indwells all those who believe in Christ, and who gives his own witness in terms of an assurance to the believer that he belongs to God's chosen people, just as Israel was God's inheritance under the old covenant. Believing means not only accepting the good news as a fact, but staking one's whole life upon it.

A seal was a common sign of ownership. Devotees of various pagan gods sometimes branded themselves with the name of the deity to whom they belonged and by whom supposedly they were protected. The seal of the Holy Spirit is not only God's stamp of his possession of us upon our hearts, but also the outward act of baptism, the visible sign of our incorporation in Christ. Christian baptism is that time when the Christian is inwardly consecrated to the service of God and sacramentally incorporated into the body of Christ, the Church. A seal is a token of proprietorship put by the owner upon his property; or it is an authentication of some statement or engagement, the official stamp that gives it validity; or it is the pledge of inviolability, guarding a treasure from profane or injurious hands. Here the thought of possession dominates, but it can scarcely be separate from the other two, protection and ratification. The signature and seal on an agreement guarantee its binding force; the experience of God's Holy Spirit in the lives of Christians is the guarantee of God's favor. The sealing implies a full impression of the image of God on our soul, and a full assurance of receiving all the promises, whether relating to time or eternity.

The Holy Spirit was the phrase which the Jews used to describe the creative power of God. The work of Christ brought about a greater opportunity for the working of this power in the world. The gift of the Holy Spirit is the first instalment, not simply a sign or pledge, of the promised kingdom, which shall be inherited in its fullness in the day of redemption (Ep 4:30). This blessing of God in Christ is not a static but a dynamic reality capable of growth and development. The gift of the Spirit is a down payment to guarantee full payment. The inner sanctifying presence of the Spirit is a guarantee that God has accomplished his promise and will carry it out to completion. The reference to inheritance also points to a future fulfillment. Inheritance expresses the totality of future blessings to which the obedient Christian may look forward when the kingdom of Christ and of God (Ep 5:5) is fully present.

We already have redemption in the radical sense of acceptance, rescue from condemnation into sonship. But we still look forward to redemption in the developed sense of actual emancipation from the last effects of sin, which is to come when the body is glorified along with the spirit. The present possession of the Spirit is the guarantee of the coming full possession of our heritage. Then the redemption of God's people will be complete. It is already inaugurated in a mysterious way but will only be fully realized when the kingdom of God is established gloriously and definitively at the time of Christ's Parousia.

God made his own the people of the elect, at the price of the blood of Christ. After the terms, blessing, saints, election, adoption, redemption, portion, promise, comes another Old Testament notion, possession, which Paul extends and applies to the new Israel, the Church, the community of the saved. The Church is peculiarly God's own possession, redeemed by Christ. At the close of his hymn of praise, the idea of God possessed by God becomes dominant. The gift of the Spirit crowns the execution of God's plan in its Trinitarian form. From all eternity the Father decrees our adoptive sonship (Ep 1:3-6); this sonship is merited by the incarnation and sacrifice of his Son (7-12); it is effected in us by the Holy Spirit (13-14). The formal and efficient cause of our predestination is the love of the Father, his will and good pleasure; Jesus is the meritorious cause; divine sonship is the immediate final cause; the manifestation of God's glory, the supreme final cause.

With the explicit mention of the Holy Spirit (13) the author completes the Trinitarian structure of God's blessings, and the third reference to "the praise of God's glory" reemphasizes their God-oriented character. Just as everything comes from God, so everything must return to him. Each refrain represents as the final purpose of man's salvation in its various parts, an admiring recognition by God's creatures of his essential grandeur. The threefold refrain makes this final purpose very conspicuous: God will formally be the only center of worship forever.

Ep 1:13-14 marks the bridge between the introductory hymn and a prayer (15-23). In the hymn the stress lies on the wealth of the inheritance which is the present possession of the baptized believer. The prayer asks that this ideal may be realized in the future consummation. The link between this life and the salvation to come is the seal of the Spirit. The doxology (14) shades off into prayer that the readers may have wisdom to understand the glory of their inheritance, and the great power of God, a power manifested in the raising and exalting of Christ (20-23) and in raising and exalting us (2:1-10). Paul is summarizing in prayer what he has said this far, a prayer that we may understand the glories of membership in the Church. The Christian life can never be one of standstill. It must be a growth in wonder at the privileges which God has given, and a growth in full understanding of all their implications. Hence Paul's prayer.

There are three points where Christians are to have insight: into the sureness of their hope, the wonderful privileges they possess, and the all-sufficiency of God's power to help and strengthen those who are committed to him. "May the God of our Lord Jesus Christ, the Father of glory, give you a spirit of wisdom and revelation in the knowledge of him, having the eyes of your hearts enlightened, that you may know what is the hope to which he has called you, what are the riches of his glorious inheritance in the saints, and what is the immeasurable greatness of his power in us who believe, according to the working of his great might" (Ep 1:17-19). Wisdom does not come by human ingenuity and cleverness in excogitating divine truth from man's mind, but is a gift from God; and revelation is the name for this gracious self-disclosure of God who always takes the initiative in this action. This gift is what we understand as actual grace.

The moral and spiritual meaning of the heart in the Old Testament, where it is the center of religious conscience and moral life, are found also in the New Testament. It is in his heart that man seeks God, hears him, serves him, praises him, loves him. The simple and pure heart is the heart that is undivided by any reserve or afterthought or sham in relation to God or man. Man should love God with all his heart. God deposits in man's heart the gift of his Holy Spirit. Christ also dwells in it. Simple, right, and pure hearts are open without reserve to the presence and action of God. Believers have but one heart and one soul.

The term saints is generally used in Ephesians and Colossians to designate Christians and replaces the term brothers. Our inheritance from God the Father is what we share with his Son Jesus. We who believe have our lives opened to divine, dynamic energy. To suggest the immensity of God's power, Paul uses a battery of words: immeasurable, greatness, power, energy, strength, might.

"This he accomplished in Christ when he raised him from the dead and made him sit in the heavenly places, far above all rule, and authority and power and dominion, and above every name that is named, not only in this age but also in that which is to come" (Ep 1:20-21). Paul delights to think of the power of Christ's resurrection. Men set him at nought, but God made him supreme. He was set at God's right hand, the place of divine power. Christ's enthronement signifies that Jesus in his humanity has now reached a position of equality and association with the Father where all God's power can act through him. Exaltation at God's right hand connotes co-regency and the exercise of cosmic authority. God exalted him in his human nature to a quiet, everlasting possession of all possible blessedness, majesty, and glory. The power on which believers lay hold is that which was deployed in God's act vindicating his Son by his resurrection after men had done their worst. Christ alone installed by God himself and endowed by him with power, has dominion over all created things. There can be no other claimant to this title. In his exaltation Christ became absolutely supreme over all beings everywhere. Paul is not attempting to classify definitely different kinds of beings; he often heaps words together to indicate that he wishes to exclude nothing. Christ is Lord of all cosmic agencies that men may care to name, because he is both their creator and rightful ruler. He excels all these forces throughout the whole time-span of the universe.

"And he has put all things under his feet and has made him the head over all things for the Church which is his body, the fullness of him who himself receives the entire fullness of God" (Ep 1:22-23). The subjection of all to Christ is expressed by a paraphrase of Ps 8:6, one of the favorite texts of the early Church. The Psalmist uses these words in exhibiting mankind as the crown of God's creation; Christ in his own person has fulfilled this true human destiny. What the Psalmist asserts of man in poetic idea St. Paul claims to have been fulfilled in Christ. As Son of Man he is heir of whatever belongs to man. Christ is seen as the ultimate Adam who enters upon his promised reign as Lord of creation.

The climax of God's power is manifest in the creation of the Church. The Church is, in a sense, the locus of Christ's cosmic reign, the focus of his power, the place of his sovereign rule. Christ's headship over all things is designed entirely to be of service to his Church. In Mt 28:18-20, Christ said that all his power was for the Church and that he is always with the Church. She needs him only, and he holds power for her; nothing else on earth possesses such power as does the Church. The Church is not just a consequence of the gospel, an organization to fulfill the institutional requirements of the Christian mission, but is rooted in the original purposes of God, and is part of his plan for the fullness of time.

Christ is the invisible leader and head of a visible community. The Church is his body, as the instrument of his purpose in the world. The Church is represented passively as the temple of God, actively as the body or organ of Christ's manifestation; the former as the sphere of divine worship and holy influence; the latter as the instrument of Christ's manifold operation on earth. The Church is the vessel of his Spirit, the organic instrument of his divine-human life. As the spirit belongs to the body, by the like fitness, Christ in his surpassing glory is the possession of the community of believers. The body claims its head, the wife her husband. Christ and the Church form one unity; he as head guides and controls the body by his Spirit. Christ is head both of guidance and government, and likewise of life and influence to the whole and to every member of it. All stand in the nearest union with him, and have as continual and effectual a communication of activity, growth, and strength from him, as the natural body from the head. This almighty Christ and his Church are not separate, but organically and eternally united. She is his body. That is why all his power belongs to her. Paul's letters ceaselessly return to this idea. He had deeply absorbed the fact that Christ has been incarnated in the Church. Christ had said, "I am with you always," and had emphasized his vital union with his Church (Jn 15:1-5, 17:20-23).

It is important to note in Ephesians a further development of the body metaphor as applied to the Church. In Rm 12 and 1 Cor 12 St. Paul's emphasis is rather on the unity of many members in one society, the head being then included as one member of the body (1 Cor 12:21). In 1 Cor 12:12 Paul thinks of Jesus as the body, while Christians form the parts of the organism. Here the

Church is the body and Christ is the head. Paul is stressing that the only loyalty that matters is that to Jesus, who alone can bring men into a living relationship with God. Paul has extended the view of the Church functioning in a coherent fashion (Rm and Cor) to that of its functioning as an expression of its head, Christ (Col and Ep).

Christ in the fullness of God and the Church here is conceived as the fullness of Christ. All that Christ has from God, the power, the gifts, the grace, he passes on to the Church which is filled with him (Ep 3:19), becoming a partaker of all that he owns and is, for the purpose of continuing his work. Jesus as God's Word receives the entire fullness of God. In turn the Church receives the entire fullness of Jesus, in the sense of being his sphere of influence and his operations center. The Church is filled with the riches of the divine life by Christ who is filled by God (Col 2:9-10). This parallels what John says: the Father is in the Son, the Son in the disciples, and the disciples in the world (Jn 17:11, 20-26). It is Christ's presence and power as head which fills the Church, builds it up, makes it one, and nourishes it for growth.

28

CHRIST, OUR PEACE

Salvation in Christ is a free gift from God (Ep 2:1-10). Christ is our peace, reconciling Jews and Gentiles with each other and with God (Ep 2:11-22). Christians are so many stones building up God's Temple, the Church, Christ being the chief stone of this new spiritual building (Ep 2:19-22).

Ephesians 2 is filled with sharp contrasts between human weakness and the result of the operation of God's mighty power. Paul evokes the great turning point brought about by Christ: what was dead now lives (Ep 2:1-10), and what was divided reconciled (11-22). Jews and Gentiles are reconciled with each other and with God. Having shown what God's power accomplished in Christ, Paul proceeds to show what it accomplishes in us (2:1-10). The power of God repeats in us a likeness to what it did in Christ. The power that raised Christ from the dead makes us spiritually alive (5). So mighty is this work of God in us that it is like his creative activity (10). It also lifts us up into heavenly existence in Christ. We even now are citizens of heaven (6). There are two levels at which people live. There is the lower level where God is ignored, and self looms large (2:1-3), and there is the higher level of trying to keep in step with God and his purposes (4-10).

"But God who is rich in mercy, out of the great love with which he loved us, even when we were dead through our trespasses, made us alive together with Christ (by grace you have been saved), and raised us up with him, and made us sit with him in the heavenly places, in Christ Jesus, that in the coming ages he might show the immeasurable riches of his grace in kindness toward us in Christ Jesus" (Ep 2:4-7). God's love describes his sense of responsibility for the human race. It has been experienced at its closest in the mission of Jesus Christ. Notice that it is a love resulting in practical action.

The entire history of the Son of Man is reproduced in the man who believes in him, not by a simple moral analogy, but by a spiritual communication which is the true secret of our justification, as well as of our sanctification and ultimate salvation. The resurrection, ascension, and heavenly enthronement of Christ are mystically reproduced in the experience of the Christian. By baptism we were raised from the death of sin to the new life of righteousness and glory, that life which is truly lived even now in the heavenly sphere where Christ is. This is the salvation bestowed on us in Christ by the grace, the free gift of God. Grace is God's unmerited favor shown to mankind in Christ. The final aim of redemption is the revelation of God's grace.

Central features of Jesus' life were his obedience to the will of God, his selflessness, and his love for his fellow human beings. This is the higher level of life to which we can rise through our relationship with the risen Jesus. To be raised up and enthroned with Jesus is to be committed to the God-centered way of life. Eternal life is already our assumed possession; and the witness of it is the Holy Spirit, the breath of immortality already moving our hearts with the pulse of divine life and prompting all Christian activities. The believer's new life is in and with Christ. It is not a thing apart; it is a participation in Christ's life. It is a share in Christ's risen life and also in his reign in the heavenlies. Christians are witnesses to what the love of God has achieved in men's lives, and this results in an even greater vision of what we owe to God.

"For by grace you have been saved through faith: and this is not your own doing, it is the gift of God, not because of works lest any man should boast" (Ep 2:8-9). No merit of our own has earned these spiritual privileges; we receive them by faith, but they are the gift of God, bestowed by his free grace on recipients altogether undeserving. Even our faith itself is a gift of God. Salvation originates in the grace and saving love expressed in Christ Jesus; it enters human experience by the receptivity of faith or trustful acceptance, through faith as the channel, but Paul never says because of faith. Faith, with an empty hand and without pretence to personal desert, receives the heavenly blessing. Christian activity consists less in man's action than in God's action through Christ. Man's role is to respond to that action.

"You are his workmanship, created in Christ Jesus, for good works, which God prepared beforehand, that we should walk in them" (Ep 2:10). God's workmanship means a creative product, a new creation in Christ, in whom mankind is given a fresh start. God is here seen as the artist or craftsman who has created our present status with himself. It is made possible in Christ Jesus through being linked to him and what he has achieved. But out of this relationship of love must spring the responsibility for good deeds, action and conduct worthy of God. Salvation by grace alone and by faith alone can be misrepresented. Hence the call now to good works, not as a ground for claiming God's favor, but as the necessary consequence of our new life in Christ as his new creation. Good works are the result, not the cause of salvation. "Beforehand" ascribes the whole matter to God. St. Paul was the last man in the world to undervalue human effort, or disparage good work of any sort. It is the end aimed at, in all that God bestows on his people, in all that he himself works in them. But man's doings are the fruit not the root of his salvation.

Ep 1:11-22 focuses on the unity of all mankind in Christ. It describes the reconciling work of Christ (13-18), the full enfranchisement of the Gentiles, and their place as stones in the spiritual temple of God (19-22). The Gentiles were without Israel's Messianic expectation, without the various covenants God made with Israel, without hope of salvation and knowledge of the true God (Ep 1:11-12), but through Christ, all these religious barriers between Jews and Gentiles have been transcended (13-14) by the abolition of the Mosaic covenant-law

(15) for the sake of uniting Jew and Gentile into a single religious community (15-17), imbued with the same Holy Spirit and worshipping the same Father (18).

"But now in Christ Jesus you who once were far off have been brought near the blood of Christ. For he is our peace, who has made us both one, and has broken down the dividing wall of hostility, by abolishing in his flesh the law of commandments and ordinances, that he might create in himself one new man in place of the two, so making peace, and might reconcile us both to God in one body through the cross, thereby bringing the hostility to an end. And he came and preached peace to you who were far off and peace to those who were near; for through him we both have access in one Spirit to the Father" (Ep 2:13-18).

The phrases, in the blood of Christ, in his flesh, by the cross, clearly call attention to the crucifixion, the death of Christ, as the source of the Church's unity. The cross of Christ has brought together Jews and pagans, and reconciled both with the Father. "In the blood of Christ," that is, by a new covenant sacrifice, and that the only perfect sacrifice ever offered to God, which includes all mankind in its scope, irrespective of external distinctions. All distinctions among men vanish at the cross. Christ has triumphed over death and all its power of division and disintegration. Jesus is the meeting-point with God for all mankind. To bring men together was a costly business. It is a deep, fathomless truth that the death of Christ is the source of the Church's unity, that out of death comes life. Paul does not explain nor can man really plumb the depths of this mystery. Christ, when he spoke of the unity of the Church, spoke also immediately of his death (Jn 10:15-18); and approaching his death, he also spoke of life out of death (Jn 12:23-24). At the Last Supper he saw his coming death as the way of bringing all men into fellowship with God. He said, "This is the blood of the new covenant shed for the multitudes."

The center of the discussion is the statement, "He is our peace." We find an exulting repetition of the word peace four times in four verses (14-17). The word peace recalls the Messiah as Prince of peace (Is 9:6). It means more than absence of hostility; it connotes well-being and security at every level.

Peace, the fullness of Messianic salvation, becomes concrete in the Church. Christ's religion is a new religion. The Jewish law is considered in its pejorative aspect, as being a dividing wall of hostility, symbolized probably by the wall in the Temple which separated the court of the Gentiles from the court of the Jews. Incorporation in Christ does not erase the differences among men, but for those in Christ such differences no longer alienate men from one another. The Mosaic law gave the Jews a privileged status and separated them from the pagans. Jesus abolished it once and for all on the cross.

It is this incorporation of the Gentiles which makes the Church something new on the stage of history: they are incorporated in one new man, the mystical Christ. The new man is in place of the two; new in status, privilege, and relationship, but its core is the elect remnant of Israel. This new man is the prototype of the new humanity that God recreated in the person of Christ, the second Adam, after killing the sinfully corrupt race of the first Adam on the cross. This new Adam has been created in "the goodness and holiness of truth" (4:24); he is unique for in him disappear all divisions among men. It is through the cross and resurrection of Christ that the whole Christ is created and so reconciled to God in one body. The one body is first of all the individual, physical body of Christ, sacrificed on the cross, but also his mystical body, which unites all the members, once they are reconciled. It is first Jesus, the common point of meeting, and then the Church which rises above divisions of nationality, color, class or birth, and is all-inclusive.

Christ came to the Gentiles through his apostles who in his name preached the gospel of salvation and peace. The exalted Christ is now present on earth through the Spirit in the Church. Pentecost may be regarded, as apparently it was in the fourth gospel, as the fulfillment of the early Church's hope of the coming of Christ; at the very least it is the earnest, the first great instalment of that fulfillment. The unity of Christians in one body, the Church, is based on their participation in one Spirit.

The reconciliation does not take place on Jewish ground, for Christ rent the veil of the Temple, as he broke down the fence. Both have a real access to God in the Holy Spirit. To have access to God is to be introduced into his presence, to receive his Spirit or influence into our life. The one Spirit who gives life to the one body of Christ, who is one with his Church, is the Holy Spirit who transformed Christ's risen body, and now extends his action to the members of Christ. Note the prepositions: it is an access to the Father, through the Son, in the Spirit. Quite incidentally the recognition of Son, Spirit, and Father comes to the surface. This Trinitarian structure is repeated in verse 22. The phrase "in one Spirit" corresponds with the "in one body" of verse 16, and also with the juxtaposition, in the Apostles' Creed of the Holy Spirit and the Holy Catholic Church.

From the idea of the Father, Paul easily passes to that of household and thence to that of house and temple. "So then you are no longer strangers and sojourners but you are fellow-citizens with the saints and members of the household of God" (Ep 1:19). The Gentiles are now fully enfranchised members of the chosen people of God, members of God's family; it is not merely to a divinely patronized society that their baptism into Christ has admitted them. The idea is not of domestic service but of the child at home. The word household depicts God's Church as God's family, kinsfolk, bound together as one under his paternal will and care. In the Old Testament "house of Israel" describes God's people.

"You are built upon the foundation of the apostles and prophets, Christ himself being the cornerstone, in whom the whole structure is joined together and grows into a holy temple in the Lord; in whom you also are being built for a dwelling place of God in the Spirit" (Ep 2:19-22). The symbolism now changes abruptly from that of body to that of building. St. Paul introduces a new metaphor to emphasize the unity and solidarity of the saints; the Church is the new temple of God. The apostles and prophets form the first foundation course, and all other believers find a place as stones in the building; Jesus Christ himself is the chief stone on which the whole building depends. This is a Messianic designation (Is 28:16). The New Testament prophets (preachers) together with the Apostles, are the witnesses to whom the divine plan was first revealed, and who were the first to preach the Gospel. That is why the Church, as well as being founded on Christ (1 Cor 3:10), is also said to be founded on them. The Apostles constitute the first layer in which Peter is the first stone. Being keyed into Christ as they are added, the many stones are added to each other to complete the shrine.

The building metaphor is expanded by a reference to Christ as the vital component of the Church's structure. The Greek word used may mean either cornerstone or capstone. The first meaning refers to the stone situated at the corner of a foundation from which the builders take their bearings for all the other walls. Thus Christ would be presented as the one who by his presence defines the shape and scope of the Church, points it in the way it is to go, and enables its sturdy construction. A keystone, capstone, or coping stone, on the other hand, is the topmost stone of a wall, the last to be put in place. Christ would then be described as both effecting and symbolizing the completion and wholeness of the Church, as the crowning element under which the structure is held together united and strong. Both interpretations are probably suggested since the latter accords with the other metaphor of Christ as head of the Church, even if the former is more in keeping with the immediate context, which speaks of the Church's foundation and its continuing construction. In any case, Christ is the one in whom the whole structure is joined together. The Church owes everything to Jesus and is entirely dependent on him. His position and function give his Church cohesion and unity.

The Church is composed of different communities and of different kinds of people, and can only be bonded together by a common allegiance to Jesus Christ and by recognition that he alone is the source of the Church's power. But it is a building that cannot be static, it must be growing more and more fit to carry out the task for which it exists. The picture before Paul's mind is a temple in process of being built. Frequently a great building is begun at different points, and in the earlier stages its parts appear to be independent erections; but as it advances all are united into one whole. The united Church is seen as a great pile of buildings accurately and gloriously entering into one mighty temple. The realization of the whole is a development, a process, a growth. The whole fabric of the universal Church rises up like a great pile of living materials, into a holy temple dedicated to Christ and inhabited by him, in which he displays his presence, and is worshipped and glorified.

The Church is to become a holy temple. The Greek word for temple (naos) denotes the shrine or sanctuary as distinct from the precincts or courts. A temple had important associations for people at that time. For example, the Jewish Temple at Jerusalem was thought of as the place where God met his people and was worshipped by them; here too the worshipper was faced with God's claim upon his allegiance. So the Christian Church is to grow into a temple or center of worship; it is to become a community in whose life and behavior the power and presence of God are to be seen and his will acknowledged.

The Church is conceived not as a static mass, but as dynamic and living. Its true being is a *becoming*. As it is in the Spirit that we have access to the Father, so also it is in the Spirit that he comes to dwell in his shrine, the Church. The Holy Spirit is the supreme builder of the Church, as he is the supreme witness to Jesus Christ (Jn 15:26-27). The words "in the Spirit," closing the verse (Ep 2:22) with solemn emphasis, denote not only the mode of God's habitation, but also the agency engaged in building this new house of God.

29

GROUNDED IN LOVE

The doctrinal section of Ephesians ends with a prayer of adoration, which sings the immeasurable love of Christ (Ep 3:14-19), and with a doxology (20-21). Ep 4:1-16 is a call to unity. Living the truth in love is the principle of our unity in Christ.

In Ep 3:8 Paul presents himself as the servant of "the unsearchable riches of Christ." This is just another designation for the comprehensiveness and power of the gospel, though like the word mystery it suggests that Christian wisdom has depths and dimensions unmatched by any other. It is unsearchable in its nature, extent, and application. So too it is unfathomable because God's love for us in Jesus Christ never ceases to cause wonder, and has a depth of meaning that can never be exhausted.

The first part, the doctrinal section of Ephesians, ends with a prayer of adoration, which sings the immeasurable love of Christ (Ep 3:4-19), and with a doxology (20-21). The substance of the prayer is that God, out of his abundance, may give the Ephesians spiritual strength (16); the indwelling of Christ in their hearts through faith, in love (17); and once again strength to know the divine love which surpasses knowledge (18-19). The purpose of prayer is to draw closer to God and his will, and here Paul's prayer is that his readers may more and more appreciate the love of Jesus and respond to it.

"For this reason I bow my knees before the Father, from whom every family in heaven and on earth is named, that according to the riches of his glory he may grant you to be strengthened through his Spirit in the inner man" (Ep 3:14-16). Jesus taught his disciples to begin their prayer with "Our Father," which describes God as one who is accessible and has a loving responsibility for the human race. Paul emphasizes the Father's transcendent causality as the starting point and motivation of his prayer. In Greek the family (patria) is literally named from the father. With a play on the Greek words for father and family, Paul stresses the relationship of God to all his creation. The families in heaven are the angels. Family is used for any social group descended from a common ancestor; God, the supreme Father, is at the origin of all families of beings. St. Paul's point is that God is the author of all imaginable fatherhood; his fatherhood is no mere metaphor, but the divine reality of which the human relationship of a father to his children is but a reflection. The Church is a family in a unique sense, as sharing God's very life and nature. The main notion here is that the Church as God's family is a society that must ultimately be conterminous with humanity, because creation is the ground of redemption.

The two verbs to be strengthened and to dwell (17), are parallel, and so there is no great difference between the action of the Spirit on the inner man and Christ's habitation in our hearts. God's Spirit is his activity in giving people extra trust to carry out his will. Even if a man by faith receives Christ into his heart, he will need the inner divine might of the Spirit of God in order to hold that glory within himself. God's glory in the Bible is often connected with God's making himself known and coming to the help of man. The riches of God's glory are the immense fullness of his glorious wisdom, power, and mercy manifested in Christ. The inner man is the Christian as he is recreated in Christ. Man's interior being is meant, his essential personhood, which when yielded to the powerful working of God's Spirit, can become thoroughly new. One's inmost self is made new by the Spirit, as Christ is received therein, and the life which is opened to Christ's presence is rooted and grounded in love.

Paul's prayer is that Christians may be like a mature tree that has thrust deep roots, or like a building that has a solid deep dug foundation: "That Christ may dwell in your hearts through faith; that you, being rooted and grounded in love" (Ep 3:17). Love is both the soil in which the plant thrives and the firm ground on which the building rests. In the New Testament the heart never means the affections only, but the sum total of inner faculties, will, conscience and intellect. It corresponds to the inner man (16). Usually Paul refers to the Spirit dwelling in men, here he says Christ; the risen Christ is the source of the Spirit. Faith and love are the media of Christ's indwelling. The dynamic aspect of the Christian life is emphasized; the Christian must not only have love but must be rooted and grounded in it. Christ's indwelling in our hearts will be seen in the love we have for him and for our fellow human beings.

"May you have power to comprehend with all the saints what is the breadth and length and height and depth, and to know the love of Christ which surpasses all knowledge, that you may be filled with all the fullness of God" (Ep 3:18-19). The universal and all-embracing character of Christ's love is the widest, longest, highest, and deepest knowledge of all, the very fullness of God. The four dimensions represent the vastness of the love of Christ towards us; they suggest that this love surpasses all human knowledge. Paul uses this enumeration, which in Stoic philosophy designated the totality of the universe, to suggest the universal role of Christ in the regeneration of the world. More precisely these are the dimensions of the mystery of salvation, or better still of the love of Christ which is its source. Paul prays that we might comprehend God's redemptive plan in all its richness and profundity, and know Christ's love of which this redemption is the consummate expression. So amazing is that love, which God's purpose for his Church in the world reveals, that it eludes our full grasp, yet at the same time, it beckons us on to a progressive experience as we are more and more filled up to the measure of God's fullness.

The Church as a whole comprehends the deep things of God in a way and to an extent impossible for the isolated individual. And the individual's fellowship with the other believers in the one body increases his own powers of comprehension. The incomprehensible vastness of God's love in Christ is the thought. And even if the words are not to be pressed too literally, we may think of it as wide as the furthest limits of the universe; long as the ages of eternity through which God's love to his people will endure; deep as the abyss of misery and ruin from which he has raised us; and high as the throne of Christ in heaven where he has placed us.

The love of Christ is both the love which Christ has for the Church and that which the Father has manifested in Christ. This love for us that Christ showed by accepting death is identical with the love the Father has in Christ. To know that love is to have experienced it in a way that transcends mere intellectual awareness. The consequence of this knowledge of Christ is to be filled with the fullness of God. This clearly forms the climax of the prayer and corresponds to the meaning of redemption. What God has achieved in Christ still has to be fully realized. There is question of knowing with a religious, mystical knowledge penetrated with love, which goes much further than any intellectual knowledge. And it is more knowing that one is loved, even if it is impossible to penetrate the depths of this love. The experiential knowledge of the love of God manifested in the person of Christ, infinitely surpasses all human knowledge. Only the believer reaches to the fullness of God's nature, as a loving person, and all its transforming power.

An audacious paradox suggests that we may reach to the perfection of the divine attributes (Mt 5:48), the fullness of God with all his light, love, wisdom, holiness, power, and glory. There is always more to be expected from God, more to be known of his love. If the sea were filled with empty containers, the containers would be filled with the fullness of the sea. By the fullness of the divine life, which he receives from Christ, in whom it dwells, the Christian enters into the fullness of the total Christ, the Church, and ultimately of the new cosmos which he helps to build. The fullness of God is attainment of purpose and realization of ideal. Later St. Paul speaks of spiritual growth as progressing "to the stature of the fullness of Christ" (4:13). Becoming a Christian is instantaneous but our moral change is progressive in several ways: by the strengthening of our inward spiritual life; by the indwelling of Christ in our heart; by the firm foundation in love which provides power for further knowledge; by experiencing the love of Christ; by being filled with all the fullness of God.

The doxology (Ep 3:20-21) celebrates God's boundless generosity and his glory both in the Church and in Jesus Christ. It makes explicit that the end of redemption is God's glory. It takes up several of the themes found in the first part of the epistle: the superabundance of God's gifts, God's power at work within the Christian, the parallel between Christ and the Church, and glory. God has manifested his glory in Christ and in the Church, Christ's Body. It is the Christian's highest duty to recognize, and to respond to, this revelation in the prayer of praise.

"Now to him, who by the power at work within us, is able to do far more abundantly than all that we ask or think, glory in the Church and in Christ Jesus, through all generations, for ever and ever. Amen" (3:20-21). God can give superabundantly quite inconceivable boons. The boldness of the prayer which St. Paul has uttered is justified by the greatness of God's power and the fact that it is actually at work in human lives.

It is in the Church that God's kingship and majesty are acknowledged in the present, and confront the world. But the Church's witness is dependent on Christ Jesus, in whom God's nature and being are revealed. The order Church/Christ stresses that the honor of Jesus is in the hands of the Church; for the impression of him that people receive is that given by the Church and individual Christians. In the Church as in Christ, in the body as in the head, the glory of God is focused and shown forth. The Church is the extension of the incarnation, and no long treatise could emphasize its dignity so powerfully as this short sentence of St. Paul.

This juxtaposition of the Church and Christ Jesus is unique in the New Testament, yet it flows naturally from the image of the Church as the Body of Christ. The Church and Christ are necessary complements of each other. In the bride and the bridegroom, in the redeemed and the redeemer, in the many brethren and in the first-born, is perfect glory paid to God. There will be endless glory for God through the Church, inasmuch as it is a vehicle for the display of all the glories of Christ. The Church completes Christ, reveals God's wisdom, and is with Christ, the sphere in which God is glorified. It is indeed a glorious Church (Ep 5:27).

In his call to unity (Ep 4:1-16) Paul lists three different threats to Church unity: discord among Christians (4:1-3); the necessary diversity of ministries (7-11); and heretical doctrines (14-15). These threats are avoided by applying the principle of unity in Christ (4-6, 12-13, 16). "Be eager to maintain the unity of the Spirit in the bond of peace. There is one body and one Spirit, just as you were called to the one hope that belongs to your call, one Lord, one faith, one baptism, one God and Father of all, who is above all and through all and in all" (Ep 4:3-6). The Church is one even as the Spirit is one: all its members acknowledge one and the same hope, one and the same Lord Jesus, one and the same faith in him, one and the same sacrament of new birth into him, one and the same Father. The Spirit is the single inner source of the Christian life and as such is continually moving all members towards what promotes peace and harmony. Each of the seven expressions bring out an aspect of the basic unity. There is one external visible community, one body; a single inner source of life, one Spirit; Christians pledge obedience to one Master, one Lord, in their baptismal profession of faith; we are bonded together as brothers, children of one Father. Finally, God is qualified with the notions of transcendence and omnipresence.

Various gifts are made available to men by the Spirit to equip all the faithful for work in Christ's service. The Church's ministers and leaders only exist to help the whole body of Christians to be true to their task of loyalty and witness to Jesus. They labor "for the equipment of the saints, for the work of the ministry, for the building up the body of Christ, until we all attain to the unity of faith and of the knowledge of the Son of God, to perfect manhood, to the measure of the stature of the fullness of Christ" (Ep 4:12-13). Christ's body is built up as its members attain unity in Christ, founded on a common faith in him. Paradoxically the Church is the fullness of Christ (1:23), its basic unity is already existent, but it has yet to be completed. The full stature of Christ, or his perfection in his earthly life, consisted in his unswerving belief that the cause of God would win the day, and in his unshakeable obedience to God's will. This is the perfect manhood demanded of Christians. The fullness of Christ, however, does not refer only to the Christian arrived at maturity of Christian life and thought, but also to the perfect man in a collective sense: the perfection of the total Christ, head and members making up the mystical Body, a maturity that will be completed at the end of time.

The unity of the Church, though perfect when viewed as a divine gift, has yet to be striven for by redeemed mankind. True unity depends on corporate faith in and perfect knowledge of the Son of God, that is, the full realization of what and who Christ is. The unity towards which the Church moves is one of personal knowledge of the Son of God, full acquaintance with the mind of Christ. Knowledge of the Son of God means acquiring the image of the perfect man, who reaches maturity in Christ by living the type of human life that was characteristic of Jesus. This embodies a new relation to God as Father and a new relation of brotherly respect and love to one's neighbor. Son of God is one of the earliest titles of Jesus. First and foremost it describes his unique relationship to God and his unique place in God's plans. The term suggests the closeness to God of the person so described, and thus brings out the price paid by God in sending Jesus on his earthly mission. Jews would see in the title, Jesus as the true representative of Israel (Ex 4:22). Among Gentile Christians, the term would suggest the divine status of Jesus.

"Living the truth in love, we are to grow up in every way into him who is the head into Christ, from whom the whole body, joined and knit together by every joint with which it is supplied, when every part is working properly, grown and upbuilds itself in love" (Ep 3:15-16). The Church maintains the truth and grows up in love as it conforms its life more and more to that of its head, Christ himself. There is no life without growth and spiritual growth comes from Christ. To grow up into Christ means an ever deepening understanding of how he and all that he has made known to us of God, apply to our situation and life here and now.

Each member exercising his gift and function for the benefit of all, contributes to the growth of the whole body of Christ.

The growing is both from and towards the head. Christ is the vital source to which the whole complex organism wholly owes its existence and action. The increase is all from Christ and yet inexorably conditioned by the faith and due working of his people. The Church grows by the action of Christ on its behalf. He exerts a unifying action on the body by imparting his risen life and bestowing his gifts by the Spirit; Christ's people make the contribution needful for Christ's designs to be realized. And so the whole is edified, built up, as love becomes the atmosphere in which the process of mutual encouragement and responsibility is exercised. The phrase *in love* is equivalent to *in Christ*. Love is the recipe for Christian growth; it is its acting directive force. The Church can grow to be an effective instrument of God, only if it is dependent on its head, its controlling power, Jesus, and if the spirit of Christian love informs its activities. Language cannot express the full truth. Christ is the head. He is also the whole organism. He is the source of its unity, growth, and energy. Consistency of thought and language is lost in this divine psychology.

30

THE BRIDE OF CHRIST

Ep 4:17-5:20 describes the new life of a Christian in Christ. Paul gives faimly life a very high ideal: the love of husbands for their wives should correspond to Christ's love for his Bride, the Church (Ep 5:23-27). Ep 6:10-20) is a description of the Christian's panoply.

In Ep 4:17-5:20, Paul describes the new life of a Christian in Christ. "You were taught what the truth is in Jesus. Put off your old nature. . . and be renewed in the spirit of your minds, and put on the new man, created after the likeness of God in true righteousness and holiness" (Ep 4:21-24). These verses combine admirably both the objective aspect of redemption, new creation in Christ; and the subjective, the personal, responsible assimilation of the new creation by each individual. The discarding of the old man and the wearing of the new are two halves of one action. The old man and the new are the old Christless self and the new Spirit-guided self, which reflects and reproduces Christ. The old man denotes the type of life led with merely the resources belonging to human nature. In baptism the Christian puts aside his former life, beginning in Christ a new manner of life. One's whole attitude to living is given a new twist. This involves accepting the new character which is portrayed in the human Jesus, the qualities that made up his life: selflessness, obedience to God, and love for people.

The radical newness of life in Christ is emphasized with the metaphor to put off and put on, which recall the total transformation of character symbolized and inaugurated at the time of one's baptism. The imagery of divestiture and investiture probably reflects the early baptismal ceremony. The revolution described here was vividly depicted in early Christian baptism when the candidate was immersed beneath the water as a sign of death to the past, and came up from the water as the sign of a new life in company with Christ. The new man is incorporated into Christ himself, the new Adam, the head of a new humanity, sharing his Spirit. Each believer puts on the New Man and is re-created in Christ, after the likeness of God.

"Be imitators of God, as beloved children. And walk in love, as Christ loved us and gave himself for us, a fragrant offering and sacrifice to God" (Ep 5:1-2). Christians imitate God in forgiving (4:34) and in loving. The perfect model of a child of God is found in Christ. The new life is a life of love modeled after God's love revealed in Christ's sacrificial death for us. The love thus revealed and bestowed, forms the substance of the Church's interior life. Children are expected to bear their father's likeness; and loved ones are influenced by those who love them. It is the mark of beloved children to become imitators of a loving father; Christians will practice the self-sacrifice of Christ, which shows how he loved us and the Father. The Old Testament terminology of sacrifice is applied to Christ's personal offering. In Ezk 20:41 God promises to accept the people themselves as a sweet odor of sacrifice. In the Old Testament the individual needed a go-between, a priest who would make an offering to enable the worshipper to gain access to God. Christ is that priest and mediator in the New Testament and the offering is the gift of himself for men. The Christian is called to participate actively in Christ's priesthood by joining his own sacrifice of love to that of his Master.

Uncontrolled lusts, especially lust for money, render to creatures the worship due to God, and so turns them into idols (Ep 5:5). Of the baptized, "It is said, Awake, O sleeper, and arise from the dead, and Christ shall give you light" (Ep 5:14). The exalted Christ awakens men from the sleep of death and brings them back to life in a new act resembling the very creation of light itself. This seems be an extract from an early Christian hymn, on baptism as an enlightening, based on Is 60:1. Baptism was known in the early Church as enlightenment, and depicted as the rising of the convert from the death of sin to union with the living God. Paul harks back to this experience as a reminder to fulfill now our baptismal profession by walking in Christ's light and by stirring ourselves to active witness.

"Do not be foolish but understand what the will of the Lord is, and do not get drunk with wine but be filled with the Spirit" (Ep 5:17-18). The stimulus for effective Christian living comes from allowing the Holy Spirit full possession of our heart. We must establish as a law of our religion that our whole being must be pervaded by the spirit of consecration. Being filled with the Spirit is connected with joy, courage, spirituality, and character. The Christian alternative to the fun of getting drunk is not solemn dullness but spiritual exhilaration. The Christian is not to escape into a world of artificial gaiety. The right kind of intoxication and joy is that inspired by the Holy Spirit, the power of God at work in Christians to make them feel near to him. This is religion, daily detailed walk in the will of the Lord. Religion is not some passing enthusiasm like the intoxication of the drunkard. If we are to know fullness, let us be filled with the Holy Spirit. There was abundant use of wine in the current mystery cults, and at times abuses in Christian gatherings (1 Cor 11:21). Joyful fellowship should rather result from being filled with the Spirit, who prompts us to encourage one another and sing hymns to the exalted Christ.

Our best moments of special enthusiasm and exaltation, come from spiritual joys, by our being filled with the Holy Spirit. The effect of this inspiration is prayer and praise. Thus the Spirit is seen to be the source of Christian prayer. "Addressing one another in psalms and hymns and spiritual songs, singing and making melody to the Lord with all your heart, always and for everything giving thanks in the name of our Lord Jesus Christ to God the Father" (Ep 5:19-20). We have here one of the rare passages in which, side by side, there is mention of prayer addressed to Christ, and the common structure of Christian prayer to the Father through Christ in the Spirit. One hallmark of the Spirit's filling will be the expression of the heart's devotion to our Lord in canticle and song. We are not merely to sing with our lips in religious gatherings, but constantly to have worshipful hearts. The highest prayers are nothing but thanksgiving, knowing that God understands us and always does what is best for us.

Paul gives family life a very high ideal. The love of husbands for their wives should correspond to Christ's love for his Church. "For the husband is the head of the wife as Christ is the head of the Church, his body, and is himself its savior" (Ep 5:12). Christ is the head of the Church, his body; he requires the obedience of his people who are rightly subject to him; he has set his love upon the Church and shown the extent of that love in all he has done for the Church's redemption; he looks upon his Church as part of himself, as his body, and cares for it. Being head of the wife or Church involves responsibility for cherishing and protecting. The forethought of the head preserves the body; control implies obligation to protect. Savior of the body indicates further the sense in which Jesus can claim to be head of the Church. He is the one who has pioneered the way to union with the true God. The title marks him out as the true and lasting benefactor of mankind, guardian and protector.

"Husbands love your wives, as Christ loved the Church and gave himself up for her, that he might sanctify her, having cleansed her by the washing of water with the word, that he might present the Church to himself in splendor, without spot or wrinkle or any such thing, that she might be holy and without blemish" (Ep 5:25-27). Christ's lordship over the Church is closely related to his love for it, exhibited and bestowed especially in his death. The Church is thought of as the bride of Christ to whom she is presented properly washed and clothed in matrimonial attire.

The husband's love is patterned on that greater love of Christ for his bride. The background here is the Old Testament. Paul in particular is drawing from Yahweh's marriage with Israel described by the prophets (Ho 2:16), in the light of the rabbinic practice of eulogizing the covenant at Sinai as a marriage between Yahweh and his people. The Torah became the marriage contract, with Moses as the one who led the bride to God. Christ's relationship to his bride, the Church, is for Paul one further way of saying that the Torah-age has given place to the new age of Messianic fulfillment. Christ showed his self-giving love by becoming man, by serving us in his earthly life, and by dying for us. The purpose and effect of his work for the Church are given in terms of sanctification; the Church is taken from the sphere of sin and placed in that of holiness. The means by which this is accomplished is baptism.

The aim of Jesus' love is described in language taken from the baptism ceremony. His purpose is to sanctify, consecrate the Church, make it a perfect reflection of his mind and purpose. This involves cleansing it, wiping away its sins through the assurance of God's forgiveness. Such cleansing is symbolized and effected in the rite of baptism. Baptism is seen as the mystical bath preparing the bride for her husband. Baptism is accompanied by the proclamation of the word, expressed by the evangelization provided by the minister and the profession of faith of the baptized. The word may also refer to the liturgical formula, including the invocation of the name of Jesus, pronounced over the candidate at baptism.

Christ is head of the Church in several senses. First he is the Church's founder. It was his appearance, alive from the dead, that assured his disciples that he was undefeated, and transformed them into a community committed to his cause and service. Secondly, he is the Church's head in the sense that he is the driving force behind the Church's life and work. Thirdly, he is the head in that he claims complete loyalty and obedience from his Church. Finally the conjugal relation between man and wife is based on the relation Christ-Church which it illumines. The theme body of Christ receives here its most perfect expression. Better than the idea head, the theme of husband and wife underlines the authority of Christ based on his sacrifice, the responsibility of the Church, and the mutual intimacy of Christ and the Church, without confusion or separation.

This presentation of Christ's love for the Church is unique in the New Teastament. In 2 Cor 11:2 Paul used the image of the Church as the chaste bride of Christ. "I feel a divine jealousy for you, for I betrothed you to Christ, to present you as a pure bride to her husband." Paul, the friend of the bride-groom, presents him with his bride. Since the prophet Hosea, the love of Yahweh for his people was presented as the love of the groom for his spouse. The idea of God's love as a burning ardor, demanding an exlusive love in return, is a commonplace in the Old Testament. The relationship of the Jewish people and Yahweh is now predicated of the New Testament faithful and Christ. The loyalty Christ claims is exclusive, as in the marriage relationship.

According to the customs current in the ancient Orient, the bride was prepared and brought to her husband by "the sons of the wedding," the bridegroom's attendants. As applied mystically to the Church, Christ himself washes his bride in the bath of baptism, and presents her to himself. The picture is perhaps that of Jesus, the king, receiving acceptable people into his court. The idea is very similar to that in Rv 21:2. It is remarkable that whereas in Ep 1:4 the Church is depicted as being holy and blameless before God, here it is holy and blameless before Christ. This shows the source of the Church's holiness to be in Christ, as both priest and sacrificial victim.

The Church is to be glorious, bright with God's glory, a center of light reflecting God's will and purpose. Stain, spot, or wrinkle are ways of talking about disfigurement. Holy means set apart, given over to the service of Jesus. Without blemish is a phrase taken from the language of animal sacrifices. It describes the perfection required in the animal victim. Here it is used of the perfect obedience required of Christians. The Church is the indefectible Bride of Christ, joined to him in an indissoluble union. To see all that mars her outward manifestation on earth, in various periods and places, in the true light, we must look upon her with the eyes of Christ. The husband ought to love his wife as part of himself. The pattern for this conduct is found in the relationship between Jesus and the Church. Christ treats the Church with tender loving care because it is his body of which we are the members. Here as in 1 Cor, Paul thinks of Jesus as the body or organism to which his followers belong as the living parts. The Church is part of the very being of the risen Jesus, and as such is cared for and loved.

In Ep 6:10-20, Paul describes the Christian in terms of the dress and equipment of the Roman soldier. The main features of the picture are taken from two passages in Isaiah: 59:17 where God himself does battle, and 11:5-5 where the warrior is the Messianic king. The significance of the various parts is not to be stressed. Each member of the Church is to be a spiritual warrior, fully equipped with the weapons of the divine Warrior himself, as he aligns himself with God against God's enemy. This is God's armor given to us, and therefore the equipment does not denote primarily human qualities. Thus the truth is that which God reveals, the righteousness is that which is bestowed upon us in Christ, the peace is that which we possess through the gospel.

"Be strong in the Lord and in the strength of his might. Put on the whole armor of God that you may be able to stand against the wiles of the devil. . .Stand having girded your loins with truth, and having put on the breastplate of righteousness, and having shod your feet with zeal to propagate the gospel of peace; above all taking the shield of faith with which you can quench the flaming darts of the evil one, and take the helmet of salvation, and the sword of the spirit, which is the word of God" (Ep 6:10-17).

There are forces at work in the world, opposed to God and his purposes. The Church is the scene of a conflict between God and the forces of evil. In this conflict Jesus is victorious, and so assures us that God is king and will achieve his purposes. Those who belong to Jesus are of necessity involved in the same struggle; they are God's center of resistance against evil. The Christian's new wardrobe includes a war suit. The use of this outfit enables him to overcome the enemy, the devil being the great general of the besieging host. The instructions are explicit as the Christian takes up his stand. He is to tighten his belt with sincerity. His personal integrity will be linked with that moral rectitude which guards the heart as a breastplate. God's soldier is equippped with the gospel of peace for sandals, suggesting that his movements are dictated by the needs of gospel witness. With all this a shield is required and this is provided by personal faith. Salvation, the helmet is a gift provided by the Lord. His weapon of attack is the spoken word of God, that is, all the teaching that God has given about himself and the mission of Jesus.

"Pray at all times in the Spirit with all prayer and supplication" (Ep 6:18). Intensity, constancy, and universality of prayer are underlined together with the mention of the Spirit. The efficacy of the Christian's war against wickedness comes, finally, from prayer, ceaseless, tireless prayer. Although having no counterpart in the soldier's equipment, prayer is evidently intended to be included in the Christian's panoply. It is his vital communication with headquarters.

Ep is given a worthy conclusion, returning to the fundamental thought of 1:3-14. "Peace be to the brethren and love with faith from God the Father and the Lord Jesus Christ. Grace be with all who love our Lord Jesus Christ with love unending" (Ep 6:23). We find here all the themes of the epistle: peace, love, faith, grace, God the Father, and the Lord Jesus Christ. The letter closes with the mention of unending love, which describes the incorruptible endurance of all that God establishes in our heart. Imperishable is the characteristic of our new life in Christ and of our love for him. Devotion to the Lord will endure imperishably for ever.

31

JESUS CHRIST IS LORD

The introduction to the epistle to the Philippians (1:9-11) is an example of joyful Christian prayer. The epistle is especially famous for its passage on the kenosis or self-emptying of Christ (2:5-11).

The letter to the Philippians is one of the most cordial and affectionate we have from Paul's hand. The entire letter breathes Paul's radiant joy and serene happiness in Christ. This Christian joy is due to fellowship with Christ and one another, through the Holy Spirit. Paul rejoices in prayer, in the fruit of his labors, in the knowledge of the preaching of the gospel, in suffering even if it should mean death. He exhorts his readers to rejoice in the Lord. He wants them to have joy in believing, in fellowship, and like him to rejoice even in trial and suffering. The introduction (Ph 1:9-11) is an example of prayer with joy. Its keynote is growth, that their love may grow and grow. Paul would have his pilgrims progress. And their progress should be in love, which exercised in knowledge and perception, enables them to approve things that excel. This concept of love is notable. Christian love is not blind, or misguided enthusiasm, but discriminating.

''I pray for all of you with joy . . . You have a permanent place in my heart . . . It is my prayer that your love may abound more and more with knowledge and discernment, so that you may approve what is excellent, and may be pure and blameless for the day of Christ, filled with the fruits of righteousness which come through Jesus Christ, to the glory and praise of God" (Ep 1:9-11). Paul asks three things: love increasing and overflowing; knowledge, in particular the gift of true discrimination where there is need to distinguish different values; and righteousness, goodness filling their whole lives. Love is the heart of the religious life, the quality without which all good works and noble endowments are as nothing; a truth which Paul develops more completely in 1 Cor 13. Christians are reminded that love is more than sentiment or bare emotion. It must be guided and controlled by knowledge and discernment. Nothing so reveals people as the things they instinctively approve. Our lives are to abound in the qualities of love, joy, peace, long suffering, goodness, meekness, kindness which are the fruits of a true and living inward religion.

Heart and head must grow together. Progress and growth in union with Christ should bring an increased personal knowledge of the Christian reality, marked by a refined and keen awareness of its meaning. Knowledge refers to the new awareness of God available to those who have become Christians; discernment, the ability to make moral decisions. The ability to see what is morally good is one of the consequences of mutual love. Distinguishing wherein one thing differs from another, the Christian is able to choose what is of superior quality. Love will then be keen-sighted for each other's good.

The term of Christian growth and development is the status of uprightness before God, yet it is not a status that one achieves by oneself; rather it is begun by God and has its fullness in that which comes only through union with Christ. The harvest does not consist in righteousness but is produced by it, and Jesus is its source. To be acceptable to God the Christian must bear fruits of righteousness: all inward and outward holiness, all good tempers, words and works, and so abundantly that he is filled with them. These fruits must derive both their virtue and their very being from the all-supporting, all-supplying source, Jesus Christ; and as all these flow from the grace of Christ, so they must issue in the glory of God.

Philippians is famous for its passage on the kenosis, or self-emptying of Christ (Ph 2:5-11), a periscope of inestimable value as reflecting the early Christian understanding of the mystery of the incarnation. This is the earliest extant statement of the threefold division of Christ's career: preexistence, life on earth, subsequent exaltation. This hymn represents an early Christian kerygmatic confession. It is a panegyric presenting the self-effacement of Christ as the model for Christian service (2:1-5). The poem begins by invoking Christian faith in Jesus' divinity and by recalling that paradoxically, his divinity was concealed throughout his mortal life (6). Divesting himself of his divine prerogatives, not indeed of his divinity itself but of the state of glory rightfully his, and assuming the role of a slave, he presented himself simply as a man (7). Having fully accepted the human condition, he followed it in obedience to the Father even to death on a cross (8). The Father responded by raising him from the dead and placing him at his right hand. God endowed him with his own name (9) so that the name Jesus (Savior) would be identified, in the knowledge of every creature, with the very same name (Kyrios, Lord) that is addressed to God the Father (10-11).

Each strophe deals with one stage of the mystery of Christ: his preexistence, his divine dignity (6), the emptying of the incarnation (7), his further kenosis in the humiliation of the cross (8), his exaltation and glorification in heaven (9), the worship of all creation (10), and the confession of Jesus Christ as Lord (11). The hymn holds before us the whole sweep of the Christ event, which begins and ends beyond time-space. It exalts the saving work of Christ. Paul quotes this ancient Christian poem to set forth Christ as the primary example of the humility which he here urges upon the Philippians. There is first a downward movement from heavenly preexistence to human life. Christ's supreme example of self-humiliation, self-abasement (2:6-8); then an upward ascent describing the exaltation of the obedient Christ, his subsequent elevation to supreme Lordship by God (9-11). In the first part Christ is the subject; in the second the subject is God. The hymn deals with the historical Christ, God and man in the unity of his concrete personality. Paul never separates the humanity and divinity of Jesus, though he does distinguish his various stages of existence.

The hymn follows a very ancient tradition for acclaiming Near Eastern kings: first addressing them as divine persons, then praising their graciousness in visiting their people and acting for their benefit, and finally describing the universal praise that is their due. But when we observe the kind of honor that is ascribed to Jesus Christ, we are compelled to ask questions about the relation of Christ to God and to mankind, and so worship leads to theology. The original setting of this hymn was the Church's worship. It is not in any obvious way concerned with the redemption of humanity but with the honor to be given to Christ Jesus. It is the same kind of hymn as those that are sung in the revelation of John (Rv 4:11, 5:12). Worship becomes the basis of action, and praise a motive for ethics. Paul is saying: act in accord with your praise.

The Greek Fathers saw in Christ's example the quality of humility, the Latin Fathers a self-denying concern for others: both lessons are discernible in the preceding context, as well as in that which follows, and both find their perfect expression in Christ's obedience unto death. This majestic passage (Ph 2:6-11) reminds one of 2 Cor 8:9 in that in both the self-humbling of Christ is presented as supreme stimulus to that self-abnegation, that spending of oneself for others which must ever be the distinctive glory of the Christian character. That the Son of God has loved him and given himself for him is an ever-present and ever-dominant note in Paul's consciousness.

"If there is any encouragement in Christ, any incentive of love, any fellowship in the Spirit, any affection and sympathy, complete my job by being of the same mind, having the same love, being in full accord and of one mind . . . and humble" (Ph 2:1-3). This is a friendly but powerful appeal, in the name of all that is most sacred; an appeal by all their deepest experiences as Christians, to preserve peace and concord. If there is anything that can move you in Christ, anything that the love of the Father can stir in your heart, if there is any sharing of the Holy Spirit among you, or any affection or sympathy for me, then fill up my joy through your mutual charity. There is a veiled reference to the Trinity, love being given as a characteristic of the Father. The "if" is rhetorical; with Christ's encouragement, and moved by

God's love for them, they are to complete Paul's joy. The word humble, which is echoed in verse 8, "he humbled himself," introduces a very important moral attitude, though it is open to exploitation and self-deception, if it is thought merely as self-depreciation. In Greek life the word humbly meant the subservient attitude of a lower class person; in Christianity, by reflection on the work of Christ, it is used to mean the lowly service done by a noble person.

"Have this mind among yourselves which was also found in Christ Jesus, who though he was in the form of God, did not count equality with God a thing to be grasped, but emptied himself, taking the form of a slave, being born in the likeness of men. And being found in human estate, he humbled himself and became obedient unto death, even death on a cross" (Ph 2:5-8). Humility, a characteristic virtue of Christianity as contrasted with paganism, is traced to its source in the voluntary self-humiliation of Christ. As often with Paul, a profound statement of doctrine emerges out of a piece of practical exhortation. The best way Paul can inculcate humility is by turning to the example of Christ, that the thought of his condescension and self-giving may shape all our attitudes. The imitation of Christ is presented as the way to peace within the community and to the highest final attainment for the individual. St. Paul relates the experience of the head to teach the members a lowly, self-renouncing love. For this purpose he shows how much Christ had to forego, and to what lengths his abnegation went. The passage is really an illustration. Paul's primary purpose is not to present a reasoned and carefully phrased doctrine but to enforce a plea with the strongest object lesson possible. Every self-emptying by men, should be a small pattern of the great act of Jesus. Humility, self-renunciation was the essential spirit of his life, and is the spirit and motive that should rule the life of a Christian. This passage is one of the chief scriptural foundations of the doctrine of the incarnation. It brings out the deity and humanity of our Lord, but throws little light on the problems connected with the coexistence of two natures in one Person.

The synonymous connected phrase, form (of God, of slave), equality (with God), likeness (of men), fashion (estate as a man), all denote resemblance in different aspects or degrees. The first signifies essential form, the mode of existence proper to the person in question; the second, the footing on which he stands or might stand; the third, his visible features; the fourth, the guise or habit of life in which he moves. Form means not mere appearance but the manifestation of a reality. Here it is practically equivalent to nature. Thus the whole phrase, "being in the form of God," asserts the Godhead of the Son before the incarnation, just as "taking the form of a slave," asserts his true manhood after it. In the form of God means having divine prerogatives, being God's virtual equal, that is preexistent and divine. Form means all the essential attributes that express and reveal externally the nature of God; Christ being God had all the divine prerogatives by right.

Equality with God refers to being on an equal base or footing, equality of rights and attributions which, of course, suppose equality of nature or essence. The phrase describes the object of Christ's kenosis. Christ could not have surrendered equality of nature, but he could and did give up in his human life equality of treatment, of dignity manifested and recognized. One should think of the opposite attitude of Adam who wanted to become like God (Gn 3:5). The outward appearance of God in the Old Testament is God's glory. Jesus did not treat the status of divine glory as a privilege or possession to be held at any price; he did not stand on his dignity. Christ pre-existent in the glory of God did not view it as a privilege that could not be forsaken—something to be grasped and never relinquished. He set no store by his position of equality with God, but willingly surrendered it. He did not hold it tight but renounced it for the benefit of others. Christ freely chose on earth humility and obedience.

The heart of the matter is the change of roles from divine authority to slave status, from the highest thinkable to the lowest known. He became not only a real human being but one like all others, sharing all the weaknesses of the human condition apart from sin. He emptied himself, that is, reached the extreme limit of self-denial. The verb emptied supplies the theological term kenosis for the deprivation of divine attributes or powers involved in the incarnation of our Lord. The verb has no metaphysical connotation but indicates the abyss of humiliation to which renunciation led the Christ. However far this diminution went, and we cannot pretend to define its limits, since it was a self-emptying, an act of our Lord's sovereignty, it involved no forfeiture of intrinsic deity. What Jesus freely gave up was the privilege of divine glory which he enjoyed in his pre-existence (Jn 17:5) and which normally should have been reflected in his humanity. He chose to strip himself of this glory so that he could receive it from his Father in the glorious resurrection as the prize for his sacrifice.

All the phrases for his slavery, humiliation, and obedience mean that he willingly accepted the human condition of powerlessness and mortality, whereas the rest of us are unwilling victims. Slave is opposed to the title Lord. Christ as a man led a life of submission and humble obedience. Paul is apparently thinking of the Isaian Servant of Yahweh. Christ proved obedient to his Father's will, even when it involved death, and no ordinary death, but one of horror and shame. To us the cross is a sacred object. In ancient times the word suggested only degradation, much as gibbet does now. He not only died but did so ignominiously on the cross, the lowest depth of his humiliation, the point farthest removed from his celestial and glorious status. From this nadir the upward movement of the hymn begins. We now start the ascent of the exaltation of Christ. Notice the style on an enthronement, including the acts of mounting the throne, the proclamation of new dignities, genuflection, and adoration.

"Therefore God has highly exalted him and bestowed on him the name which is above every name, that at the name of Jesus every knee should bow, in heaven and on earth and under the earth, and every tongue confess that Jesus Christ is Lord, to the glory of God the Father" (Ph 2:9-11). Christ's humiliation was the pathway to his exaltation. Service is the law of attainment. The exaltation is presumed as achieved in the resurrection, the divine work par excellence of God's mighty power. The acknowledgement will come at the Parousia. The passage is modelled on Is 45:23 which proclaims the purpose of Yahweh to bring all nations to obedience to himself. The universe gives glory to God and thereby attains the goal of its creation and redemption.

To give a name is to confer a real quality. This name is Lord (Kyrios), the equivalent of the sacred name Yahweh, the ineffable and divine name, the supreme name which claims and secures universal homage, and which, because of the triumph of his resurrection is now Christ's to enjoy. The three cosmic divisions cover the entire creation. To bend the knee is an expression of adoration; the figure expresses the universal submission of all creation to Christ.

The phrase "Jesus Christ is Lord" was the earliest and simplest confession of faith when people became Christians. Each of the three names indicates one of the aspects of the person of our savior: Jesus (the man), Christ (the Messiah), Lord (God). This proclamation is the essence of the Christian creed and forms the climax of the hymn. The use of Is 45:23, in which this homage is addressed to Yahweh himself, is a clear indication of the divine character that is meant to be understood by the title Lord. God exalted Jesus and so finds his glory even in the humiliation of his Son. The Father who exalted Jesus receives glory when the name which he gave him is confessed and adored. This confession redounds to the glory of the Father in whom the work of Christian salvation originates. It is a proof of the Father's power, goodness, and wisdom that he has begotten such a Son who in no way is his inferior (Chrysostom).

St. John Chrysostom underlines the dogmatic richness of the passage. It teaches the preexistence of Christ as God; the unity of nature with the Father, and the distinction of persons; the mystery of the incarnation uniting the immutable divine nature and the form of the slave in the same person; the identity of that person in its triple existence (eternal, terrestrial, and celestial); the merits of Christ's sacrificial death; the reality of his human body; the adoration due to Christ the Lord. The humiliations of Christ give us our model; his glorification is our encouragement.

32

CHRIST, THE ONE MEDIATOR

The Pastorals throw much light upon the organization and discipline of the early Church. 1 Tm 1:12-17 is a burst of praise of Christ's mercy. In 1 Tm 2:1-6 Paul asks for prayer for all men, who all have the one mediator between God and men, Christ Jesus. 1 Tm 3:16 is an ancient Christian hymn to the glory of Christ; 1 Tm 6:14-16 is a solemn doxology; 1 Tm 1:9-10 a summary of the Christian vocation and message; 2 Tm 2:11-17 a baptismal hymn. The introduction to Tt (1:1-3) is a summary of all the theology of salvation and of the apostolate. Tt 2:11-14 decribes God's saving action, its effects and demands; Tt 3:4-7 the consequences of the incarnation and the effects of baptism.

The main purpose of the *Pastorals* is to set up a high standard of Christian character and to inculcate loyalty to apostolic teaching. But a great part of their value lies in the light which they throw upon the position and duties of Christian ministry, and upon the organization and discipline of the Christian Church. To the clergy these books are some of the most valuable which the New Testament contains; they form part of that Bible within the Bible which belongs especially to them.

Listen to the first part of Paul's First Letter to Timothy. "From Paul, an apostle of Christ Jesus by command of God our

Savior and of Christ Jesus, our hope" (1 Tm 1:1). Jesus is our hope, as he is our life, our peace, our righteousness, because from him these and all blessings proceed. 1 Tm 1:3-20 describes the struggle for faith, the defense of the truth. "Divine training is in faith" (1:4). Training pictures the Christian life as the discipline of a servant in a large household. God's steward is charged with the mysteries of faith, and it is in the atmosphere of faith that his work is done. He must not waste the time and attention of his hearers.

"The aim of our charge is love that issues from a pure heart and a good conscience and sincere faith" (1:5). The gospel which Timothy had to preach consists of love springing from purity of heart, an elightened conscience, and a sure faith. The foundation of Christian teaching is faith; the end, love. But this can only subsist in a heart purified by faith and is always attended with a good conscience. The nature of Christian love is defined by its three sources: a pure heart is the single-minded intention to serve God; a good conscience is the constant desire to do right; a sincere faith accepts Christ as its guide. The four characteristics are acquired in reverse order. Faith is the foundation. It issues in the inward enjoyment of a pure heart, and the concern to preserve a good conscience, and in the practice of love towards God and men. Such love is the end in view, the proper goal and completion of saving faith and of Christian preaching.

1 Tm 1:12-17 is a burst of praise of Christ's mercy. "The grace of our Lord overflowed for me with the faith and love that are Christ Jesus" (1:14). Grace greater than his sin enabled Paul to show faith and love acting in a soul united to Christ. "The saying is sure and worthy of full acceptance, that Christ Jesus came into the world to save sinners. And I am the foremost of sinners" (1:15). The introductory formula, "The saying etc.," is proper to the Pastorals and probably introduces traditional material: a current, primitive credal phrase that states the purpose of the incarnation of God's Son as Messiah. "But I received mercy for this reason, that in me, as the foremost, Jesus Christ might display his perfect patience for an example to those who were to believe in him for eternal life" (1:16). After

the pardoning of such sin as his, no one need despair. The recounting of so great a mystery of mercy leads to a spontaneous outpouring of adoration. "To the king of the ages, immortal, invisible, the only God, be honor and glory for ever and ever. Amen" (1:17). This doxology stresses that God alone is supreme. It is noteworthy for the attributes ascribed to God. He is eternally sovereign, immune from decay, not observable by human eyes, the one and only true God. And when such words are publicly uttered it is for all to assent and say, Amen.

Paul asks for prayer for all men (1 Tm 2:1-6). He justifies his universal exhortation by pointing to the character and will of God as the universal savior; to God's unity as the one God for all men; to his provision of the human Christ Jesus as the single mediator between God and the whole human race; to the universal scope of Christ's redeeming act which was for all. "God desires all men to be saved to come to the knowledge of the truth" (1 Tm 2:4). Universal prayer is in accord with the revealed will of God. For God's will to save is as wide as his will to create and protect, as his creative power and providence. This points to the universality of the Christian community grounded on God's saving will. This is one of the strongest affirmations of the universality of God's grace. It is not said that God has determined that every single person must be saved; but simply that his general desire for mankind is that all alike shall enjoy salvation by coming to the knowledge of the truth, by direct and intimate apprehension. Redemption is universal yet conditional; all may be saved, yet all will not be saved, because all will not conform to God's appointed conditions. Paul affirms clearly the universal salvific will of God, without entering into the problem of its relationship to free will in man's salvation. On God's part is desire, on man's part responsibility.

"For there is one God and there is one mediator between God and men, the man Christ Jesus" (2:5). This is a short creed, a Christian version of the Jewish Shema (Dt 6-4-9), the great creed of Judaism, repeated daily by pious Jews. The very humanity of Christ and his appointment as the only mediator between God and men, supply added indication that the salvation provided in him is for all men alike. This universality arises from God's oneness. As the only God, he deals in the same way with all men. And the unity of God calls to missionary activity. If there is but one God, we lead all men to him. "He gave himself as a ransom for all, the testimony to which was borne at the proper time" (1 Tm 2:6). Ps 49:7-9 explains the meaning of ransom to be redemption from death. This underlines the vicarious nature of Christ's sacrifice. By his willingness to die for all men, Christ showed us that God wants everyone to be saved. Jesus is the redeemer who loved and died when God's plan came to maturity; he is the subject of the preaching now during the period of the Church. The witness begun in the Old Testament was continued by Jesus and is now perfected in the Christian gospel. Christ was the Father's witness all through his life, but especially, at the moment of his death on the cross.

"I desire then that in every place the men should pray, lifting holy hands without anger or quarrelling" (2:8). To raise the hands, with the palms open and facing upward, as if to receive a divine gift, is the ancient Christian gesture for prayer, and is perhaps the most natural gesture in very earnest prayer. The standard of conduct is conveyed by the holy hands, and the disposition of heart by freedom from anger and its consequence, quarrelling. To be at peace with one's neighbor is a necessary condition of effective prayer. Anger and quarrelling are contrary to love, which is the motive of intercession. The atmosphere of controversy is not congenial to devotion. And ill will and misgiving respecting one another are incompatible with united prayer to our common Father.

1 Tm 3:16 is an ancient Christian hymn to the glory of Christ, a confession of faith, a summary of Christian truth. The mystery is Christ now revealed and the basis of Christian holiness. "Great indeed, we confess, is the mystery of our religion. He was manifested in the flesh, attested by the Spirit, seen by angels, preached among the nations, believed in the world, taken up in glory" (1 Tm 3:16). The hymn expresses the profound nature of Christianity. It centers in Christ, preexistent but appearing in human flesh; the goodness of his mortal existence was verified by the Holy Spirit; the mystery of his Person was revealed to the angels, announced to the Gentiles and accepted by them in faith.

He himself was returned, through his resurrection and ascension, to the divine glory that is properly his.

Jesus was vindicated in his claim to be the Christ by virtue of the Spirit of holiness which dwelt in him (Rm 1:4), through the declarations which the Father himself made at Jesus' baptism and transfiguration, and especially in the great fact of the resurrection. The clauses present three contrasts: he Lord was manifested in his earthly life and declared to be righteous by the resurrection, when his humanity became quickening spirit (Rm 1:3-4). He was seen by angels who declared the resurrection, they witnessed, to his Jewish followers, and preached by them to the Gentiles. He was believed on in the world and received up into abiding glory in heaven. Faith shows his acceptance with men, and glory his acceptance with God.

"The appearing of our Lord Jesus Christ will be made manifest at the proper time by the blessed and only sovereign, the King of kings and the Lord of lords, who alone has immortality and dwells in unapproachable light, whom no man has ever seen or can see. To him be honor and eternal dominion" (1 Tm 6:14-16). This solemn doxology was probably part of the prayers used in the synagogues of the Greek world. The assertion of the universal kingship of God is in opposition to the pagan worship rendered to the emperors; and the affirmation of God's transcendence and inaccessibility contradicted the Gnostic pretensions. King of kings was a not infrequent Oriental title, adopted first by the Jews as a deliberate challenge to heathenism, and taken over by Christians, in face of the claims made by the Roman Emperors. The poem's theme is the incomparable glory of God. He is unique in his supremacy. He is also transcendent in holiness, dwelling in unapproachable light. The hymn provides a significant description of the unique sovereignty of God. In his absolute bliss and unending life he is completely self-contained. Such attributes belong to him and him alone. He is thus the exclusive Lord of all else. So to him should all honor be rendered and all power or rule ascribed.

2 Tm 1:9-10 is a summary of the Christian vocation and message. "God saved us and called us with a holy calling, not in virtue of our works but in virtue of his own purpose and the grace

which he gave us in Christ Jesus from all eternity, and now has been manifested through the appearing of our savior Christ Jesus, who abolished death and brought life and immortality through the gospel." The Christian's holy call is to a consecrated life dependent on God's eternal purpose manifested in the incarnation of Christ. The call is holy because it comes from a holy God and takes us away from the wickedness of the world and sets us apart for the service of God. It is a call to godlikeness. God's will, love, grace are the ground of redemption; works are the means employed by man with faith. Good works are an intended fruit of salvation not its cause. It is the Lord in his risen life who reveals God's agelong purpose for ourselves. We are to be what he already is.

"Remember Jesus Christ, risen from the dead, descended from David, as preached in my gospel" (2 Tm 2:8). Here is the great incentive of Christian service, and the central subject of the Christian message. Paul directs attention to two great facts concerning Jesus Christ. He is the living, victorious Lord risen from the dead, and he remains what in time he became, the man Christ Jesus descended from David.

2 Tm 11-13 may well be an extract from a hymn sung at baptismal services, and if so, it would remind us of those basic principles of Christian life and service which the rite signifies. "The salvation which is in Christ Jesus goes with eternal glory. This saying is sure: if we have died with him, we shall also live with him; if we endure, we shall also reign with him; if we deny him, he also will deny us; if we are faithless, he reamins faithful, for he cannot deny himself." Through baptism Christians die spiritually with Christ and live with him forever, but not without giving witness to him through suffering in the present life. The faithfulness of God, even when our heart is weak and faint, is greater than our heart. God's nature is to love and to save whatever can be saved, and to this he adheres even though men prove inconstant.

"God's firm foundation stands, bearing this seal: 'The Lord knows those who are his', and, 'Let every one who names the name of the Lord depart from iniquity'... Aim at righteousness, faith, love, and peace, along with those who call upon the Lord from a pure heart" (2 Tm 2:19-22). The firm foundation laid by God is the Church of Christ which is the ground story of the glorious temple of the future. The Church is only the first and early story of that glorious building which the divine architect has planned, and will complete in heaven. The solid foundation which God has laid, his Church, stands unmoved. On it is the stonemason's mark denoting ownership and workmanship. This seal and inscription should serve as a perpetual reminder to all the members that they are not their own, and of their consequent obligation to holiness of life.

Those "who are his," "who name the name of the Lord," "who call on the Lord" are those who believe in Christ and worship him as Lord. The phrases are synonymous for Christians. The Church is immovable and bears God's seal and inscription stating its specific dedication to God. A twofold truth stands as a permanent inscription upon the Church's foundation; the inscription involves quotations from Nb 16:5 and Is 26:13, one bearing on predestination, the other on free will. The two biblical texts complement each other; God guards those he loves and they live in righteousness.

The introduction to Tt (1:1-3) is a summary of all the theology of salvation and of the apostolate. Christianity is the divinely ordained means to lead men to faith, to the salvation promised by God and now revealed in Christ. The stress is on God's initiative and sovereignty, on his choice of the Church to carry his truth to the world, and on the need of a spirit of godliness or active reverence of God.

Tt 2:11-14 describes God's saving action, its effects and demands. The Christian moral life is based on the contemplation of the loftiest mysteries of God. "The grace of God has appeared for the salvation of all men" (Tt 2:11). This gives us the substance of the Christian faith. God's grace is his love imparting itself and producing its own image. It appeared in the incarnation and redemptive work of Christ. God's grace is a real and active force, a power that works in us illuminating the intellect, warming the heart, and strengthening the will. It is the might of the everlasting Spirit renovating man by uniting him to the sacred manhood of the Word Incarnate. The Spirit teaches us a sober self-control, justice toward our neighbor, and reverence toward God. "Training us to renounce irreligion and worldly passions, and to live sober, upright, and godly lives in this world" (Tt 2:12). Recreation of character and conduct is the main purpose of the incarnation. The final cause of the revelation in Christ is not creed but character. "Awaiting our blessed hope, the appearing of the glory of our great God and Savior, Jesus Christ" (Tt 2:13). This is an eloquent expression of Paul's belief in the divinity of Christ. The strength in which the Christian life is to be lived is the grace revealed in the first advent. The hope to which it presses is the glory of the second advent. "Who gave himself for us to redeem us from all iniquity and to purify for himself a people of his own who are zealous for good deeds" (Tt 2:14). This is the simplest possible statement of the atonement and its purpose: on the negative side, redemption from sin, and on the positive side, purification of life. We are saved by faith in order to do good works, to follow the example of Christ who went about doing good.

Tt 3:4-7 describes the consequences of the incarnation, the effects of baptism: rebirth, justification by the grace of Christ, communication of the Holy Spirit, and right to the inheritance of eternal life of which the gift of the Holy Spirit is the pledge. Man's salvation is viewed only from the side on which it is wholly God's work. "When the goodness and loving kindness of God, our Savior, appeared, he saved us, not because of deeds done by us in righteousness but in virtue of his own mercy, by the washing of regeneration and renewal in the Holy Spirit" (3:4-5). Washing may be said to describe a change of condition; regeneration, a change of status; and renewal, a change of disposition, restoration of the relationship to God which was lost through sin. Baptism to be efficient must be both by water and by the Spirit. It is not a mere outward act. "Which he poured out upon us richly through Jesus Christ our Savior, so that we might be justified by his grace and become heirs in hope of eternal life" (3:6-7). This gift of the quickening and indwelling Spirit has been made ours by God through Christ and his saving work. And so the whole Trinity is active to make salvation ours. To the ideas of salvation, cleansing, and justification, is added that of eternal life. Already heirs, and in part, possessors of the inheritance, believers look forward in hope to its full enjoyment. The full gospel includes not only the gift of God's Son for our justification, but also the gift of God's Spirit to make us heirs who can, by the life he makes ours, hope to enjoy salvation eternally.

33

CHRIST OUR HIGH PRIEST

Hebrews' teaching on the heavenly priesthood of Christ is a special feature of the epistle; Christ is the High Priest of the heavenly tabernacle (3:1). Hebrews opens with a reflection on the climax of God's revelation to mankind in his Son (1:1-4).

The epistle to the Hebrews, addressed to a Jewish-Christian community, presents an elaborate proof of the preeminence of Christianity over Judaism. It emphasizes three points: the superiority of Jesus Christ to the prophets, the angels, and Moses himself; the superiority of Christ's priesthood to the Levitical priesthood; and the superiority of Christ's sacrifice to the sacrifices offered by the Levitical priests. The notions of covenant, priesthood, and sacrifice are the backbone of the epistle.

The idea of a covenant, a solemn contract between man and man, in which each party made a formal promise to the other, was adopted into the religion of Israel to explain the relationship between Yahweh and his people. Fellowship with God is the object of all covenants between God and man. God's side of the contract was the promise of salvation, "the promise of entering into his rest" (Heb 4:1). On the side of man, fellowship is expressed supremely in worship. Reverent adoration is the right and natural attitude of the creature in the presence of the creator; and in the ancient world worship took the form of offering sacrifice. In the Old Testament to "draw near" is used of coming to offer sacrifice. So the covenant with Moses was inaugurated by a sacrifice, and under the covenant, the law ordained and provided sacrifices, a sanctuary and a priesthood, all of them ineffectual in themselves, but typical of higher and better realities.

In the world, already now, Christians are citizens of the heavenly kingdom and worshippers with Christ in the heavenly sanctuary. The mind of the author of Hebrews is so concentrated upon the work of our Lord in heaven that he has no explicit reference to the worship of the Church upon earth. The Church's worship is one and the same with the eternal worship of the heavenly shrine. The emphasis laid upon the sacrifice of our Lord as being made once and for all and its strong assertion that "by one offering he has perfected for ever those who are sanctified" (Heb 10:14), greatly clarifies the nature of our Eucharistic celebration. A true conception of the Eucharistic sacrifice must put it in one line, not only with what Christ did once for all on the cross, but also with what he is continually doing in heaven.

Hebrews' teaching on the heavenly priesthood of Christ is a special feature of the book. On the cross our Lord, as sacrificer and victim, laid down his life for us and endured that shedding of his blood apart from which there is no redemption (Heb 9:22). In the heavenly sanctuary as priest and victim he offers himself for us in his ascended life. His appearing before the face of God for us, and his intercession and his offering of himself there, would lose all its meaning and power, if he had not first laid down his life on Calvary. The heavenly offering is an offering of life whereof to have died is an ever-present and perpetual attribute. Christ's death is the source from which all the virtue of his priestly work, cleansing, sanctifying, perfecting, is derived. Our writer's mind is fixed upon the vision of our High Priest at work in the heavenly temple, and this fact accounts for the rare occurrence of direct references to the death of Jesus. But the cross fills the background of his thoughts throughout the whole epistle. It is never forgotten or overlooked.

In Hebrews Christ is chiefly regarded as the High Priest of

the heavenly tabernacle (3:1). This is the only New Testament book that gives us a distinct conception of the priesthood of Christ. This is exercised after his resurrection and ascension. His sacrifice on the cross is actually presented to God in heaven. To our author the whole present interest in Christ is in that later sphere of his heavenly life, in what he is now as our priest and intercessor, though that rests on what he was on earth in his obedience and sacrifice. The death of Christ is the one sacrifice for sin (9:12). The sacrifice consists in his offering himself to God in death "by the eternal spirit" (9:14), that is apparently, in virtue of his divine spiritual nature, which being eternal confers eternal efficacy. The essence of the sacrifice consists in the attitude of Christ's will, namely, in his delighting to obey God's will, even to the extent of dying, when the course of obedience involved that extremity.

Hebrews has a direct bearing upon Christian worship in general and Eucharistic worship in particular. It offers to us the sublime vision of a worship in which earth and heaven are united: men are bidden here and now to step through the veil that separates the two and enter into fellowship with the angels and the saints (12:22-23), and above all with the High Priest and leader of the heavenly liturgy, "The great priest over the house of God." As in the Apocalypse, a door is opened into heaven and a voice bids, "Come up higher." "Sursum Corda" might well be taken as the motto of the epistle. It is from this uplifting vision that the glorious interchanges of earth and heaven in the Eucharistic liturgies have sprung. Time and space are done away with, and redeemed humanity on earth and in Paradise is revealed in union with its High Priest engaged in their unceasing offering. At each Eucharist on earth we step, as it were, into his heavenly land, and enjoy the privileges of citizenship.

Christ's great act of obedience in death was offered as the deed, not of a mere man, but of the leader and high priest of men, whereby he enables us to participate with himself in doing the will of God, in which our sanctification stands. Still, this is only to be enjoyed on condition of trust and fidelity; and the counterpart of Christ's sacrifice is his people's faith, the triumphs of which are celebrated as a conclusion of the whole argument (Ch 11).

Thus the new covenant predicted by Jeremiah is established by Christ.

Another treasure-house of truth is opened to us in the teaching of the epistle upon atonement. By the blood and the risen life of him who died, the token of his victory over sin and death, the new covenant was inaugurated. We have the clearest New Testament exposition of the very heart and essence of the atonement in the statement of this truth in 10:8-10: "We have been sanctified through the offering of the body of Jesus Christ once for all."

Hebrews opens with a reflection on the climax of God's revelation to mankind in his Son (1:1-4). This grand opening statement indicates the great theme of the writer: "Christ, the apostle and high priest of the religion we profess" (3:1). It indicates in a few pregnant phrases the central significance of Jesus Christ in the working of the purpose of God. This vision of the absolute supremacy and sufficiency of Christ, his transcendence as revealer and redeemer, dominates the thought of the whole epistle. Instead of the ordinary epistolary introduction, stands a prologue which announces the great themes to follow: the superiority of the new order of revelation to the old, which it perfects; the divinity shared by the Son and manifested to us in him; his place in the cosmos; his role in achieving salvation for us by his passion and transitus to the heavenly world; his superiority to the angels. The prologue is a stately declaration of the superiority of Christianity to Judaism. Note the contrast between "of old" and "in these last days;" to the fathers and to us; by prophets and by the Son; yet it is the same God who spoke then and speaks now. God's Son, who is the exact counterpart of the Father, not only had part in the creation (Jn 1:13), but continues to sustain the universe. Having accomplished his priestly work of purification for sins, he was enthroned in royal splendor. Thus Christ is prophet, priest, and king.

The divine communication with men was initiated and maintained during Old Testament times through chosen men, the prophets (1:1). But now, in Messianic times, the final period of man's religious history, God the Son, creator and end of all things, is the communicator with men (2). He is the perfect and exact representation of the Father's being, even to the divine creative power, who entered human existence to destroy the power of sin. After accomplishing this he returned, through his resurrection and ascension, to his natural place with the Father (3). No creature, not even angels, can match the unique dignity of his Person (4). In his eternal being, Christ is genuine, absolute Deity, the visible outshining of God's glory, himself an exact expression of the divine nature, the eternal Son of the Father, "very God of very God." In the divine ordering of the universe he is its creator, sustainer and end. By him it was made; he upholds it; he is its heir. In relation to men he is men's prophet, priest, and king. In him God spoke his final word of revelation; so he brings God to men. In his own Person he made our purification for our sins, and so he brings men to God. He now sits enthroned at God's right hand, and as exalted God-man has obtained by inheritance a position far above all others.

"In many and various ways, God spoke of old to our fathers; but in these last days he has spoken to us by a Son, whom he appointed the heir of all things, through whom also he created the world" (Heb 1:1-2). God first acted and spoke not man. This fact is the ground of true religion and of true worship. Men communicate with the God who first revealed himself to them. God's revelation is also continuous, gradual and progressive, an expanding revelation. The old revelation was preparatory and transitory; the new, in and through God's Son, is final, complete and absolute. The contrast implies not only the superiority of the new revelation but also its finality. No later revelation can go further than this. The superiority of God's revelation in Christ is due to the transcendent character of the person, the rank, status, and authority of him through whom and in whom it comes.

The author stresses complementary aspects with a unifying principle behind them: God, author of the old revelation and of the new; Christ, God and man; Christ as the one in whom creation finds its beginning and its final consummation. Christ's coming brought in the final era of the world's history, which will end when he appears a last time. His life and mission comprise

God's last word to the world. But what he had to say could not be expressed in words alone but took the form of a human life, a life whose obedience and dedication mark the turning point of human history, and embody the love of God for us. The decisive revelation of God is given, not only in a document, but also in a person.

After the prophets God sends a messenger who is not a mere spokesman like the others; he is a Son, the very Word of God. God sent us *a* Son. The indefinite article bespeaks nature and character, all the depth and breadth of what that Son is in relation to the Father. The Son is one who has a unique relationship to the Father, one who carries out the will and purpose of the Father, and who therefore has a unique and supreme revelatory function. To be son implies to have the right to inherit. Here the possession of all things is attributed to a divine initiative because there is question of Messianic and eschatological benefits.

The Son's preeminence is described partly in terms of the Old Testament personification of divine Wisdom, and partly with reference to the royal psalms (e.g. Ps 2:8) which find fulfillment in his work. He is the eternal creator, the mediator of God's revelation in time, and the heir of all things at the end of time. When Hebrews says that God made the Son heir of the universe, his perspective is still that of eschatology already begun; when he goes on to say that through the Son God made the universe, his gaze turns back to the other end of time. The first attribute belongs primarily to Christ's humanity, the second to his divinity. The Son was not made heir, for the universe belongs to him from eternity, but Christ as man actually came into possession of his dominion over the universe when he entered the heavenly world in glory.

"He reflects the glory of God and bears the very stamp of his nature, upholding the universe by his word and power" (Heb 1:3). The glory of the Lord in the Old Testament means a manifestation of God as a bright light. The Son derives from the Father the nature of divinity, as the radiancy of the sun, though derived from the sun, is what the sun is. The two figures, reflection and image or stamp, are complementary the one to the other, the former expressing the unity of the Son with the Father, the latter his perfect revelation, reproduction of the Father to man. The Son is "Light from light" as the Nicene creed puts it. "The sun is never without effulgence, nor the Father without the Son" (Theophylact). Reflection contains the double notion of derivation and manifestation. It indicates the divine origin of the Son from the Father and at the same time his personal independence. It suggests that "the Son can do only what he sees the Father doing" (Jn 5:19). Christ is also the exact representation of God's nature, his real being. All the essential characteristics of God are brought into clear focus in him; he who has seen the Son has seen the Father also (Jn 14:9).

The Son conserves the universe, harmonizes it, governs it, and leads it to its ends, by his powerful word; the divine might is such that no effort is necessary, a word suffices. The whole course of nature and of human history is in Christ's hands and he is conducting both to their destined end, the goal of creation, which is the establishment of God's kingdom. This demands purification from sin, the redemptive work for the sake of which the Son came to earth. With his mediatorial work accomplished, Christ ascended to heaven and sits at the right hand of God, the place of honor and power. This session denotes the acceptance of him and his sacrifice by God the Father, and also his exaltation as heir, and his enthronement as king. The Father spoke in him as prophet; the Son made expiation for our sins as priest; and he sits at God's right hand as king. The session is the resumption of his original dignity, but it is in the character of prophet, priest, and king that he is there seated and functions.

"When he had made purification for sins, he sat down at the right hand of the majesty on high, having become as much superior to angels as the name he has obtained is more excellent than theirs" (Heb 1:3-4). Purification expresses the work of Christ in priestly language; it summarizes the achievement of the Son of Man on earth. The main theme of the letter is broached with the idea of the priest who made purification for sins. The writer of Hebrews understands the priestly service to be the essential activity of the Son, and the real reason for his coming to earth. The word and the idea of purification are derived from the Jewish sacrifices, and particularly from the sin offerings on the Day of Atonement, when the priest made a purification of sins by the sprinkling of blood on the mercy seat. The author seeks to show how Jesus fulfills the Levitical priesthood, thus bringing to light the reality which the priesthood symbolizes or foreshadows. But in this passage his chief concern is to assert the glory of Christ. When he finished his work of purification, he achieved authority and power, symbolized by the image of the session at God's side.

The enthronement of Christ at God's side, an echo of the words addressed to the Davidic king in Ps 110:1, is a regular feature of the apostolic preaching. It indicates the completion of Christ's work and its acceptance by God, and also that his position is one of divine dignity (equality with God) and dominion (repose, power, triumph). The Son, both human and divine, shares God's sovereignty; he has attained his appointed destiny.

The contrast of the Son with the angels is for the purpose of showing his superiority to all created beings, even the highest. He does a more perfect work: the fulfillment of Old Testament prophecy, including the institution of sacrifice. He brings the perfect and complete revelation, the disclosure of God's love in the cross. The context suggests that the name Jesus obtains is Son; but name means in general rank or status and that is the writer's real point. So far as the human nature is concerned, Jesus became Son of God in the fullest sense at his resurrection; until then he existed in that condition which Paul calls the likeness of sinful flesh. But the sonship he received when he was glorified is based ultimately on the relation he had with the Father before the incarnation. As the preexistent One, the title, Son, belonged to him always ("God sent his Son" Rm 8:3); thus the name properly belonged to the incarnate Jesus, even before his exaltation.

34

THE PERFECTER OF OUR FAITH

Heb 10:19-25 is an exhortation to worship with Christ as our great priest. The author gives a description of faith (Heb 11:1-2, 6) and then presents Christ as the pioneer and perfecter of our faith (Heb 12:1-2).

Heb 10:19-24 is an exhortation to worship. The scene is the heavenly sanctuary into which the people of God are admitted. Leading the worship at the head of the Congregation is Christ, the great priest with his perpetual offering. Behind him the body of the faithful are bidden to draw near, prepared in heart and life for their worship. The passage states the benefits of Christ's priesthood and urges us to respond in faith. We have access to God through Christ; we should respond in worship (22), faith (23), and fellowship (24-25). The author recalls what Christ has accomplished and what the Christian should do in response. He uses the language of worship, adapting the terminology of the tabernacle to the new world of realities inaugurated by the sacrifice of Christ. The impulse to worship has a twofold source: the confidence made possible by Christ's self-giving, and the living presence of the great priest who presides over God's house. The traditional language of Old Testament worship is given heightened meaning. The sanctuary is the true sanctuary, the presence of God. The blood of Christ is his self-offering as sacrifice for sin. The new and living way through the curtain means that access to God is now the prerogative of every

Christian, and that it has been won for him through the obedience of Christ in offering up his flesh, that is, his life.

"Therefore, brethren, since we have confidence to enter the sanctuary by the blood of Jesus, by the new and living way which he opened for us through the curtain, that is, through his flesh, and since we have a great priest over the house of God, let us draw near with a true heart in full assurance of faith, with our hearts sprinkled clean from an evil conscience, and our bodies washed with pure water. Let us hold fast the confession of our hope without wavering, for he who promised is faithful; and let us consider how to stir up one another to love and good works not neglecting to meet together" (Heb 10:19-25). This is a call to steadfastness in faith, hope, and love. It summarizes the positive appeal of the whole epistle. It is based on the doctrinal teaching already given of Christ's one sacrifice and his abiding continuance in the place of sovereign ability as our high priest. It is a call, first of all, to enter into the realized presence of God, in confident, appropriating faith (22). This is complemented by exhortations to be steadfast in the open confession of Christian hope (23), and to be active towards fellow-Christians in love, fellowship, and mutual encouragement (24-25). This brief threefold exhortation is virtually expanded in the remainder of the epistle.

God is to be worshipped through Christ. There is a way, free access to God's presence, which has been inaugurated for us by Jesus, the forerunner. The exalted Christ is our new, living way to God. The sanctuary is heaven, the focal point of union between God and man, and the goal of our pilgrimage toward salvation. Only the high priest could enter the Holy of Holies once a year. Henceforth all believers have access to God through Christ. The curtain or veil through which Jesus opened up this way was his human flesh. For when it was broken in sacrificial death, the symbolic Temple veil was rent asunder. The curtain is taken as a symbol of his incarnation; but because it is a torn curtain it symbolizes his crucifixion also. Both are necessary to open our way to God. As the Jewish priest entered not without blood, and as Christ entered through his own blood, so Christians admitted to the privilege of the priesthood enter by the blood of Christ. The blood of Christ is a theological symbol for his saving work and its fruits. The union of believers with Christ admits them to share in the privileges of his priesthood, namely, the right to enter into the Holy of Holies. To draw near is used of all approach to God for worship, particularly in reference to the priest's work of offering sacrifice. In union with the High Priest, the priestly house of God enters the Holy of Holies to offer their sacrifice of good works.

The writer describes the manner in which worship is done: the Christian is to worship with a true heart, that is to say, he is to come with sincerity in his inmost being; he is to worship in full assurance of faith, to have done with all doubt and misgiving, reflecting continuously on the basis of his faith, the person and work of Christ; he is to worship with his heart sprinkled clean from an evil conscience, and his body washed with pure water, that is to say, he is to assemble for worship only after he has gained a consciousness of sins forgiven through faith in the atoning work of Christ, and only after he has participated in Christian baptism. These last two requirements for worship are cast in language suggestive of the ancient ritual and are intended to show that the Christian stands in the high place of being a priest himself, ordained for the worshipful service of God.

Confession is the New Testament technical term for the praise of God. We are urged not only to maintain the creed but also to keep a firm grip on the worship of God, which is the content of our confession. The characteristic New Testament emphasis on the close interconnection of divine and human activities is also present here. The ground of our worship is the faithfulness of God. We can hold our confession without wavering because underneath and behind us is God's covenanted reliability. And the experience of worship is a community affair. We do not respond automatically to the full meaning of worship; we need to be stimulated, as we meet together in worship. Love and good works are of the essence of Christianity. And since their maintenance is dependent upon the mutual interaction of the Christian community, it is absolutely essential that one assemble with other Christians, if he is to be assured of continued spiritual development. Any type of go-it-alone Christianity is unthinkable. The meeting of Christians gives the opportunity to exercise love and good works, and also to make the confession of the Christian faith and hope which is to be held fast. Probably the gathering together of the community for the celebration of the Eucharist is meant.

Heb 10:26-31 is a warning against the sin of apostasy or deliberate revolt against God. The warning is given in terms of sacrifice. If a Christian persists in sin, he is repudiating Christ's sacrifice and bringing judgment on himself. "He has spurned the Son of God, and profaned the blood of the covenant by which he was sanctified, and outraged the Spirit of grace . . . It is a fearful thing to fall into the hands of the living God" (Heb 10:29, 31). It is a frightful thing to meet God apart from Jesus Christ. There is a sternly severe side to God's character as well as a tenderly gracious one.

"Now faith is the assurance of things hoped for, the conviction of things unseen. For by it the men of old received divine approval" (Heb 11:1-2). Faith is the anticipated and assured possession of heavenly realities. The author is not setting out to give a definition of faith, but only to point out some of the effects it must necessarily produce in those who possess it; it makes the unrealized future and the unseen things of the present into solid certainties. Instead of defining faith comprehensively, the author describes those aspects of it which bear upon his argument. The examples taken from the lives of Old Testament saints (Ch 11) are meant to illustrate how faith is the source of patience and strength.

The terms underline the paradoxical character of faith which possesses without holding, knows without seeing. Assurance is used in ancient commercial documents in the sense of title deed. Faith as the title deed of good things to come combines the elements of hope, confidence and trust, and parallels Paul's understanding of the presence of the Spirit as earnest money guaranteeing the inheritance or full possession, or as first fruits assuring the imminence of the harvest. By faith the believer has the title to good things to come and also a solid conviction of the reality of the divine realm. Faith is equally sure of the coming fulfillment of things hoped for and of the present reality of heavenly things. The very being of God is the supreme unseen reality with which faith has to do; and his faithful fulfillment of his promises (11:11) and his certain rewarding of those who seek him (11:6) are the great future goods for which faith hopes.

This is a descriptive definition, based on metaphor, and it is existential rather than essential. It is concerned not with the articles of faith which must be believed, with God as the formal object of faith, or with the components of intellect and will and grace that go into the making of an act of faith but with the assurance that faith is a guarantee of the unseen realities in which we hope, the celestial homeland which we are approaching. Faith looks upward and forward, and so it is akin to hope. Indeed the definition's existential approach here blends faith and hope into one, but faith stands out as the basis of hope. Faith is that by which we already have a title to the things we hope for. It is plain that in faith as our author conceives it, hope plays a prominent part; faith is the firm assurance, the basis of the fulfillment of our hope; it persuades us of the reality of what is not seen as yet, and enables us to act upon it.

Faith is that by which the invisible becomes real and the future becomes present. They exist apart from faith, but it is by faith that they are realized. Faith based upon the firm word of God is not really a leap into the dark. Faith has no possibility of rational proof; it is based uniquely on God's word: his promises and revelation. There are other complementary points of view in the New Testament. Paul represents faith especially as a personal relation between God and the believer. James affirms the insufficiency of a purely conceptual faith in the existence of God, and insists on the necessary link between faith and good works.

Heb 11:6 is a general axiom referring to the existence and moral government of God, corresponding to the two aspects of faith. "Without faith it is impossible to please God. For whoever would draw near to God must believe that God exists and that he rewards those who seek him." The faith that is essential for salvation has a double object: belief in the existence of one, personal God, who by his very nature cannot be seen, and belief in a remunerating providence, the foundation of the hoped for happiness, since God must give a just recompense for all effort spent in searching for him. No mention of Jesus is made here because the context deals with the time of Henoch.

The Christian life is to be inspired not only by the Old Testament men of faith (Heb 12:1), but above all by Jesus. As the architect of Christian faith, he had himself to endure the cross before receiving the glory of his triumph (2). Reflection on his sufferings should give his followers courage to continue the struggle, if necessary even to the shedding of blood (3-4). This is a call to serve God acceptably. The exhortation is based first of all on the supreme example and complete sufficiency of Jesus himself as the pioneer and *perfecter of our faith.*

"Therefore since we are surrounded by so great a cloud of witnesses, let us lay aside every weight, and sin which clings so closely, and let us run with perseverance the race that is set before us, looking to Jesus the pioneer and perfecter of our faith, who for the sake of the joy that was set before him endured the cross, despising the shame, and is seated at the right hand of the throne of God" (Heb 12:1-2). This expresses the pattern of death and exaltation, suffering and glory, which in its various forms is general in the New Testament writers' thought about Jesus' death and resurrection. The many heroes of faith mentioned in Ch 11 become to the writer an amphitheater of spectators cheering the Christian runner on toward the goal. Once they were themselves runners; now they are promoted to the rank of spectators. Their presence and example ought to be a stimulus to those running now. The author has a fertile mind for appropriate metaphors. He sees the Christian life as movement towards a goal. He uses the image of a race with runners stripped and resolute. We are runners in a race Godward and heavenward. We must get rid of whatever imperfection or sin that would weigh us down and slow our progress.

Jesus, however, is the supreme example of faith and the climax of the list of heroes. He is the one who completed the race of faith and reached the throne of God, arriving at the goal before us. He is the leader in the way of faith, and he leads to the very end, exhibiting the perfection and triumph of faith. He is the pioneer and perfecter of our faith who needed the utmost of courage and stamina for his strenuous ministry. He has opened the trail for us, and he also enables us to follow his path. His mission in life required great personal effort. He needed motivation even as we do. His motivation was the joy of doing God's will, a joy which comprises the completion of his work, his exaltation at the Father's right hand, and the consequent blessing of his people. He endured the cross and thus won the victory and now shares God's sovereignty. Christians fortify themselves by recalling what Jesus endured and by recognizing that, in the face of the extreme shame and suffering of crucifixion, he had regard for the heavenly reward which he now permanently enjoys enthroned in heaven. The manner and success of his achievement not only make possible our pursuit of the same pathway of faith, but also guarantee that he will be able to complete what he enabled us to begin. In this way he is both the initiator and consummator of our faith.

Christ alone has fully realized all that is involved in faith and in keeping the faith. His faith included faith in the grace of God and the salvation of men, and enabled him to endure the cross and led him to the reward of heavenly enthronement. The Christian's goal is Jesus who participated in our human experiences. He is not only the object of faith's vision, he is also its greatest encouragement. As pioneer he blazed the trail of faith for Christians to follow. But he is also faith's perfecter, for all that faith hopes for finds its consummation in him. Jesus is a further example of encouragement to faith in that the endurance of the cross was the price he willingly paid for the joy that was set before him. Thus believers are encouraged to regard their sufferings (less, in any case, than Christ's) as a small price to pay for the prize to be secured at the end of the race set before them. Choosing the cross resulted in Christ being exalted in glory. With Christ's exemplary life before their eyes, believers will finish the race though weariness may tempt them to give out and quit. The life of Jesus, therefore, is a call to perseverance, for the contest is not a short dash to glory, but a distance race calling for endurance.

"Consider him who endured from sinners such hostility so that you may not grow weary or fainthearted. In your struggle against sin you have not yet resisted to the point of shedding your blood" (Heb 12:3-4). Our sufferings are light compared with those of Jesus. Christ's obedience was unto death; he has not promised to let his disciples off more easily.

35

JESUS CHRIST ALWAYS THE SAME

Heb 12:18-29 compares the two covenants of Moses and of Christ. The appendix contains a call to faithfulness (Heb 13:7-16); this is introduced by a kerygmatic confession of faith (Heb 13:8). The epistle concludes with a prayer (Heb 13:20-21).

The true worship of God is enabled by the new covenant, not by the old. As a final appeal for adherence to Christian teaching, Heb 12:18-29 compares two covenants of Moses and of Christ. The Mosaic covenant is shown to have originated in fear of God and threats of divine punishment (12:18-21). The covenant of Christ gives men direct access to God (22), makes them members of the Christian community, God's sons, a sanctified people (23) who have Jesus as mediator to speak for them (24). A contrast is established between the assembly of Israel gathered for the striking of the old covenant and the giving of the law, and the assembly of those who have entered the new covenant. The scene of the former is on earth, the scene of the latter is the heavenly sanctuary, the place of Jesus' completed sacrifice on which the new covenant is based. The former covenant was established in an atmosphere of dread. Not so the new: there is about it an atmosphere of joy and peace and confidence, though at the same time awe. The frightening events which accompanied the giving of the old covenant are contrasted to the graciousness and tenderness of God's love in Christ. Yet though we are invited to a glad and glorious fellowship in contrast to the dread warnings and threats of the old covenant, to refuse is on that account even the more heinous crime. This last warning is linked with a final encouragement in the bright vision of the glories of the new fellowship.

"You have come to Mount Zion and to the city of the living God, the heavenly Jerusalem . . . to the assembly of the first-born who are enrolled in heaven, and to a judge who is God of all, and to the spirits of just men made perfect, and to Jesus, the mediator of a new covenant, and to the sprinkled blood that speaks more graciously than the blood of Abel" (Heb 12:22-24). The approach to God is no longer in a terrifying theophany as at Sinai but in a city built by God, the one hoped for by the fathers, one that is already heavenly. With the angels all Christians are gathered around their triumphant mediator, in whom they find sanctification and fulfillment. The meeting place of God and his covenant people is heaven itself. It is better than the old Sinai because it is heavenly, not earthly, and glorious, not terrifying. It is not called the heavenly Sinai, but the heavenly Jerusalem, because it is not the place from which we are setting out, but the end at which we are arriving. At Sinai God spoke, but not finally; in Jesus he has spoken his last word, and the present choice of obedience or refusal is the final choice.

In the Christian dispensation everything is spiritual and heavenly. Because of God's presence in the Temple, Jerusalem became thought of as the earthly counterpart of heaven, and was consequently used as an image of it. Restored Jerusalem belongs to the heavenly world of valid spiritual realities, and of man's meeting with God. We have already come to this heavenly city because we share already in the reality of the good things brought by Christ (10:1), but at the same time we are still on the way to the heavenly city which is to come (13:14). The inhabitants of the heavenly Jerusalem are the angels in their myriads, the first-born, God the judge of all, the departed saints, and Jesus the mediator. It is to this festive gathering that Christians are invited to come and worship. The first-born are the elect in general, Christians who, unlike Esau, value their birthright. First-born expresses the idea of privilege and heirship. It describes all who belong to the Church. They are the company who have peculiar rights to the heavenly Jerusalem and whose names are therefore enrolled in the register of its citizens.

The last mentioned reality of the heavenly sanctuary is that which has opened it to the faithful, the sacrifice of Christ. The blood of Abel cried out for vengeance (Gn 4:10); that of Jesus brings forgiveness and access to God (Heb 10:19). Abel's blood demanded Cain's banishment from God's presence; the blood of Jesus brings us into God's presence. Jesus' blood has better things to tell than that of Abel. Jesus' blood signifies his sacrifice for sins and his covenant with those sprinkled with it (10:22); in fact, it signifies obedience, redemption, salvation, the whole work of bringing many sons to glory. Abel's blood signifies rebellion, hatred, sin, all causes of Christ's work. Jesus' crowning and comprehensive work in heaven, is to minister to all who come to him, all the promised blessings of the covenant now established and sealed for ever by his shed and sprinkled blood. This is the literary and theological climax of this eschatological scene. The context is that of Christ's heavenly liturgy, and the connection reappears here with the sprinkled blood speaking before God, that is, in the symbolism drawn from the liturgy of the Day of Atonement. Christ's blood effects the reconciliation between God and his people, a union which is the consummation of that peace and holiness which Christians strive after as their goal (12:14).

"Let us be grateful for receiving a kingdom that cannot be shaken and thus let us offer to God acceptable worship, with reverence and awe, for our God is a consuming fire" (Heb 12:28-29). This is the conclusion of the epistle and includes its cultic application. The unshakeable kingdom is the heavenly city where the Son reigns with God over the angels and the saints. Even now Christians live there and their life is a liturgy of thanksgiving under the purifying fire of God's holiness. The kingdom is a common New Testament description of the destiny of Christians in heaven. It was the main theme of Jesus' preaching. God is king, Jesus at his right hand shares his kingdom, and Christians are given it. We will enter the kingdom at the Parousia, but it is ours now in principle. God's kingdom is unshakeable and will have no end.

The proper response to such a gift is worship with reverence and awe, with a sense of God's holiness and transcendence. Not only in the Old Testament but also in the New, God is a consuming fire. In other respects there may be a wide difference between the law and the gospel, but the one God of both, though now revealed in Jesus Christ as the God of all grace, is still a consuming fire; his justice burns those who reject his grace. Fire is a symbol of God's living and purifying holiness.

The appendix to Hebrews contains a call to faithfulness (13:7-16) introduced by a kerygmatic confession of faith (8). The greatest of all patterns to imitate is Jesus Christ. Human leaders may pass away, but Jesus Christ, the supreme object and subject of their faithful teaching remains, and remains the same; no novel additions to his truth are required. "Jesus Christ is the same yesterday and today and for ever. . . It is well that the heart be strengthened by grace" (Heb 13:8-9). It is the inward heart that matters, and it is essential that the heart be established by the grace of God, for grace is the active principle of Christian faith and by it the conscience is cleansed and communion with God is secured.

Christ is the one all-sufficient guarantee of salvation. The Christ who was to the saints of old the object of their faith and the source of their strength is the same to us today and will be to all others in the days to come. The same in his person and offices, in his love and power, in his truth and grace; the same object of faith; and the same in all respects, to all believers, in all ages. This declaration brought about by the mention of the word of God and of faith, underlines the central truth preached by the heads of the community. The teachers may disappear but Christ remains, and it is to him that Christians bind themselves. In this declaration the divinity of Christ resounds. From Ch 2 onward the humanity of Christ has been uppermost in the thought of the author, sometimes a suffering humanity, sometimes a glorified one, always a humanity acting in the power of the eternal spirit (9:14). But Jesus Christ who in the stages of his life, suffering, death, and glorification was subject to the changes of historical development and ultimately of glorification, is also Jesus Christ, the Son of God, timeless and unchanging, transcending the world of past, present, and future in the sphere of eternal existence which belongs strictly to God.

"We have an altar from which those who serve the tent have no right to eat" (Heb 13:10). The altar is here put for the sacrifice on the altar; the Christian altar is the Christian sacrifice, which is Christ Jesus with all the benefits of his passion and death. We have an altar which is neither the cross of Christ, nor the Lord's table, nor Christ himself, but all of them; and of it they who cling to the outmoded sacrifices of the old law cannot partake.

"For the bodies of those animals whose blood is brought into the sanctuary by the high priest as a sacrifice for sin are burned outside the camp. So Jesus also suffered outside the gate in order to sanctify the people through his own blood. Therefore let us go forth to him outside the camp, bearing abuse for him" (Heb 13:11-13). This describes the genuine liturgy of Christ and our participation therein. Jesus suffered as a perfect sacrifice for the purifying of his people; but his people who follow him outside the closed circle of Judaism, know him as alive from the dead, one to whom they may go, and from whom they may by faith derive abiding sustenance. The sanctification or purifying consecration of Christ's people by the blood of his voluntary sacrifice, corresponds to the sprinkling of the atoning blood on the propitiatory by the high priest. On the Day of Atonement the high priest went into the Holy of Holies and sprinkled it with blood of the victims, but the bodies of these animals were burnt outside the camp. Jesus as expiatory victim realized this type by being crucified outside the walls of Jerusalem. We Christians must leave the camp of Judaism and of the world. Quite after his usual manner the writer lays hold of a casual word or phrase to introduce a new theme. The only point of strict analogy between the two cases is seen in the words, outside the camp. Pressed further the comparison breaks down, for the burning of the carcass in the one case presents no parallel with the crucifixion.

Jesus was content to be excommunicated from the earthly Jerusalem in order that he might build the city which is to come, the heavenly Jerusalem.

Sanctification is not to be had in the earthly liturgy of the Old Testament, but in the liturgy of grace, the heavenly liturgy of Christ's saving act (Heb 9:11-28). "For we have no lasting city, but we seek the city which is to come" (Heb 13:14). To receive the benefits of Christ's work we must not cling to the earthly Jerusalem, but to Christ the living Lord of grace; we must find our hope in the true city of the living God, which is the city of the coming heavenly order which will remain. Christians are a pilgrim people, consecrated by Christ, seekers after the new Jerusalem. Although this city is yet to come, the Christian by faith is already a citizen and a worshiper within it.

Christ must be the heart and the center of the Christian community. "Through him then let us continually offer a sacrifice of praise to God, that is, the fruit of lips that acknowledge his name" (Heb 13:15). We have here a glimpse of the sacrificial theology of the apostolic age. The expiatory sacrifice itself is that of Christ, who sanctifies the people with his blood; this sacrifice has been made once and for all, never needing to be repeated because the forgiveness of sins it achieved is totally sufficient. Christians living in the space of historical time, between the historical sacrifice of Christ and his return at the end of time, associate themselves personally with this sacrifice, and they have something of their own to bring to their celebration of this mystery: a liturgy of praise. Unlike the single and unique sacrifice of Christ, this liturgy of praise continues throughout the ages of redemption and is the same kind of liturgy as that of the angels and the elect in heaven: praise sung to the glory of God and the saving work of Christ. But even this role of creatures in the sacrifice is carried out in power and virtue which comes through the grace of Christ. The historical sacrifice of Christ, his passion and death, ascension and session, is all-imporant and all-sufficient; the liturgy of Christians is derived from it and made in its power, and the role proper to Christians in that liturgy is praise.

Citizenship in the heavenly city consists in paying homage

to its king in worship. That worship is offered through Christ, by means of, in union with, and through the grace supplied by his sacrifice. Our sacrifice finds a higher and truer expression than in the offering of an animal sacrifice; it is the offering of the heart out of which the mouth speaks. This sacrifice is a continual one, not occasional as under the old covenant. It is offered through Christ, possible only through him, acceptable only through him, as the high priest over the house of God (1 P 2:5). Like Heb 10:19, this verse presents a picture of the perpetual offering in the heavenly sanctuary. But it adds two new thoughts: we have an offering of our own to make, and that offering is a praise offering not an offering for sin as our priest does.

The sacrifice of praise or thanksgiving had been the highest form of peace-offering under the Levitical law (Lv 7:12), and the Psalmists (Ps 107:22), had adopted the term to describe that truly spiritual worship, which the atoning sacrifice of Christ does not supersede, but deepens and assures. Christ's sacrifice of atonement shall never be repeated; but an offering to God is, in its highest form, sacrifice or sacred service, whether it be of words or charity, or of the duties of ordinary life (Rm 12:1). Such sacrifice is now to be offered continually, and through the one true High Priest, who has really opened the way for such worship to be brought to God, by the one real sacrifice of atonement which is effectual for ever.

The word name is a shorthand expression for all the deeds of God by which he discloses himself to men. To acknowledge his name is therefore more than giving a passing gesture of recognition. It is to relate oneself seriously to God's self-disclosure, to accept Jesus Christ as God's definitive word to men. It is to recognize God as the true God. It means to worship him as such and recognize the greatness of his grace. The proper faith response of Christians is to worship God and live in Christian fellowship. This is the Christian life. It is our writer's equivalent of Jesus' two commandments, to love God and to love one's neighbor. The true sacrifice of praise is offered by Christians and is manifest in their conduct. Our sacrifices are our continual offerings of praise and thanksgiving. together with ministries of practical kindness to men.

"Do not neglect to do good and to share what you have, for such sacrifices are pleasing to God" (Heb 13:16). The worship and praise of God includes acts of mercy, kindness, love, and service. Praise must be accompanied by deeds of kindness and charity; these also are sacrifices that bring pleasure to God. The whole round of the Christian life, in fact, is sacrificial in character. Worship with the lips is not enough. It must be accompanied by good deeds; sharing, in particular is singled out. Praise to God is one kind of sacrifice; service to men is a second which arises from the first and is like unto it.

Hebrews concludes with a prayer. "Now may the God of peace who brought from the dead our Lord Jesus, the great shepherd of the sheep, by the blood of the eternal covenant, equip you with everything good, that you may do his will, working in you that which is pleasing in his sight, through Jesus Christ, to whom be glory for ever and ever. Amen." (Heb 13:20-21). The prayer assumes the collect form and order: title and address; mention of divine attributes appropriate to the thing asked for; the petition; the ground of asking, through Jesus, the Mediator; ascription of praise. It sums up ideas expressed at great length earlier: the sacrifice of Christ, the establishment of a new covenant, and the life of the Christian as at once the work of God and a matter of our own exertions. The words "brought from the dead" refer not only to Christ's resurrection but also to his entrance into the heavenly sanctuary and his exaltation as head over the household of God (3:1-6).

The focus is on the doings of God. What God has done is the ground of assurance and hope and the substance of the prayer. God brought up Jesus from the dead; he did this to him not only personally as his Son, but more particularly as the leader of his people, that is, as the great shepherd of the sheep and as our Lord. He did it to him in relation to the new and eternal covenant secured and ratified by his death. His resurrection is, therefore, decisive proof that man is reconciled to God, or able to enter glory, and that God is now active to fulfill for his people all that is promised to them under the new covenant.

An Interesting Thought

The publication you have just finished reading is part of the apostolic efforts of the Society of St. Paul of the American Province. A small, unique group of priests and brothers, the members of the Society of St. Paul propose to bring the message of Christ to men through the communications media while living the religious life.

If you know a young man who might be interested in learning more about our life and mission, ask him to contact the Vocation Office in care of the Society of St. Paul, Alba House Community, Canfield, Ohio 44406 (phone 216/533-5503). Full information will be sent without cost or obligation. You may be instrumental in helping a young man to find his vocation in life.
An interesting thought.